Breaking *the* Mirror *of* Heaven

"This is a book that needed to be written . . . and I can't imagine a better writing team to have taken on the challenge. Robert Bauval and Ahmed Osman have expertly untangled the history of the Egyptian Antiquities Organization, in all its guises, and successfully exposed the trauma of the Zahi Hawass years. This is a story that should be read by all those interested in Egyptology and everyone who cares passionately about Egypt . . . a tour de force in modern historical investigation."

DAVID ROHL, EGYPTOLOGIST, HISTORIAN,
BROADCASTER, AND AUTHOR OF *A TEST OF TIME*

"Egyptology has lied to us for too long. Now a meticulous investigation by two top authors reveals the disturbing truth. This book is dynamite."

GRAHAM HANCOCK, AUTHOR OF *FINGERPRINTS OF THE GODS*

"Due to Robert Bauval's influence, as well as that of many other great authors, false beliefs on the origins of civilization will be studied well into the future. The observations and approaches in Bauval's books are dazzling."

JAVIER SIERRA, *NEW YORK TIMES* BESTSELLING
AUTHOR OF *THE LOST ANGEL* AND *THE SECRET SUPPER*

"Breaking the Mirror of Heaven is a hugely important book. In a time when we can all see 'the rise of idiot experts,' this book focuses our attention on the political games that are played with the honest interpretation of our past. Self-serving individuals seek to bury new information by pretending that claimed academic rank outweighs cold evidence. Bravo, Robert and Ahmed, for such a delightful and persuasive blow for reason."

CHRISTOPHER KNIGHT, COAUTHOR OF
THE HIRAM KEY AND CIVILIZATION ONE

Breaking *the* Mirror *of* Heaven

The Conspiracy to Suppress the Voice of Ancient Egypt

Robert Bauval and Ahmed Osman

Bear & Company
Rochester, Vermont • Toronto, Canada

Bear & Company
One Park Street
Rochester, Vermont 05767
www.BearandCompanyBooks.com

Text stock is SFI certified

Bear & Company is a division of Inner Traditions International

Library of Congress Cataloging-in-Publication Data
Bauval, Robert, 1948–
  Breaking the mirror of heaven : the conspiracy to supress the voice of ancient
Egypt / Robert Bauval and Ahmed Osman.
      p. cm.
  Includes bibliographical references and index.
  ISBN 978-1-59143-156-5 (pbk.) — ISBN 978-1-59143-813-7 (e-book)
  1. Egypt—Antiquities. 2. Excavations (Archaeology)—Egypt. 3. Egyptology. 4.
Hawass, Zahi A. I. Osman, Ahmed, 1934– II. Title.
  DT60.B385 2012
  932—dc23

                                                                        2012007964

Printed and bound in the United States by Lake Book Manufacturing, Inc.
The text stock is SFI certified. The Sustainable Forestry Initiative® program
promotes sustainable forest management.

10   9   8   7   6   5   4   3   2   1

Text design by Priscilla H. Baker and layout by Virginia Scott Bowman
This book was typeset in Garamond Premier Pro with Arepo used as the display
typeface

To send correspondence to the authors of this book, mail a first-class letter to the
author c/o Inner Traditions • Bear & Company, One Park Street, Rochester, VT
05767, and we will forward the communication, or visit the authors' websites at
www.robertbauval.co.uk or **ahmedosman.com/home.html**.

Contents

Acknowlegments   vii

Introduction: A Cross between a
Peacock and a Scorpion   1

1   The Making of Egypt's Indiana Jones   12

2   Out of Darkness   51

3   The Pasha   91

4   Saving Ancient Egypt   136

5   The End of an Era   152

6   Secret Chambers   194

7   Revolution!   225

    Postscripts   243
       "A Message to All My Friends"   243
       November 2011   244
       March 2012   246
       May 2012   246

APPENDIX 1   The Paris Obelisk: How and
             Why Freemasonry Came into Egypt   247

APPENDIX 2 Discoveries and Achievements—
            or Personal Agenda?   271

APPENDIX 3 "LIVE" Egyptology   287

APPENDIX 4 The Death of Tutankhamun:
            The Cover-up   305

APPENDIX 5 Egypt, My Native Country   331
            Out of Egypt by Ahmed Osman   331
            Losing Alexandria by Robert Bauval   334

            A Last-Minute Update   341

            Notes   342

            Bibliography   348

            Index   352

Acknowledgments

Writing this book has been a special experience for me. Having studied and researched the history of ancient Egypt for nearly three decades, it was now extremely rewarding to have the opportunity to write a book about the birth and rise of modern Egypt and the biographical events of one of its most colorful and controversial figures in Egyptology, Zahi Hawass, the world-famous chief of Egypt's Antiquities. I hope you will enjoy reading it as much as I enjoyed writing it with my coauthor, Ahmed Osman. My gratitude goes to my wife, Michele, for her love, her ever-enduring patience, and her tolerance for sharing living quarters with an author who is gestating a manuscript. This is the eighth time she has had to go through such intellectual pregnancy, but as always she has done it with grit and good cheer. Special thanks go to my brother Jean-Paul Bauval for also being a good friend and neighbor, and to my children, Candice and Jonathan. It has often been the case in my writing career that an exceptional person comes along to be my intellectual and spiritual haven from the long hours of solitary grind an author inevitably goes through. This time my good fortune was to meet Maria Fernandez Garcia. Thank you dear Maria; you are a true friend.

ROBERT BAUVAL

We also give thanks to Pauline and Fiona Bauval (Torremolinos), Gary Evans (England), Andy Collins (Avebury, Wiltshire), Sherif el Sebai (Cairo), Tamer Medhat (Cairo), Yousef and Patricia Awyan (Nazlet el Saman, Giza Pyramids), Gouda Fayed (Sphinx Guest House, Nazlet al Saman), Hillary Raimo (New York), Richard (Fuzzy) Fusniak (Cambridge, England), Geoffrey and Therese Gauci (Sydney, Australia), Juliano Fernandez (Uruguay), Naco Ares (Madrid), John (Nany) and Josette Orphanidis (Athens), and many other friends, Facebook "friends," and colleagues too numerous to list here. A big thank you also goes to our U.S. publisher Inner Traditions • Bear & Company, especially our editor Mindy Branstetter for her professionalism and friendship. As ever, we are eternally grateful to our readers around the world for their support and for their loyalty over the years. Without you all this hard work would have no meaning or satisfaction.

ROBERT BAUVAL
AND
AHMED OSMAN

Introduction

A Cross between a
Peacock and a Scorpion

Switch on your TV, and there's Zahi Hawass . . . turn on a different show and there he is again. . . . The affable archaeologist is here, there and everywhere—on CNN, the BBC, the History Channel, the Learning Channel, the National Geographic Channel and your local PBS outlet, to name but a few.

"I am already famous and powerful. What I do I do for Egypt. It is the first time that Egypt has been correctly explained to the public. . . . No one in the history of archaeology has helped Egypt more than I."

NEVINE EL-AREF, QUOTING ZAHI HAWASS,
"ZAHI HAWASS: A HAT IS A HAT," *AL-AHRAM WEEKLY*

Never before in the history of archaeology has one man reached such notoriety as did Zahi Hawass, Egypt's ex-head of antiquities. Molded by the American media mill into a real-life Indiana Jones, complete with Stetson hat and denim shirt, and marketed globally as the superstar of Egyptology, Hawass became a household name, in league with his friend and compatriot, the actor and heartthrob Omar Sharif. Vilified and feared, loved and adored, Hawass's public profile fluctuated from "charismatic and passionate" to "bully and megalomaniac." Hardly known outside Egypt before the 1990s, Hawass shot to international fame after being handpicked by Rupert Murdoch's Fox TV and turned into a sort a no-nonsense-cum-kick-butt hero of archaeology—or, as more poetically minded critics saw him, a sort of oriental Dr. Jekyll and Mr. Hyde of virtual archaeology or, better still, a cross between a peacock and a scorpion. Hawass was promoted as the defender of Egypt's history, a fearless knight in shining armor fighting off battalions of enemies whom he labeled "pyramidiots, theorists, foreigners, amateurs, followers of Seth, Jews, and Zionists." With creative editing, however, Hawass's persona came across on television as charismatic and passionate. The American television-weaned generation lapped it all up—and so did Hawass himself. Lulled by a false belief that his marriage with American media would last forever, reassured that the close relationship he enjoyed with Susanne Mubarak, Egypt's first lady, would always protect him no matter what, and fooled by the daily flattery showered upon him by his office staff, his colleagues, his peers, and his numerous fans around the world, Hawass began to believe in his own larger-than-life image. He felt invincible. No one and nothing could stop him. Like an alley cat with nine lives, and perhaps a few more to spare, he brushed aside his critics and rivals and deflected scandal upon scandal like water off a duck's back. Yet those who had crossed his path and tasted his wrath knew better. They had seen his true colors. Nevertheless for a long time, they, too, were neutralized, their voices muffled by the local press controlled by Hawass's powerful mentors and the mass media apparatus controlled by Fox TV and other affiliates of the Rupert Murdoch empire.

But for all tyrants, sooner or later the proverbial rug is pulled from under their feet; tyrants must fall from the precarious and dangerous heights they ascend to. In the case of Hawass, it took, quite literally, a revolution. And even then, the entrenchment of his position was such that it also took several "resignations" and "reinstatements" from his ministerial post to bring him down, ironically at the hands of his own people—those thousands of employees in the antiquities services who protested outside his office and in the iconic Tahrir Square with angry shouts of "Thief! Thief!" and banners with slogans of "American Puppet" and "Traitor." On July 19, 2011 (ironically the Great Day of Renewal in ancient Egypt when the Star of the Nile rose at dawn before the sun), Hawass's star dimmed and was finally extinguished as he stepped out for the very last time from the headquarters of the Supreme Council of Antiquities (SCA) and was besieged and nearly lynched by an angry mob of SCA employees. Now like all prominent members of the old regime, Hawass is under a strict travel ban awaiting investigation on a multitude of charges including misappropriation of funds, theft of antiquities, corruption, and mismanagement.

To comprehend why and how such a paradoxical man became the supreme authority and controller of the world's most precious and important antiquities, one must delve far and wide, not only into his origins but also the origins of the SCA (previously the EAO, Egyptian Antiquities Organization) and the emergence of modern Egypt itself—from the Napoleon invasion in 1789 to the "invasion" of Hawass in the early 1990s. Only then can a true picture emerge—a picture that is as exotic as it is shocking and bewildering.

A special kind of research and a close involvement with Egypt was needed for this task, one that necessitated a journalistic and behind-the-scene approach. As the authors of this book, having both been born in Egypt (Ahmed Osman in Cairo in 1934, and Robert Bauval in Alexandria in 1948) and having lived in Egypt on and off over the last sixty years—from the end of King Farouk's reign in 1952 to the ousting of President Hosni Mubarak in 2011—we felt well suited for this job. We felt more so because we have been close observers of Zahi Hawass's saga for the last two decades and have, more than once, crossed paths and swords with this larger-than-life official. It is no secret that we are not the best of friends with Hawass. We have been openly critical about his methods and behavior and make no bones about it. He, in turn, has also been openly critical (to put it mildly!) about our work and our persons. Many would therefore think that we are perhaps too subjective to give Hawass a fair deal in reviewing his two-decade-long reign as "king of the pyramids." But we pride ourselves on being dispassionate evidence-driven researchers and professional in our recounting of the facts.

Since November 2011 much has happened, and Egypt is still in upheaval. In the streets of central Cairo protesters have clashed with the military, with the Health Ministry reporting several deaths and more than five hundred injured. Confusion and fear have taken hold of the nation. The Supreme Council of the Armed Forces (SCAF) finally kept its promise by allowing free and multiparty elections to take place for parliamentary seats. This brought out millions of Egyptians to vote for the first time in their lives. The results were shocking to some, and obvious to others. The Egyptian Parliament has now a 75 percent majority of Islamists, 45 percent from the Muslim Brotherhood's Freedom and Justice Party (FJP) and 30 percent from the Salafist Al-Nour (Light) Party, the latter an ultra-conservative Islamic faction modeled on Saudi Arabian Wahhabism, which is under Sharia Law. The military, however, still retains, behind the scene, an important political role. A political, social, and cultural Pandora's box has been opened, and there is no telling where all this "Islamization" of Egypt will eventually lead to. But while our concerns as native Egyptians are naturally for the well-being of our country and its people, as historians and researchers into Egypt's past we are equally concerned for the future of Egypt's antiquities. The latter is thus the main thrust of this book.

The pharaonic legacy that has miraculously survived the millennia (and, sadly, much has been destroyed or damaged over the last two centuries), although it is on Egyptian soil, it nonetheless belongs to humanity as a whole. It is, quite literally, the remains that were the crucible and nursery of civilization and, as such, need full protection and care. The man who was given this responsibility for the last decade was Zahi

Hawass. Many have remarked, however, that instead of focusing on protection, he has treated the pharaonic antiquities as if they were his own private property. To many now, Hawass comes across as a wolf in sheep's clothing who, on the one hand, flaunted an image of himself as protector and savior of Egypt's history while in practice, on the other hand, concerned himself more with his own political career and his media image. When, after the revolution, some journalists referred to him as "the Mubarak of antiquities," clearly they were not making quaint jest but were very serious indeed.

And yet some readers may rightly ask: "What if his accusers are completely wrong in their assessment of Hawass?"

It is to do justice to this pertinent and disturbing question that we have written this book. We did not want to simply put Hawass on trial here; we also wanted to put *ourselves on trial*. We wanted to be both the prosecution and defense of this case. And most of all, we wanted you, the reader, to be the judge and jury. In more pragmatic terms, we wanted to look at the wider picture, to examine carefully and without bias the full historical landscape in which this strange story has unfolded, and to ask the question not in one perspective alone but from different facets and directions:

- ▲ Was Hawass the person that the media portrayed him to be, or was he really someone else?
- ▲ Did Hawass work hard to save Egypt's antiquities, or did he use it for his own benefit?
- ▲ Was Hawass a hypocrite who conned the world with his charm and media savvy, or was he simply a jovial and loud roustabout, a sort of modern Robin Hood, taking money from the rich American moguls to help the poor deprived Egyptians?
- ▲ Was he manipulated by the media, an innocent victim of greedy television producers seeking to make a fast buck, or was it the other way round?

In one of his famous outbursts Hawass declared, in a London *Sunday Times Magazine* article ("King Tut Tut Tut" by Richard Girling, May 22, 2005):

> I will work with anyone who does something good for Egypt . . . I never waste my time fighting people. I have never hurt anyone in my life, but if you hurt me I will tell you to get out of my way. Some people threatened to kill me. They were jealous archaeologists who were lazy. I call them the followers of Seth, the devil god.

How true is that statement?

In order to write this book we delved into newspaper articles, reports, as well as our own memory of past events and encounters with Hawass. However, we also made great effort to block bias and avoid unverified claims and speculations, and stayed instead focused on facts and reliable evidence. Our job, we now feel, has been done with honesty and fairness. It is now up to you, the reader, to come to your own conclusions about the "man with the hat."

There is, nonetheless, another more subtle, but equally important point to consider about Hawass, which we, as authors, have been directly affected by. It would thus be hypocritical on our part if we did not mention it at this stage.

In our many years of research we have become convinced that Egypt has always been regarded as the cradle of civilization, the place where humans made the transition from childhood to maturity and where the fount of human knowledge began to flow profusely. It was in Egypt that many of the first steps in cultural and scientific advancement took place, such as the invention of writing, the development of architecture and engineering, astronomy, mathematics, and medicine. It is where some of the first true cities were built, libraries and universities established, and where it was recognized that humans have two dimensions—physical and spiritual—and belong not only to the earthly realm but to the whole cosmos. It was in Egypt that monotheist religion began and where, as the Bible and the Qur'an confirm, Moses received God's commandments on Mount Sinai. And, according to the Gospel of Matthew, it was from Egypt ("Out of Egypt have I called my son," Matthew 2:15) that God called his son. The highly sophisticated classical Greeks, among them Plato and Solon, admitted that it was from Egypt that Greece borrowed much of its science and knowledge. It would not be an exaggeration to say that believers, as well as atheists, saw—and many still do see—Egypt as the true spiritual home of all humanity. There is an old Hermetic saying that *Egypt is the mirror of heaven,* and Arabs have always proclaimed Egypt *masr om el donya,* the mother of the world. Many people all over the world feel somehow connected to Egypt and still come to the banks of the sacred Nile to seek their origins and their very souls. After Napoleon's invasion of Egypt in 1798, scientific archaeological research began in Egypt with scholars from all disciplines and from many nations diligently taking part in this noble enterprise. Academics, professionals, and even ordinary people from all walks of life felt free to do research on ancient Egypt; to seek the origin of their beliefs, myths, and religious ideologies; and, more important, to express their views openly and publish their findings without fear of retribution or censorship. In this way, Egypt began to find its lost soul, and a wonderful "Egyptomania" grew in the Western world, the latter wearied by two world wars and the dullness and insipidity of postindustrialism, and it began to take delight and find warmth in ancient Egypt. In postwar Europe in the 1940s and 1950s, the rediscovery of the Gnostic texts at Nag Hammadi in Upper Egypt injected new blood in the study of early Christianity, as well as reviving the study of the first-century Egyptian Hermetic Texts, which had greatly influenced and inspired Renaissance scholars and, later on, the scientists and humanists of the Age of Enlightenment, not least Francis Bacon, Isaac Newton, and Descartes. The late nineteenth century and early twentieth century saw the emergence of pyramidology, which, although a pseudoscience itself, nonetheless kindled a huge interest in Egypt's mysteries and its spiritual influence on the world. Then in the 1980s and 1990s sprang a new breed of researchers, loosely labeled "alternative" Egyptologists, who challenged old dogmas with radical and controversial new theories that highlighted an Egypt far older, more mysterious, and more sophisticated than previously thought. Books like Peter Tompkin's *The Great Pyramid,* Graham Hancock's *Fingerprints of the Gods,* Christopher Knight's and Robert Lomas's *The Hiram Key.* There were also books by us, such as *The Orion Mystery* and *Keeper of Genesis* (Robert Bauval), *Stranger in the Valley of the Kings* and *Moses and Akhenaten* (Ahmed Osman) and others that hit the bestseller lists and brought Egyptology out of the confines of a dry academia and pushed it into the lap of a wider international audience, drawing the interest of the popular press and television. Egyptology and ancient Egypt and its mysteries spread like wildfire or, more aptly, like a wonderful and invigorating breath of fresh air in the general public around the world. Healthy debate ensued, articles filled magazines and periodicals, television documentaries dominated the channels, and even Hollywood joined in with blockbusters such as *Stargate* and *10,000 BC.* And even though these movies grossly fictionalized ancient Egypt, they nonetheless excited the collective consciousness, especially of the young, and drew many into more serious studies of this golden civilization and its intellectual, cultural, and spiritual legacy. Yet, sadly, Zahi Hawass, instead of jumping on the bandwagon, or at the very least letting it be, fumed in silence at the growing success of the alternative Egyptologists and then, finally like some angry volcano, erupted and lurched himself against any attempt to understand Egypt's past as the fountain of universal knowledge. Thus began Hawass's private war of attrition against "alternative" authors and intellectuals, and indeed against anyone, even professional Egyptologists, who dared to disagree with his own interpretations of Egypt's ancient history and its artifacts. However, that was only the beginning, mere verbal scuffles, compared to the full-scale war that was to follow; for when Hawass finally had clawed (some would even say bullied) his way up the Supreme Council of Antiquities (SCA) in 2002 and took control of all antiquities in Egypt as Director General, he initiated his own reign of terror, which impeded—sometimes censored, or even banned—works and research that did not meet with his approval. Acting as the personification of Egyptology itself, Hawass was so eager to announce "major discoveries" that he even sometimes took over discoveries and claimed them as his own, interpreting the evidence to suit his own views. And so it was that Hawass used his political weight as Director General of the SCA and Vice Minister of Culture, as well as his huge media image, to force himself on the scene, bulldoze all opposition, and simply brush aside all new ideas that he did not like or approve. Under the claim that he was promoting Egyptian tourism, he was seen on nearly all television channels, not just locally but on mega-media such as Fox TV, National Geographic Channel, and satellite giants like History Channel and Discovery Channel with sensational "discoveries" and exploits. Playing up to nationalistic sentiments, Hawass fed the local media with the notion that he was "defending national pride" and "Egyptian culture" against its enemies, which he labeled "pyramidiots," "Zionists," and "Jews." And abroad, specifically with American television media, he fed the image of himself as a real-life Indiana Jones, making dramatic discoveries and heroically defending Egypt's history from "amateurs" and "cranks." It is well known that we, as independent researchers and authors, were often at odds with Hawass, as we represented the very opposite of what Hawass stood for.

Having been born in Egypt and having published several bestsellers that re-examined the deeper aspects of Egypt's ancient past in the light of new research and evidence, we were particularly targeted by Hawass and regularly subjected to media attacks by him. It is well known that before Hawass's takeover of the Supreme Council of Antiquities (SCA), our books had roused a huge interest all over the world in Egypt's mysterious past, its influence on the Bible, and its prehistoric origins. Translated into more than twenty-five languages, our books pricked the interest of people from all walks of life and generated wide debate and discussion. But as Hawass became more and more influential with the high position he held in the Mubarak regime, the less and less Egyptologists felt comfortable—indeed some seemed terrified—to comment on, let alone condone, any new ideas that they knew conflicted with Hawass's own. So feared was Hawass by his Egyptian colleagues and employees (and even by many Western Egyptologists), that most of them preferred to remain silent rather than face his wrath. And so the real and noble purpose of Egyptology (i.e., to understand the mind and soul of ancient Egypt) was pushed aside and replaced by ad nauseum appearances of Hawass on television flaunting this or that "discovery" or seen "protecting" Egypt from this or that "enemy." The upshot of all this was that new research and ideas in Egyptology—albeit some very radical but nevertheless stimulating—were forced into a kind of intellectual limbo for many years.

There still is today a strange silence from Egyptologists, both in Egypt and elsewhere, perhaps still spooked and intimidated by two decades of authoritarian rule and control from Hawass. And thus one of the purposes of this book is for us to speak out and break this barrier of fear. We also hope that now, with Hawass gone, Egyptology in Egypt will be democratized again, and that new ideas, no matter how controversial, will be allowed to be expressed and debated. It is hoped, too, that politics will not enter scientific Egyptology ever again as it did during Hawass's tenure, and that new research will be reviewed and debated only on its merits and not based on biased, personal vendettas, racism, or idiosyncratic nationalistic attitude. It is perhaps befitting that we conclude our introduction with this message of hope coming from ancient Egypt itself, or, to be more specific, from the *Hermetica* (Asclepius III, 26a).

> But when all this has befallen, Asclepius, then the Master and
> Father, God, the first before all . . . will look on that which has come

to pass, and will stay the disorder by the counterworking of his will, which is the good. He will call back to the right path those who have gone astray; he will cleanse the world [Egypt] from evil . . . and will bring it back to its former glory . . .

Now on with our story . . .

1
The Making of Egypt's Indiana Jones

We [Egyptians] are the only ones who really care about the preservation [of antiquities]. Foreigners who come to excavate, maybe some of them care about preservation, but the majority care about discoveries.

ZAHI HAWASS

They call him the Pharaoh, the keeper of the pyramids. He rules Egyptology with an iron fist and a censorious tongue. Nobody crosses Zahi Hawass and gets away with it.

RICHARD GIRLING, "KING TUT TUT TUT,"
SUNDAY TIMES MAGAZINE

The story we are about to tell is as intriguing as it is fascinating. It is not merely the story of a man who dominated and controlled Egyptian antiquities for several decades as if they were his own but also the story of Egyptian archaeology itself and the way modern Egypt created such a man. These topics need to be properly reviewed, first to understand how, and why, Zahi Hawass became what he is and, second, to provide a new vision that is desperately needed to save Egyptian antiquities from decline and perhaps even total destruction.

We begin, however, with the man himself.

BACKGROUND AND FORMATIVE YEARS

Zahi Hawass was born on May 28, 1947, in Abeyeda in the Eastern Delta—a small village not far from the busy port of Damietta and one hundred twenty miles north of modern Cairo. It is important to understand the context in which young Zahi grew up, for it was those early formative years that set the mental, emotional, and intellectual foundation of the man who would become the "king of the pyramids." Egyptians who came from such villages and not from principal and chic cities such as Cairo, Alexandria, Damietta, Ismaileya, or Port Said were regarded, rightly or wrongly, as coarse and clumsy by the sophisticated city dwellers. To put it in another way, the young Hawass grew up with a big chip on his shoulder, and this, we believe, coupled with his renowned aggressive and ambitious character, installed in him a burning desire to become "somebody famous." When he was only thirteen years old, Hawass mourned the death of his father. This traumatic event may indeed be at the root of Hawass's ambition to prove himself to his village and eventually to the whole world.

In a National Geographic special in 2002 titled *The King of the Pyramids* we are shown a young Hawass playing football in a dusty field with the village kids, kicking and dribbling a football, and clearly being admired as the leader of the pack. In the same TV documentary, Hawass, now in his fifties and head of the SCA (Supreme Council of Antiquities), is shown returning in triumph to his village and being greeted like a national hero. Various famous guests and celebrities appear in this TV documentary, such as the actor Omar Sharif and the Egyptologist Salima Ikram who lauded Hawass's qualities while brushing aside his bullying and his bombastic rude manners, seeing them, instead, as the ways of a passionate man. To these eminent "friends" Hawass is a kindhearted, generous, and fun-loving man, although admittedly sometimes a bit of a bull in a china shop when he blows his top at colleagues or vents his anger in public. This was the "Indiana Jones butt-kicking tough guy with a big heart" that National Geographic and other media wanted the world to see. The truth, however, could well be very different indeed, as we shall see.

To Zahi Hawass, like most young men living in coastal villages of the Egyptian Mediterranean, Alexandria was the hot spot, the place to make a career, and, in his particular case, the stepping-stone to much loftier goals. There, in this ancient city, which gave the world geniuses like Euclid and Archimedes, heroes like Alexander the Great and Mark Antony, and romantic characters such as the legendary Cleopatra and the beautiful and gentle Hypatia, things were happening in postwar Egypt. It is worth noting that just a century and a half ago during the French occupation of Egypt (1798–1801), Alexandria had but a mere six thousand residents and that the great universal city of the ancient world had been totally wiped away, with little more than a shanty fishing town remaining. It is said that many of Napoleon's scientists, when they disembarked on the shores of Alexandria, openly wept at this pathetic sight.

When Muhammad Ali, Egypt's first modern ruler, came to power in 1805, he welcomed foreigners, as well as Jews, to settle in Alexandria and help him rebuild the city. A massive reconstruction program was launched, and by 1927, Alexandria had regained much of its ancient glamour and prestige, becoming one of the major shipping and trading centers of the world. After World War II, although the vast majority of the Alexandrians were native Egyptians, they hardly made any impression on the large and elite cosmopolitan community made up of wealthy and powerful European families—Greeks, Italians, Maltese, Armenians—who monopolized and ran the major commercial activities.

Alexandria, until the early 1950s, was dubbed the Nice of the south Mediterranean. It boasted a large contingency of intellectuals, a high society of educated and multilingual Europeans, and a steady stream of cultural and societal events. Looking like a dainty and sophisticated belle epoque city of the French Riviera, Alexandria's breezy *corniche* (the coastal road) was bejeweled with splendid villas and public gardens overlooking the azure Mediterranean Sea. British novelist Lawrence Durell, who had lived in Alexandria during World War II, describes the city in his opus masterpiece *The Alexandria Quartet* as being a highly cultured and stylish metropolis, with a splendid sporting club, beautiful public parks and city squares, a plethora of chic nightclubs and music houses, wonderful coffeehouses and high-class restaurants, and fancy casinos and luxurious hotels. But all this was soon to change for the worse.

In 1952, when Hawass was only a tiny tot, Egypt's so-called Free Officers Movement toppled the monarchy of King Farouk and began purging the country of its feudal rich landlords, the *pashas* and the *beys*, seizing their land assets and redistributing them in smaller parcels to the

Figure 1.1. Modern Alexandria: View of the Corniche of the Eastern Harbor

fellahin, the poor peasantry. The so-called *khawagas,* a term referring to Europeans and other foreigners living in Egypt, were also targeted, with many of their assets sequestrated, and after the 1956 Tripartite War, many of them (especially the British and French) were expelled from Egypt. From 1952 to 1956, a deep-rooted resentment for the khawagas, which had been fermenting for almost a century in Egypt, was suddenly unleashed, especially among the young Egyptians, and those khawagas who chose to remain in Egypt—including many families, such as that of coauthor Robert Bauval, whose lineage goes back several generations in Egypt—were subtly and even openly persecuted and disfavored. Along with the khawagas were also the Copts (Egyptian Christians) who were now regarded as second-class citizens. Such was the mood in Egypt while Hawass was growing up and reaching manhood. By the time Hawass went to Alexandria in 1964, the quarter-million-strong population of the khawagas had dwindled drastically, with only a hard-core group remaining. The city then underwent some major changes in its social and economic life.

On the ninth anniversary of the Free Officers 1952 coup, Nasser announced a vast nationalization program, which cut deeply into the private sector, including shipping and export companies. This had a devastating effect on the lifestyle in Alexandria, and the city began to quickly lose it eminence and charm. Between 1960 and 1964, the private sector was all but eliminated with the nationalization of factories, banks, insurance companies, and export and import traders, which forced many foreigners who owned these enterprises—Greeks, Italians, French, British, and Jews—to pack whatever they could carry and leave Egypt for a new life in Europe and the New World. A massive brain drain took place, leaving behind a city now run by a corrupt, uncouth, and inexperienced gang of young officers who, overnight, were given high positions in the government and the public sector. Within months, the economy and infrastructure of the city was in chaos. A rampant black market, coupled with widespread corruption, set in and brought daily life to almost a standstill.

Figure 1.2. Robert Bauval's parents, Gaston (1905–1966) and
Yvonne (1915–2009), in Alexandria in 1939. They were typical
Khawagas in Egypt. They were both born in Alexandria.
They both rest in the Latin cemetery outside
the eastern gates of the ancient city.

At the University of Alexandria, where Hawass studied Greek and Roman history for a few years, the textbooks that were in English and French had been burnt by zealous Nasserites and replaced by a new Arabic curriculum that, in the case of the humanities, history, and archaeology, was designed to laud the virtues of the revolution and denigrate the era of the monarchy and foreign control. Each morning before lectures, students would gather in the open court of the university and participate in a lengthy salute of the new national flag (the black, white, and red banner designed by Nasser himself and now made world famous by the Tahrir Revolution of 2011). They stood at attention, listening to pep sermons on the virtues of Nasser and his reformation programs and ending with the chanting of the new national anthem. A new ultranationalistic anti-Western mood befell most Egyptians (and almost certainly young men such as Hawass, who had a chip on his shoulder), and a deep-rooted resentment toward foreigners was fostered, which affected their perception of the Western world. Added to this national psychosis was the rife and virulent hatred for Israel, which encouraged a profound anti-Semitic attitude among the students. This anti-Semitism emerged in later years when Hawass became head of the SCA.

The bachelor's degree that Hawass pursued was not, oddly enough, in Egyptology or archaeology but in Greco-Roman studies. He graduated in late June 1967, a time of huge turmoil in Egypt as it was but a few days after the catastrophic defeat of Nasser in the Six-Day War with Israel. The Egyptian army was totally annihilated in the Sinai, and the holy sites in Jerusalem (Al Aqsa Mosque and the Dome on the Rock) were occupied by the Israelis, led by General Moshe Dayan. This was the (almost) last nail in the coffin of Egypt's hero, President Gamal Abdel Nasser, who was forced to make a humiliating public apology to the nation by assuming all the blame and handing over his resignation (which, as it turned out, was not accepted). One can just imagine the state of mind of Hawass, now in his early twenties and poised to start a career; Egypt's future looked very bleak, indeed, with the economy almost at a standstill and the Suez Canal, which was controlled by the hated British, closed to all shipping. Egyptian national pride—and by extension Hawass's own—suffered a huge and devastating blow.

So what possible career was now open for Hawass? In an interview he gave *Al-Ahram Weekly* in 2005, Hawass reminisced on his early career days, stating that he had not really enjoyed his time at the university because, he said, the studies were "too passive" for him. As for his career ambitions, Hawass admitted that he originally thought of taking up a diplomatic career but failed the admittance examination because "they were not convinced of my sincerity." He, therefore, took the next logical route for a graduate in Greco-Roman studies: Hawass decided to join the Egyptian Antiquities Organization (EAO), forerunner of the SCA, as a junior inspector. At this point begins Hawass's alleged love affair with Egyptology and archaeology.

Even though Hawass was fired up with high hopes and ambition, he hadn't really expected to get a senior job at the EAO as his qualifications were not in Egyptology or archaeology but in Greco-Roman studies. Furthermore, to land a senior job at the EAO one had to have a Ph.D., whereas, Hawass had only managed to get a D average in his bachelor's degree, which was too low for entry into a Ph.D. course of study. So, at this stage, it looked like the road to any senior post was cut off from him. The best he could do at this time was to get a job at the Sound and Light Show at the Giza Pyramids. This show had been introduced in the early 1960s and was becoming a popular tourist attraction. Hawass figured that this job, even though not quite the archaeological posting he had hoped for, was close to the activities around Giza and, more important, was a good place to be, should an opportunity arise. Such an opportunity did come in 1974 when, as luck would have it, he met a young American named Mark Lehner.

THE SCHOLAR AND THE PSYCHIC

In 1972, Mark Lehner, then in his early twenties, had been a chemistry major at UCLA, Berkeley, but apparently had dropped out to pursue a

Figure 1.3. Mark Lehner (right) and a friend, Mohammad Nazmy,
President of Quest Travel

young lady who led him to, of all places, the Association of Research
and Enlightenment (ARE), an organization better known as the Edgar
Cayce Foundation (ECF). The ARE/ECF was the creation of the
world-famous American healer, psychic, and seer Edgar Cayce (1877-
1945). Lehner's parents had been members of the ARE/ECF and presumably Lehner was attracted to this organization, as well as the young
woman he was pursuing. At any rate, Hugh Lynn Cayce, Edgar Cayce's
eldest son, took a keen interest in Lehner and decided to groom him
for an important mission that had been in the planning for many years:
to find the legendary Hall of Records in Egypt, which his father had
predicted would soon be found under the Sphinx. Apart from Edgar
Cayce's alleged psychic and healing abilities, he also gave readings while
in a trance state, which mainly dealt with Egypt and how survivors of
the lost continent of Atlantis had come to the Giza Necropolis in 10,500
BCE and there had concealed their advanced scientific knowledge in a

secret repository, which Cayce called the Hall of Records. According to Cayce, this Hall of Records was somewhere under the Great Sphinx, and now in 1973, nearly three decades after Cayce's death, his eldest son, Hugh Lynn, was determined to have a shot at finding it with the help of Lehner.

Lehner's first task at the ARE/ECF, however, was to compile the Egypt readings of Edgar Cayce into a book titled *The Egyptian Heritage*. Lehner, at least at this early stage in his career, seemed to give full support and credence to Edgar Cayce's readings on Atlantis and the Hall of Records. Hugh Lynn was much impressed with Lehner's work ethic and enthusiasm and quickly saw in him a potential scholar who, when groomed, could provide serious credibility to Cayce's readings. To this end, Hugh Lynn convinced some wealthy ARE/ECF members to put up the funds for Lehner's further education and got him enrolled, through his connections, in an archaeology and anthropology course at the American University in Cairo (AUC). Lehner's real mission, however, was to make contact with high officials at the EAO and obtain permits for the ARE/ECF to search for the Hall of Records at Giza. It seemed like an almost impossible assignment (psychic organizations and professional Egyptology make strange bedfellows and are as apt to mix as oil and water). But as things turned out, Lehner did succeed well beyond everyone's expectations, even his own. While studying at the AUC, Lehner got to meet Zahi Hawass who, by then, had managed to get a job as an inspector at the Giza Pyramids. The two men took to each other immediately, and so began a friendship and collaboration that was to last several decades.

In 1976, and with the help of Hawass, Lehner was able to get a permit for the ARE/ECF to work at the Sphinx. An academic front was necessary, however, since the ARE/ECF would certainly have elicited a barrage of opposition and protest from Egyptologists and other academics. The Stanford Research Institute provided this front, but the whole project—a photometric survey of the Great Sphinx—was fully funded, and thus fully controlled behind the scene by the ARE/ECF and Hugh

Lynn Cayce. Hugh Lynn's dream had come true: a huge opportunity to work at the Great Sphinx and have a real shot at finding the legendary Hall of Records.

All went well until the Egyptian authorities caught the ARE/ECF people drilling holes around the Sphinx. A scandal ensued, and the project was cancelled before any proof of the Hall of Records could be found. Yet far from being discouraged, Hugh Lynn devised a long-term plan. Hugh Lynn's official biographer, A. Robert Smith, explains how this plan was to pan out:

> Hugh Lynn had no sense of defeat. He would stay with the search as long as it took, building alliances with other groups and individuals. One of the latter was the Egyptian inspector at Giza, [Zahi] Hawass, who he had met through Lehner in 1975 . . . If Zahi Hawass was to advance within the government, to further his own career and open doors for Hugh Lynn's project, he could do it best on the wings of higher education at an American Ivy League college. His patron [Hugh Lynn] cleared the way: "I got him a scholarship at the University of Pennsylvania in Egyptology to get his Ph.D. I got the scholarship through an ARE person who happened to be on the Fulbright scholarship board."[1]

Later, in 1984, a few months before his death, Hugh Lynn made this astonishing vow.

> I'm never giving up there. It's very important . . . we are looking for the records. This is what the "readings" say of the pyramids themselves and the sphinx. We are looking for the Atlanteans records which are buried there . . . the Sphinx is guarding them. We are playing for all the marbles.[2]

It is clear that the ARE/ECF was—and probably still is—very determined to look for the alleged Hall of Records at Giza and, as

Hugh Lynn had bluntly put it, was ready to play "for all the marbles." This almost certainly entailed, among other things, paying for Lehner's education in Cairo and, later, as reported by A. Robert Smith, for Zahi Hawass's education in the United States. In 1978 Hawass went to the United States to obtain a Ph.D. at the University of Pennsylvania. Clearly the ARE/ECF expected much from Lehner and Hawass. Their high qualifications, it was hoped, would presumably help them both advance to higher positions within Egypt and the EAO, which in turn would enable them to grant permits to the ARE/ECF to work at Giza.

It seems evident that the ARE/ECF was grooming both Hawass and Lehner to take control of the Giza Pyramids and Sphinx in order to undertake the "work" (as Hugh Lynn puts it), which, without a doubt, entailed finding the fabled Hall of Records of Atlantis. To achieve this bizarre objective, a long-term plan was set in motion. Let us note in passing that Edgar Cayce, the seer behind this ambitious work, had strong connections with important people, some of whom were senior Freemasons and, at least on one occasion, strongly implied that unfolding events in Egypt would, somehow, be connected with Masonic aspiration for a new world order.

> For, with those changes that will be wrought, Americanism with the universal thought that is expressed in the brotherhood [Masonic?] of man into group thought, as expressed by the Masonic Order, will be the eventual rule in the settlement of affairs in the world. . . . the principles that are embraced in the same [Masonic Order] will be the basis upon which the new order of peace is to be established . . .[3]

Such an incredible and lofty mission by Edgar Cayce—which apparently required for its implementation the grooming of Hawass into a high official with a Ph.D.—may not seem too strange to ordinary people in the West; but it would be unacceptable to any government to have one of its officials use his or her position to promote an outside agenda in this way. It would be unthinkable, to say the very least, that the Egyptian

Figure 1.4. Edgar Cayce
(photo courtesy of the Edgar Cayce Foundation)

government would sanction such behavior. However, we are not here judging the merits of what appears to be a sort of "Masonic" mission, nor are we putting on trial the Masonic Brotherhood We are here to investigate and review the possible clandestine activities of Zahi Hawass.

Having said this, it must be strongly pointed out that Freemasonry has been banned in Egypt since 1964, and in the eyes of many (if not all) Arabs—especially staunch Islamists and anti-Zionists—Freemasonry is synonymous with Zionism and, consequently, loathed as an evil influence. Hawass—perhaps naively—let himself get deeply involved with the Edgar Cayce Foundation and its covert search for the Hall of Records at Giza, and in doing so, especially with the pos-

Figure 1.5. John Van Auken, chief executive of the Association of Research and Enlightenment of Edgar Cayce, who often conducts tours at the Pyramids and other sites in Egypt. (photo courtesy of the Edgar Cayce Foundation)

sible Masonic and "new world order" objectives of his patrons, could be viewed by some as placing Egypt's national security at risk. For as we shall see when we review two events (one, a millennial celebration in December 1999, and the other, a ritual that was allegedly to be performed on November 11, 2011), the mere suspicion that some "Jewish Masonic" groups planned to stage events at the Giza Pyramids sparked dangerous reactions and accusations of plotting against "Islam," which resulted in forcing the Egyptian authorities to cancel both events and even, in November 2011, to call in the army and the riot police to protect the Giza Necropolis from angry Islamist protesters!

Figure 1.6. Hugh Lynn Cayce, who indirectly sponsored Mark Lehner
and, allegedly, Zahi Hawass's education
(photo courtesy of the Edgar Cayce Foundation)

Seen from a Western viewpoint, there is no real problem if certain groups wish to visit the Giza pyramids or any other ancient site on a private basis, perhaps even do harmless rituals if permission is given to them by the authorities in charge of these monuments. As long as no damage is done to the monuments or any desecration, we, too, see no real harm in this. But in the Arab world, and especially

Figure 1.7. Zahi Hawass in 1996

in Egypt, such activity, especially if it involves Freemasonry, is bound to meet with much hostility. We are aware that Zahi Hawass, notwithstanding his obvious support from the Edgar Cayce people, has given permission to many other esoteric and New Age groups to undertake private visits inside the Great Pyramid of Giza and other ancient temples in Upper Egypt. Indeed, Hawass was well aware that—and gave his approval to—the elusive Rosicrucians of the AMORC (Ancient and Mystical Order Rosae Crucis), a worldwide esoteric organization with headquarters in the United States and France, which often comes to Egypt to perform ceremonies, rituals, and probably initiations at ancient sites, especially at the sacred lake in the oasis of Fayoum. Also, as we have seen, members of the Edgar Cayce Foundation, another worldwide organization, which promotes the Cayce readings on Atlantis and ancient Egypt, also are regulars at the Giza Pyramids and other sites in Egypt. And on at least three occasions, between 2004 and 2008, Masonic groups from Britain sponsored by Masonic lodges and the *Freemasonry Today* magazine have been given special permission to have private sessions inside the Great Pyramid as well as temples in Upper Egypt. There is no doubt that Hawass was fully aware of all this and very often would come and meet the groups and even give lectures to them.

Zahi Hawass completed his Ph.D. in Egyptology in 1987 in Pennsylvania and returned to Egypt. As Hugh Lynn had hoped, Hawass was promptly appointed general director of antiquities for the Giza Pyramids on December 31 of that year. The head of the EAO at the time, the direct boss of Hawass, was Ahmed Kadri. Finally, Hawass was now exactly where Hugh Lynn wanted him to be: in control of the Giza Necropolis.

From 1990 to 1991, a direct attempt to find a "secret chamber" under the Sphinx took place using seismographs and also motorized drills. In 1996, radar explorations took place, as well as in 1997 and 1998. Also sonar tests were performed inside the Great Pyramid and in the deep shaft known as the Osiris Shaft, at the back of the Sphinx enclosure. In all these expeditions, the Edgar Cayce Foundation or some of their senior funding members were directly or indirectly involved. Often the main protagonists were two wealthy businessmen, Joseph Schor and Joseph Jahoda (see Bauval, *Secret Chamber,* chapter 10).

AHMED KADRI AND
THE SPHINX CONTROVERSY

Since 1980, the Sphinx of Giza has been undergoing a series of major repairs and restorations, mainly to deal with the alarming surface flaking of the limestone from which the monument was fashioned. There was much controversy as to what caused this, although the main consensus was that the water table had risen, causing a capillary effect on the soft and porous limestone that made up the base of the Sphinx, resulting in the saturation and eventual flaking of the surface. On February 10, 1988, while Ahmed Kadri was enjoying his morning coffee at his office in downtown Cairo, he answered his personal phone to hear the excited voice of an inspector from Giza telling him that the Sphinx was falling apart. Kadri jumped into his car and told his chauffeur to take him to the village of Nazlet El Samman (known to tourists as the Sphinx Village) double quick. Unknown to him, Farouk Hosni (Minister of Culture) and Hawass were already at the Sphinx, with the former clearly very angry at what he saw.

It should be known that Kadri had been one of the Free Officers (also among them were Gamal Abdel Nasser and Anwar Sadat) who, in July 1952, had toppled the monarchy and declared Egypt a republic. As such, Kadri commanded much respect and admiration from his colleagues and friends. Not so, however, from Farouk Hosni, the minister of culture, who disliked him intensely. Hosni wanted to have full control of Egypt's antiquities, and Kadri was in the way. Although a military man at heart, Kadri had joined the EAO in 1962, where he supervised the international efforts to save Nubia's monuments (mainly the temples of Abu Simbel and Philae) during the building of the High Dam and eventually rose through the ranks to become the director general of the EAO in 1982. All was going well for Kadri until 1987 when his archenemy Farouk Hosni was made minister of culture. Kadri, a strong man with a rather calm temperament, nonetheless managed to thwart Hosni's bids to take over the EAO. In this bitter feud between Kadri and Hosni, Hawass took the side of the

Figure 1.8. Farouk Hosni, Minister of Culture
under Mubarak from 1987 to 2011 (photo courtesy *Al-Ahram*)

latter, an act of solidarity for which Hosni would always be grateful. Both men then colluded to bring Kadri down.

The opportunity to strike came in late January 1988, following six days of fierce desert winds, which had sandblasted the Sphinx and the nearby pyramids. Known as *khamseen,* these desert sandstorms cause havoc in Cairo, turning the sky a strange ginger color and covering everything with a fine layer of reddish dust. A khamseen can last for several days, driving some Cairo city dwellers into a form of temporary mild madness and bringing to a standstill much of the city's daily commercial activity. The khamseen winds usually come in late March, but in 1988 they arrived early, and the one that hit the Giza area in late January was a particularly violent sandstorm. Whether because of this, or for other unknown reasons (the controversy was never fully settled), two large chunks of limestone from the body of the Sphinx, halfway up its right shoulder and collectively weighing seven hundred pounds, came loose and, at precisely 1:30 p.m. in broad daylight, broke off and came crashing down to the ground in full sight of the hundreds of tourists, hawkers, camel riders, and guards that normally surround this iconic monument at all times of the day.

As they gazed at the surreal spectacle of the Sphinx falling apart, it is said that someone shouted "The Sphinx is dying!" or words to that effect, sending a chilling message across the multilingual groups who, from English to French, Italian, German, and Chinese, whispered this cry. Soon rumors were rife of imaginary terrorist attacks and "aliens" breaking out from inside the bowels of the monument! The most credible and perhaps most damning rumor was that a guard had seen "someone" pushing the loose stones off the shoulder of the Sphinx, but this rumor was quickly quenched by Hawass.

What was a little odd about this whole episode was that, when Hawass was first told of the incident, rather than immediately informing Kadri, who, after all, was head of the EAO, he chose to inform Minister of Culture Farouk Hosni instead. The minister left his office and got to the scene, even before Kadri was given the news. When Kadri did eventually arrive, Hosni openly blamed him for the whole incident. A political furor ensued, resulting in Kadri's dismissal. But was Kadri really to blame or was he framed? Such a thought certainly crossed the mind of the *New York Times* correspondent Alan Cowell who, in the December 14, 1989, issue wrote an article under the headline "Crumbling Sphinx: Was It Sabotage?"

. . . others said the controversy related to the profound personality differences between Culture Minister Hosni and Ahmed Kadri, the former antiquities director, who once oversaw the restoration of the Sphinx and who lost his job when the shoulder fell off last year. Dr. Hani Hilal, a professor of rock engineering at Cairo University, said: "The whole issue is a personal conflict between antiquities officials. There have been far more drastic incidents and nobody paid any attention to them."

Was Cowell implying—as was Hani Hilal—that the incident was a pretext to get rid of Kadri? In any case, with Kadri now out of the way, Farouk Hosni did succeed in extending his direct authority over the EAO. To understand the mental state and forceful personality of Hosni, one has to only read from the English language newspaper in Egypt, the *Al-Ahram Weekly,* when, in 2008, Hosni was nominated for the post of UNESCO's director general.

When Egypt nominated Minister of Culture Farouk Hosni to be UNESCO's next director-general all hell broke loose. Hosni's supporters argued he was uniquely qualified for the job, a man of refined taste, gentle manners and profound culture, a proponent of all the arts, a champion of archaeology and of the theatre, a balletomane and patron of the opera, a lover of literature and devotee of the popular arts. Others decried him as the most corrupt minister in the Cabinet, head of a cabal that specialises in bribes, pointing out that three of his advisers are now in jail, sentenced to 10 years of hard labor after being found guilty of attempting to solicit more than 50 million Egyptian pounds in return for contracts to carry out restoration work. A painter by profession, Hosni is no stranger to criticism. During his 21-year tenure as minister of culture he has been a controversial figure, frequently locked in feuds with the National Democratic Party, Islamist politicians and left-leaning intellectuals. His latest battle, as a candidate for UNESCO's director-general, is being fought on an international front.[4]

Although it was Kadri who had appointed Hawass as director of the Giza Plateau in 1987, Hawass must have realized that his future would be better served if he took the side of Hosni in his feud with Kadri. Yet it must be asked: How could Hawass, who had started as an uncouth village boy from the Delta, befriend a highly sophisticated man such as Farouk Hosni who had spent many years as head of Egypt's cultural attaché in Rome and Paris? Reading between the lines of Cowell's article, the latter obviously suspected foul play in the 1988 incident at the Sphinx.

> The Egyptian authorities have reopened an investigation into what really happened last year when a 700-pound chunk of the Sphinx's shoulder plummeted to the ground. In a nutshell, the question is: Did it fall or was it pushed?
>
> An American visitor identified only as Larry Hunter, whose home address or whereabouts have not been made public, produced a videotape. On it was a taped confession by Ahmed el-Shaer, a guard at the Sphinx, who said he had seen two antiquities officials hammering at the Sphinx's shoulder before the slab fell down. What's more, he said on the tape, he had taken a bribe from high officials to remain silent about what he had seen. . . .

If there was any truth in this, then the implication at the very least was that Kadri had been fired unjustly. Incensed by such accusations, Hosni ordered the setting up of a committee to investigate the question of sabotage. Yet we read further in Cowell's article how Hawass dismissed outright Larry Hunter's videotape.

> "This is a ridiculous story," said Dr. Zahi Hawass, the archaeologist in charge of the Giza area, accused on the videotape of being

part of the cover-up. "Scientific reports prove that the rocks fell because of natural reasons, caused by erosion, rain and salt crystals between the outer rock and the mother rock of the statue."

Later, on his website, Hunter was to make these comments:

> During a trip to Egypt in 1989 I got involved with a story regarding sabotage against the Sphinx's right shoulder, the felling of a 700-pound stone that occurred in February 1988. Dr. Hawass, during the public outrage relating to the accusations being raised against him regarding his involvement in the sabotage, made a public disclosure to the Egyptian press that I made up the story of the sabotage against the Sphinx shoulder stone falling, because he wouldn't let me open a Secret Chamber in the bottom of the Great Pyramid whose existence I had revealed to him.

At any rate, in December 1989 the investigation committee that was set up by Hosni hastily concluded that there had been no sabotage and that the slabs had fallen from natural causes. Two years later, on October 9, 1990, the discredited ex-chief of the EAO, Kadri, suddenly died in Pittsburgh at the age of fifty-nine, and the whole affair was forgotten. Be that as it may, the fact remains that from the very moment Kadri was fired, a strong and lasting relationship developed between Hawass and Hosni, with Hawass gradually becoming the minister's most trusted adviser, and not just in matters of archaeology. It was a rather unlikely friendship to say the least—one might even say it was an unholy one, looking at it now in hindsight.

UNHOLY TRINITY
Hawass, Hosni, Mubarak

Farouk Hosni was a well-known artist with sophisticated and delicate tastes. Being unmarried at the mature age of fifty in an Arab culture,

Figure 1.9. Suzanne Mubarak, Egypt's ex–First Lady
(photo courtesy *Al-Ahram*)

Hosni's private life was looked upon with suspicion, especially as he was never seen with any intimate women partner. He did, however, have one close platonic female friend in the person of Mrs. Suzanne Mubarak, Egypt's First Lady.*

This friendship went far back to when Hosni was still a cultural attaché in Rome. Whenever Mrs. Mubarak visited Rome for a shopping spree, she relied on Hosni's artistic taste to show her around and help her choose fashionable outfits.†

In Egypt, Mrs. Mubarak's interest and appetite in antiquities had

---

*During the Tahrir Revolution of January 25, 2011, Farouk Hosni was removed from his post when President Mubarak reshuffled the Cabinet on January 30, 2011.
†In a televised interview on March 12, 2012, Farouk Hosni bluntly denied he was the "pet" of ex-First Lady Suzanne Mubarak. But the historical evidence indicates that they were close beyond normal protocol, and that Farouk Hosni was her "protégé."

become common gossip. It was said, for example, that she had asked Hosni that no new discovery should be announced before she herself had been given the opportunity to ascertain if there were any items to her liking. With such omnipotent backing, Hosni, and now also Hawass as part of this cabal, had full and unchallenged control of the world's vastest legacy of antiquities. As one Egyptian archaeologist, who is worth quoting in full because his views reflect those of nearly all Egyptian archaeologists and Egyptologists but who prefers to remain anonymous, put it:

> Two men control all archaeological work in Egypt: the first is the head of Egypt's Supreme Council of Antiquities, Zahi Hawass; the second is Egyptian Minister of Culture . . . Farouk Hosni . . . These two men keep telling us Egyptian archaeologists that the budget is too small to finance any of the projects for which we file applications. But we all know that our archaeology and monuments bring in more foreign currency than the Suez Canal, so where is all that money going? The Egyptian museum in Cairo takes in sums most people can't even imagine, so where is it all going? UNESCO gave millions to save our monuments, where did it all go? Many ancient Egypt exhibitions travel around the world, collecting millions every year. The government keeps saying the money is for restoration and conservation but we see nothing being done, while many of our monuments are falling to pieces—is it because Hawass and Hosni are stealing the restoration money? Corruption presently rules Egyptian archaeology, as can be seen in the employment of people who are not professionals in our field, while most archaeology graduates are out of work and abandon their careers because they can see that those two men won't allow them to work in their beloved field, and that even if an Egyptian archaeologist gets to work in his field, his salary will not even be enough for him to ride the bus to work. The sad truth is that the budget for archaeological projects is small because the money ends

up in the pockets of powerful players, headed by these two men.

We keep seeing Hawass on TV every day, presenting international shows and meeting beautiful women in his office, but if any Egyptian archaeologist tries to see him or complain about his policies, the security guards outside his office know exactly how to deal with them. Egyptian archaeologists are complaining every day, but the media hear only one voice: Zahi Hawass, talking about our great civilization on TV while we suffer injustice. If you go to his office, you'll see what is really important to him, i.e. you'll see how much he loves women. That's the truth, I saw eight secretaries (all of them young girls) working in his office. We Egyptian archaeologists know this reality, but others treat him as if he was one of the greatest archaeologists in the world. One day it will all be revealed, and shame will cover them like the desert once covered the Sphinx. Another situation under everyone's eyes is: who excavates in Egypt today? It is of course those who can pay more, many of them Americans who deal directly with Zahi Hawass, while scientists of other nationalities have to pay more and mention Hawass's name when writing up their work. Egyptian archaeologists are mostly employed as observers, it is nearly impossible to see Egyptians actually conducting an excavation today. That would need Zahi's permission, and he will forbid it if he can. How many Egyptians study archaeology at the universities? Well, about 250 students graduate every year from the different departments of the faculty at Cairo University, so by now there must be thousands, but because of the Supreme Council's bad politics and corruption, most of them end up staying at home or changing careers to survive, as they watch graduates from fields unrelated to archaeology take their positions with the approval of Zahi Hawass and Farouk Hosni.

Looking at the lighter side of all this, the tale of Farouk Hosni is reminiscent of something straight out of *A Thousand and One Nights*: A young abstract painter, shy and sensitive, somehow finds himself in the inner court of the caliph's (Mubarak's) palace, quickly wins the favors of this oriental oligarch's wife, and eventually rises to become the all-powerful vizier and cultural representative of the caliphate. At the height of his career, the vizier remembers how a young man from the Delta (Hawass) once stood by him against his hated rival (Kadri), and so repays him by making him Keeper of the Sacred Sites (the pyramids and the Sphinx), the most coveted and prestigious cultural post in the realm.

The reality, however, is far less romantic: the friendship between Hosni, Hawass, and Suzanne Mubarak, according to many legal complaints now lodged with Egypt's attorney general, resulted in the alleged siphoning or diverting of funds originally meant for archaeological facilities and restoration, as well as an upsurge in international black markets, as attested now by Interpol and other agencies involved in the prevention of antiquities trafficking.

GADDAFI AND THE MISSING STATUES

One incident is definitely worth reporting here and now, for it involved no other than the late deposed president of Libya, Muammar Gaddafi.

To replace Kadri at the EAO, Hosni chose Mohammed Abdel Halim Nur el-Din, a soft-spoken and highly respected archaeologist who had received his formal education in Germany. But he, too, was not to last very long. We shall encounter Nur el-Din again in a later chapter when we review the huge scandal and controversy that surrounded the discovery of a "door" at the end of a shaft inside the Great Pyramid by the German explorer and engineer Rudolf Gantenbrink. At any rate, Nur el-Din was replaced by Sayed Tawfik, who also lasted only a few months. Finally in early 1990 Mohammed Ibrahim Bakr was appointed chairman of the EAO and so began, from this moment onward, an open feud—this time between Bakr and Hawass. This feud was to last many years, for Hawass was now himself vying for total control of the Giza Pyramids and ultimately, as we shall see, of *all* the antiquities in Egypt.

Figure 1.10. Mohammed Ibrahim Bakr, General Director of the Egyptian Antiquities Organization (EAO), 1990 to 1993, and archenemy of Zahi Hawass (photo courtesy of Caroline Davies)

That there was no love lost between Hawass and Bakr is putting it very mildly. After many open clashes between them in the press, the crunch came in the spring of 1993 during a state visit by Muammar Gaddafi. A nightmare scenario was about to unfold for both men.

This very strange incident—the second in less than five years—that occurred at the Great Sphinx in January 1993 has not yet been fully resolved or, for that matter, properly understood. On January 19, a cavalcade of black limousines, escorted by motorized police with sirens wailing and red lights flashing, arrived at the entrance of the Giza Necropolis and made its way to the Sphinx. There, between the paws of the huge lion-bodied monument, were displayed several small statues on a small table. These statues, dated to the time of the pyramid builders, had only been found a few months before and were deemed priceless (the items were from the Fifth Dynasty, a period during which many of the pyramids at Abusir and Saqqara were constructed). To everyone's surprise, the man who emerged from the leading car was Libya's then president Muammar Gaddafi, accompanied by none other than Farouk Hosni. They were warmly greeted by Hawass, obviously ready for this occasion, seeing that he was wearing a fine suit and silk tie. What was most bizarre about this event was that Mohammed Bakr, the chairman of the EAO, was not present. Indeed, Bakr apparently had not been informed of this stately visit—neither by Hawass nor by Hosni—as proper protocol, or at the very least good manners, required.

So when Bakr heard the news over the radio, he jumped into his car and angrily hurried to the Giza Plateau. There was the typical pandemonium with guards and inspectors rushing left and right in obvious excitement. The confused and angry Bakr was met by a very flushed Hawass who informed him that one of the ancient and priceless statues had "disappeared!" This thirty-centimeter-high statue depicted a Fifth Dynasty pharaoh standing upright and wearing a royal wig on his head. It was an extremely rare and valuable item, wonderfully preserved with its original paint. Needless to say, Bakr was livid, more so because just a few weeks before, on November 7, 1992, he had seen a photograph in a glossy magazine of Hawass standing next to Omar Sharif, the latter holding in his hands the very same statue that had now apparently disappeared. Upon seeing this photograph, Bakr had given strict instructions to Hawass to never again remove a statue or other important artifacts from the Giza storeroom without written permission from him. Yet today, Hawass had blatantly ignored Bakr's orders and had instructed the Giza storeroom to bring this statue, along with thirteen other statues, which had also been discovered recently, to be displayed at the foot of the Sphinx for the apparently unannounced visit by Muammar Gaddafi. Bakr did the right thing to assert his authority: he immediately suspended Hawass from his post at Giza and then requested that a committee be formed to investigate this bizarre incident.

However, Hosni, clearly in a barefaced act of cronyism, demanded both a speedy end to the committee's investigation and that Hawass be forthwith reinstated at Giza. The local media, which was largely controlled by Hosni, remained silent; but the *Al Wafd* newspaper, known to be openly critical of the government, made its outrage known with these comments.

> Egyptian antiquities . . . as it seems, have become a private possession for employers and officials, whose responsibility [should be] to save these antiquities and protect them. The Egyptian public knew nothing of what has taken place [as] the Ministry of Culture has kept the matter secret . . . fearing that it might reach the press . . . [However] after the decision by the Chairman of Antiquities Organization [Dr. Bakr] . . . to transfer the Giza Antiquities Director, Dr. Zahi Hawass, to work at the areas of Cairo and Matariya antiquities, the decision number 730 on 20/3/1993, was followed by another decision number 731 of the same date to establish a stock-taking committee for the pyramid area antiquities store, details have broken out which represent a shameful disgrace and a crime against Egypt. These details almost revealed and directly made known . . . [the names of] those whose wills combine to insult Egypt and neglect its antiquities' treasure. They remain in complete protection (secret?) by some of those who have authority.[5]

According to the report of the investigation committee, Mrs. Amal Samuel, the antiquities inspector responsible for the Giza storeroom, confirmed that her boss, Hawass, on January 19, 1993, had sent her a note written in English asking that some items be taken out of the storeroom, which included the statue that disappeared. She duly carried out Hawass's instructions. Closer investigation revealed that twelve other ancient artifacts had also mysteriously disappeared from the storeroom at Giza since Hawass had been appointed director general of the pyramids. The report furthermore revealed that Hawass, on February 24, 1992, had taken out of the storeroom a statue labeled No. 188, which had not yet been returned. More damning was the fact that all these removals from the Giza storeroom were done without any authorization, written or otherwise, from Bakr, and therefore constituted, according to the investigation committee, a criminal act. Bakr insisted that the committee continue its investigations until it arrived at a definitive conclusion, and he also vehemently opposed Hosni's call for the reinstatement of Hawass at Giza.

On his part, Hosni took this as a personal affront—and also perhaps as a golden opportunity—to get rid of Bakr by demanding his resignation. Furthermore, and to everyone's bemusement, he ordered Hawass to return to his post at Giza. After much deliberation and many ugly scenes at the EAO and at the Ministry of Culture, Bakr yielded to the huge pressure put on him by Hosni (and probably by Suzanne Mubarak) and finally handed in his resignation at the end of March 1993. Hosni's muscle-flexing did not stop here: He somehow coaxed the prime minister to issue a new decree that made him, Hosni, the de facto chairman of the EAO—a very coveted position that five years ago Kadri had prevented Hosni from occupying. From that point on, all new heads of the EAO received the lesser title of secretary general instead of chairman as was previously the case.

With Hosni now in full control of antiquities, Bakr's successor, Abdel Halim Nur el-Din, who was reappointed as secretary general of the EAO but now had limited authority, had no other option but to carry out Hosni's instructions to put an end to the investigating committee's pursuit of Hawass's role in the missing statue. Nur el-Din also had to reluctantly agree to the return of Hawass as director general of Giza. There was one more thing that Hosni had to ensure for the good continuation of the EAO: before the investigating committee was dissolved, it hastily arrived (not surprisingly) at the conclusion that Hawass was in no way to blame for the disappearances of the statue and various other ancient artifacts from the Giza storeroom. The committee also determined that Mrs. Amal Samuel, the inspector in charge of the storeroom, had been negligent and so was made to pay a fine of 300 Egyptian pounds (about $60)—even though her only crime was to obey Hawass's instructions! As for the missing statue, antiquities valuators estimated its market worth at $5 million—a very lucrative deal for whoever it was that had made the statue "disappear." Some believe it may perhaps turn up one day in Gaddafi's personal collection in Tripoli.

1993: YEAR OF THE MYSTERY DOOR AND BAKR'S RESIGNATION

Meanwhile, unknown to everyone during this turbulent month of March 1993, an archaeological time bomb was about to explode. A daring exploration was taking place inside the Great Pyramid in what can be best termed "semisecrecy." Deep within an unexplored shaft in the Great Pyramid, a tiny machine that resembled a miniature tank with tracks, named Upuaut II (Opener of the Way), after the Egyptian jackal god, had climbed some fifty meters into the narrow southern shaft of the Queen's Chamber and was reaching the end of its "journey into the unknown."

With its small headlights illuminating the tenebrous tunnel and its mini-video camera rolling, it was about to record something that would soon send a shock wave around the world. At the other end of the shaft inside the so-called Queen's Chamber was Rudolf Gantenbrink, a young German man, rather handsome in a rugged sort of way, seated in front of a TV monitor. He was delicately manipulating the two joysticks of the control console of the robot, his gaze locked on the color images that were being sent deep from inside the shaft. His two colleagues, also Germans, sensed his excitement and rushed to look at the images displayed on the monitor. Gantenbrink pressed the stop button on the console. The robot halted, its beams shining on what appeared to be a

Figure 1.11. Gantenbrink's robot, Upuaut II, which was used to explore the shafts in the Great Pyramid in March 1993

small trapdoor with two copper handles. He wasn't sure whether he felt like laughing or crying. He could hardly believe his eyes. *A door?* The robot was filming a small secret door at the end of the shaft! The date: March 22, 1993. The time: 11:05.

Later, in chapter 6, we cover in much greater detail this amazing story and the huge repercussions it had for all those involved, as well as how this apparently great archaeological discovery was to be masterminded into a huge media stunt by Hawass and a giant American media conglomerate involving hundreds of millions of dollars.

As was the case with the missing statue—and before that Kadri and the falling blocks at the Sphinx—Bakr was again not informed of this discovery, at least not until several weeks after the event. And when he did find out, he lashed out at the German team and at Hawass, even going so far as to claim it was all a hoax. In the English language *Egyptian Gazette* of April 28, 1993, under this amazing

Figure 1.12. Upuaut II at the British Museum

headline "German Scientist's Claim a Hoax," Bakr was quoted saying that "the EAO never granted its approval to this German." Bakr seemed perplexed as to how "this German" (apparently even at this stage Bakr didn't know the German's name) managed to conduct such an important exploration in the Great Pyramid without him knowing of it, let alone without his approval. What Bakr did not know—but surely suspected now—was that Hawass had a hand in this. But Bakr's protests yet again went unheeded and Hawass, as always, thus got off the hook. It was amid this confusion that Bakr was forced to hand in his resignation in late June 1993, and Hawass returned to his post at the EAO with a hero's welcome. Bakr meekly took up his old teaching post at Zagazig University in the Delta, but not before, in a brief surge of bravado, he lashed out one last time at his tormentors. What follows is an extract of Bakr's most revealing interview in *Al-Ahram Arabic Daily* as reported in the *Times* (London) by Christopher Walker in July 1993.

[Mohammed] Ibrahim Bakr, the expert removed from his post as chief of Egypt's vast archaeological heritage three weeks ago, has accused an official "mafia" of controlling the Giza pyramids plateau for the last twenty years. Dr. Bakr, who is highly respected among international Egyptologists, claimed that the plateau on the outskirts of Cairo has suffered widespread theft of antiquities and widespread financial malpractices which the "mafia" wanted hushed up. "This was the main issue," Dr. Bakr said of his resignation. "I wanted these practices reported to the prosecution authorities, but my request was turned down." In an interview with the *Al-Ahram*, Bakr disclosed that his departure came after personal differences with Farouk Hosni, the Culture Minister. . . . Dr. Bakr claimed angrily that "certain people" whom he did not identify acted as if the Giza plateau . . . was their private property. "The exploitation ranged from entrance fees paid by visitors to documentaries film which they shot at Giza and sold abroad. Lately they even refused to register newly discovered antiquities."

A few years later, in early 1995, Bakr's daughter was killed by a hit-and-run motorist. Perhaps jolted by this tragedy, another surge of bravado prompted Bakr to come out again with guns blazing at the mafia—a rather courageous act (some may even say foolhardy in those dangerous days of the Mubarak regime).

This time around, however, Hawass clearly saw Bakr's attack being directed personally at him, and so Hawass immediately took a defensive position, turning the argument around and bluntly accusing Bakr of "jealousy" and "political infightings." Here are some extracts from an article that appeared in the *Middle East Times* of February 19 to 25, 1995, with the headline "Besieged pyramids' boss bites back against critics."

General Director of the Giza Pyramids . . . Dr. Zahi Hawass, has responded to criticism of corruption and lack of accountability

ST TIMES | 19 - 25 FEBRUARY 1995

Any old iron? Former EAO chief Ibrahim Bakr (left) and Zahi Hawass do not see eye to eye.

Besieged Pyramids' boss

Figure 1.13. From the *Middle East Times*, Mohammed Ibrahim Bakr (left) and Zahi Hawass (photo courtesy *Middle East Times*)

within the Egyptian Antiquities Organization (EAO): "No foreigners or other experts are stealing antiquities; it's all the work of smugglers . . . talk of a mafia within the organization is not true." He told the *Middle East Times* from his on-site office at the Giza pyramids. . . . Hawass says repeated efforts to deal with the theft were ignored by previous EAO chiefs. [Mohammed] Ibrahim Bakr was forced to resign in June 1993 following a long speech in parliament by independent deputy Galal Gharib who listed charges of malpractices and negligence.

Bakr says he was the victim of a campaign engineered to have him removed because of his attempt to rid the EAO of what he termed "the rotten apples." As EAO chief, Bakr claimed he had discovered that government employees were involved in tomb robbing at the Pyramids plateau that EAO officials were siphoning off ticket revenues, and tendering out restoration projects to favored companies for commission money.

[But Hawass says] "This is my life, my child, a part of me—how could any of us steal it?" Something of a maverick figure, Hawass says he is now free to achieve things at the Pyramids without political infighting and jealousies of the past.

It is common knowledge in Egypt that before January 25, 2011, the start of the Tahrir Revolution, the Egyptian press was almost totally controlled by the minister of culture Farouk Hosni, and the now-vilified and dismantled National Democratic Party had given its full backing and blessing to Hawass. So the beleaguered Bakr had absolutely no chance for fair treatment in the media. He became a mere voice in the wilderness and eventually gave up his fight against the alleged "mafia." In March 1995, we managed to tracked Bakr at his private residence and asked him on the telephone what he really meant by the claims he made in the press in 1993 and more recently in February 1995. Bakr's bravado, however, seemed to have withered away. Obviously shaken and perhaps even frightened, Bakr amazingly feigned a lapse of memory about the accusations against Hawass and Hosni he had made to the media.[6]

But who or what exactly was this alleged "powerful mafia" that Bakr alluded to but did not identify by name? Indeed, how and why had matters reached such a confusing and appalling state? And why was Bakr so reluctant now to speak out? An uneasy silence fell over the Giza Pyramids only to be broken by the (rather frequent) appearances of Hawass on television channels in America and all over the world. The new boss of the Giza Pyramids was now being groomed into a real-life Indiana Jones celebrity for big bucks, TV documentaries, and specials. Wearing a Stetson hat and denim shirt, he was frequently seen on the History Channel, the Discovery Channel, the National Geographic Channel, Fox TV, CNN, and many other TV channels around the globe. It seemed that the world could not get enough of Hawass. He was portrayed by the media as the world's most famous Egyptologist, the voice of modern Egypt, and the defender of Egyptian culture and prestige. All this media attention soon turned Hawass into a household name. Very early on, he had realized and appreciated the power of the press and especially television, as explained in "Tomb Yields Many Mysteries, but no Mummy" by Michael Slackman (*New York Times,* June 28, 2006).

> . . . in modern Egypt the master of ceremonies, the only man allowed to pull back the curtain for the audience, is Dr. Zahi Hawass, the General Secretary of the Supreme Council of Antiquities. . . . Dr. Hawass is fiercely protective of Egypt's past—and of his monopoly on revealing it to the world. When a tomb is discovered, Dr. Hawass insists that he be the first inside as television cameras roll.

Now, as the undisputed "king of the pyramids" and the world's most prestigious, most mysterious, and most well-known archaeological site, Hawass had the international media stumbling over each other outside his office to get an interview with him or his permission for a TV documentary and, more lucratively still, get an exclusive on new "discoveries." Riding high on this wave of publicity and clearly enjoying his celebrity status akin to a movie star, the once uncouth and clumsy young man from the rural Delta village began to believe in his "image" fostered by the media. Worse, under the protection of Hosni and the Mubaraks, Hawass began to believe he was infallible. As we shall see later, almost all the "discoveries" that Hawass claimed he made were, in fact, made earlier by other Egyptian archaeologists who were too frightened to object to this type of "archaeological plagiarism."

We shall return to Hawass and his iron-fist reign at Giza in a later chapter. But now it is important for our readers to review the history of the EAO and, more important, to understand how and why a person like Hawass managed to get full control of Egypt's antiquities and was able to manipulate events to suit his own agenda and ambitious needs.

2

Out of Darkness

From the height of these pyramids forty centuries look down upon you.

Napoleon Bonaparte addressing his soldiers
before the "Battle of the Pyramids," July 21, 1798

The nationalist and Islamist forces disfigured Egypt's history and tried their best to make average Egyptians feel ashamed of their past. . . . This was propagated in school curricula and the media, making Egyptian roots . . . a subject of ill repute inside Egypt.

Emad Gad, "Reconsidering Egypt's Identity,"
Al-Ahram Weekly

Before we review the historical events that led to much destruction and desecration of ancient Egypt's legacy, we need first to clear up a cultural and historical confusion that Zahi Hawass, whether unconsciously or deliberately, has instigated. During the past twenty years or so, Hawass, with the help of both the state-controlled media in Egypt and the mogul-controlled media in the United States, had carved a rather gratifying image of himself that extended well outside the boundaries of Egyptology and the traditional role of an antiquities chief. His ego, grossly inflated by the media attention he was receiving as director

general of the Giza Pyramids, prompted him to see himself as a spokesman for the Egyptian people and, more specifically, as the defender
of Egyptian culture, honor, pride, and prestige vis-à-vis the rest of the
world. Much like his hero Gamal Abdel Nasser, who in the 1960s had
claimed to be the voice of the Arabs (*sawt el a'arab*) against their hated
enemies, Israel and Britain (see box), Hawass made himself the voice
of Egypt against some mysterious enemies who, in his view, wanted
to steal Egyptian monuments and insult Egyptian culture. Like Don
Quixote, Hawass was fighting imaginary foes that only existed in his
own imagination. To do this, Hawass, like Nasser before him, needed
to create his own version of reality to suit his political goals—a reality
(more a propaganda, really) that he felt would appeal more to national
pride and Arab self-esteem.

Gamal Abdel Nasser, who was president of Egypt from 1954 to 1969,
was renowned across the Arab world for his passionate speeches
and rhetoric. In the 1950 and 1960s, his sonorous and agitated voice
was constantly heard on the radio by an adoring mass. After the
1956 Suez War, when a British-French-Israeli coalition that attacked
Egypt was repulsed through the intervention of America's President
Eisenhower, Nasser made hay out of this "victory" against the three
enemies (el odwan el thulata), giving Egyptians, and the rest of the
Arab world, a false sense of military strength, which finally led to
catastrophic defeat in the June 1967 war against Israel. The problem with Nasser was that he began to believe in his own rhetoric
and ignored the harsh realities on the ground. He conjured an imaginary Egypt with a perfect socialist system, efficient industries, and
a powerful organized military—whereas the reality was very different, indeed, with a crippled economy, a badly trained and poorly
equipped military, and a deeply corrupt and grossly inefficient public
sector riddled with red tape.

Similarly, Hawass had conjured an imaginary Egyptian Antiquities

Organization, where archaeological sites were efficiently admin-istered and protected, whereas in reality the very opposite took place. Indeed, such bizarre self-deception was finally made obvious to the whole world when, during the January 2011 revolution, wide-spread looting of antiquities took place across Egypt and at the Cairo Museum in Tahrir Square, and Hawass stunned everyone by insisting that little, if anything, had gone missing.

KING TUT TUT TUT

Giving but one example, in September 2002, the National Geographic Channel did a two-hour live broadcast from the Giza Pyramids aired in 141 countries, with Hawass as the star of the show. The program's much-exaggerated title "Secret Chambers Revealed" had been hyped and marketed around the world for months, raising the public's expecta-tion to a state of frenzy about the imminent opening of a "door" leading into a secret chamber in the Great Pyramid. It all turned out, alas, to be a damp squib as there proved to be nothing behind the door other than a dead-end block. Clearly flustered by this fiasco, Hawass had to face the international press—CNN, Fox News, BBC, and Al Jazeera among others—in the banquet hall of the Mena House Oberoi hotel to com-ment on the event. Sweating profusely, Hawass addressed a bemused audience with a bizarre tirade against Jews and other "bad people" who talk against the Egyptians.

This program, which was seen by 141 countries, will tell all the peo-ple about the great Egyptians who built the pyramids. . . . The most beautiful thing of this "door" when I saw it was that I told the lady presenter, I told her that I smell the scent of the Egyptians . . . the importance of the discovery and this completely discards the theory about the pyramid built by slaves [Jews in captivity], because slavery cannot build something genius like building the pyramid, and I will tell the public that everyone who tries to talk against the Egyptians should shut their mouths!*

Hawass's bombastic ways (so typical of Egyptian politicians of the old regime) were brought to attention in a *Sunday Times Magazine* feature article (May 22, 2005) by British journalist Richard Girling titled "King Tut Tut Tut." Here are some excerpts.

"They call him the Pharaoh, the keeper of the pyramids. He rules Egyptology with an iron fist and a censorious tongue. Nobody crosses Zahi Hawass and gets away with it . . . nobody of any standing in Egyptology will come out to help you," said one well-known Egyptologist of his colleagues, "because they'd lose their jobs." Sadly, people are cowering round his ankles . . . Hawass . . . holds the keys to the pyramids, the Valley of the Kings, the Sphinx, Abu Simbel, everything. No Egyptologist gets in without his permission, and few will chance his anger.

You can see why. Hawass is a one-man conflict zone who could start a war in an empty sarcophagus. In 2003, by some accounts (no fact passes unchallenged), Hawass expelled 14 expeditions from the country and, by his own account, denied access to hundreds more. He decides who digs where, and reserves for the SCA [Supreme Council of Antiqties, the new name for the EAO]—in effect, himself—the exclusive right to reveal their findings. Such is the level of paranoia that some archeological teams are scared even of their own success.

"There are people digging out there," says another UK specialist, "who are praying they won't find anything significant. If they do, they know the dig will be shut down until a certain individual arrives to take over. There are artefacts that have been excavated, only to be put back until the certain personage gets round to visit-

---

*Robert Bauval was present at this press conference and filmed the entire bizarre event.

Figure 2.1. Zahi Hawass at a press conference at Cairo's Mena House Hotel, September 2002. "Jews did not build the pyramids!"

ing the site so that he can 'discover' them for himself." But exactly who are these people? Will they talk? Can any of this be proved? No surprise: noses are tapped, papers shuffled, but nobody steps up to the microphone or hands over the evidence. What is certain is that Hawass himself feels no such inhibition. Offenders are characterized as "nuts," "amateurs," or "pyramidiots." To those on the wrong side of his outbursts, this marks him out as a bully. But to supporters he is a hero who has routed the old colonial powers of the English and French, and reclaimed Egypt for the Egyptians.

"If the British want to restore their reputation, they should volunteer to return the Rosetta stone because it is an icon of our Egyptian identity. I don't want to fight anyone now, but if the British Museum doesn't act, we will have to employ a more aggressive approach with the government. . . . The artefacts stolen from Egypt must come back." Bloomsbury may blanch, but this kind of stuff plays well in Cairo. British libel laws make it impossible to repeat much else of what he says. The curator of an internationally famous museum, possessor of another precious artefact that Hawass wants returned, is denounced as a thief. . . . All this, and more, has helped cement Hawass's reputation. Anyone who puts on an Indiana Jones hat, sticks out his jaw and faces the foreigners down is stepping straight into his own legend. . . . His life is an epic struggle of good against evil.

JUMPING ON THE ZIONIST PLOT BANDWAGON

In the Arab world, and particularly in Egypt, shouting "Zionist" (akin to Jew, *Yahud,* or Israeli to most Arabs) is like waving a red cape in front of a virile and aggressive bull. Egypt, after all, has had three wars with Israel—the country founded by Zionists in 1948—two of which, 1948 and 1967, were humiliating defeats for Egyptians. And although a fragile peace treaty has been in force since 1978, the so-called Camp David Treaty, the term *Zionist* in Egypt is almost akin to terrorist. In other words, if one wishes to draw a very negative and detrimental reaction toward a person, then you accuse that person of being a Zionist. Bearing this in mind, this tactic was used more than once by Hawass (as well as by Farouk Hosni) in attempts to discredit opponents and rivals.* When, for example, in 1992 to 1993, the "rogue" Egyptologist John Anthony West and Boston geologist Robert Schoch presented their theory for an older Sphinx, Hawass took personal affront. In an articled titled "Stealing of Egypt's Civilization," Hawass called their scientific investigation "a sort of Zionist penetration" and further stated that West "represents a continuation of this cultural invasion of Egypt's civilization."[1] In the same article, Hawass accused his archenemy Mohammed Bakr of irresponsibility for granting West and Schoch a permit.

The odd thing about all this is that although one can just about comprehend how and why the Egyptian press would revel in all these

---

*As we write these words on September 10, 2011, Egyptian protesters, brought to a frenzy by anti-Israeli slogans and rhetoric, stormed the Israeli Embassy in Cairo, burned its flag and documents, causing the ambassador and his family to flee Egypt.

imaginary Zionist and American plots "against Egypt's civilization," the same cannot be said for the normally much more sober and balanced European and American media, who should have simply ignored such hysterical outbursts and wild accusations by Hawass. Yet this was not always the case. Some foreign journalists seemed to mistake Hawass's political game for passion and bravado, and subsequently supported him in his "campaign," which only ends up fuelling his xenophobic war against Zionists, foreigners, pyramidiots, theorists, and Jews. The angle that the foreign press took, however, was that Hawass and, by extension, Egypt's antiquities and civilization were being attacked by aggressive "New Agers" bent on distorting and manipulating Egypt's historical past and culture to suit their own dark agendas.

Here is what happened: on May 7, 1997, Hawass called an international press conference in Cairo to vent his frustration and to solicit the help of the international media to combat his enemies, namely a group of "pseudo-scientists" (he actually named Robert Bauval, Graham Hancock, and John West) whose "personal attacks through television and other media has recently escalated to the point where it has become threatening" (*New York Times,* May 24, 1997).

Reporters seemingly falling for Hawass's charms, including reporters of the influential *New York Times* and the *Times* (London), took up Hawass's call for a counterattack with gusto. The first media salvo against Hawass's "enemies," as to be expected, came from the English language *Egyptian Gazette* concocted by a rather confused and ill-informed reporter called Mohsen Arichie. Under the weird headline "Nauseating Headache over Great Pyramids' Monster Guard," Arichie made the word *theorists* sound like terrorists in a wild and hysterical tirade.

The ancient Egyptians are probably turning in their tombs following growing calls by some Western and Jewish scientists about the real builders of the Great Pyramid and the world-famous monster, the Sphinx . . . Some of these theorists went so far in their zeal to excavate under and inside the Great Pyramid that they snapped at and insulted Dr. Zahi Hawass, director general of the Giza antiquities when he refused to listen to their lousy suggestions. . . . The Orion-inspired theorists scanned the Sphinx and the Pyramids with a special camera in 1992 and insisted that the extraterrestrial beings left data and secrets of their visit in Egypt . . . the theorists Graham Hancock and a colleague named Robert Bauval made a television movie . . . Hawass was also attacked by unknown theorists in Chicago and South Africa . . . The Minister of Culture Farouk Hosni explained that such ridiculous claims wanted to deprive Egypt of its glorious ancient history. He also mocked an Israeli attempt to attribute the ancient Jews as the real builders of the Great Pyramid and the Sphinx . . . [Hawass] didn't exclude the possibility that the commotion was suggested by Israel after its humiliation . . .[2]

Totally out of character, the London *Sunday Times* joined this counter-attack charade against the New Agers with an article on June 22, 1997, by Steve Negus, the Cairo correspondent, under the banner "Egypt Plagued by New Age Pyramidiots."

As dawn breaks over the Pyramids, chanting New Age worshippers dance naked in the empty desert watched by a few incongruous camel drivers. But other Egyptians are beginning to suspect that a sinister agenda lies behind the increasing numbers of outlandish foreigners who claim to be in search of pharaoh's ancient wisdom. . . . Hawass is particularly incensed by the writings of Robert Bauval, a Belgian architect, and Graham Hancock, British author . . . and John West, an American tour guide, who argue that the pyramids were built by superior beings from Atlantis, extraterrestrials or angels. In response to growing concerns about the activities of the New Agers, Egyptian authorities have vowed a public relations counter attack. "This is piracy," said Farouk Hosni, the Culture Minister. "Our history and our civilization must be respected!"

In 1977, Israeli prime minister Menachem Begin visited Egypt's National Museum in Cairo. Talking to the press, he stated, in a tongue-in-cheek manner, that it was the Jews during their captivity in Egypt who built the Giza pyramids—admittedly a lame Jewish joke, which no one with the most basic knowledge of Egyptology and ancient history should have taken seriously let alone been offended by. The "Jews in captivity built the pyramids" theory had been popular in the late nineteenth century with the Bible-crazed so-called British-Israelites and various British pyramidologists, such as John Taylor, David Davidson, Charles Piazzi Smyth, and, more recently, Peter Lemesurier who saw in the Great Pyramid a prophetic monument designed by Jehovah and built by the sweat of the Israelites during their alleged captivity in Egypt. But this nonsensical theory has long been debunked, and no historian, let alone an Egyptologist, takes such things seriously at all. In any case, Begin, realizing that he may have ruffled some Egyptian feathers, quickly retracted his comment. The matter should have ended there and then had not Hawass and Hosni converted this storm in a teacup into a monumental clash of civilizations, keen to display their patriotism and show their outrage against the Jewish plot supposedly masterminded from the United States. This attention-grabbing political card was to be used more than once over the years by Hawass and Hosni, and recently in the *Asharq Al-awsat* newspaper of June 20, 1999, and also the *Al-Ahram* of January 16, 2001, when it was reported in the latter.

> Dr. Zahi Hawass, the Deputy Minister for Culture, has confirmed the existence of a suspicious campaign on the internet against Egyptian history, the pyramids and the Sphinx. In a telephone conversation Hawass told *Asharq Al-awsat* "a group of half-educated people interested in Jewish history is leading the campaign from the United States, in order to undermine Egyptian civilization." Hawass explained that "the Jewish campaign against Egyptian history started some years ago, on more than one Internet site. It became more

intensified during the last few weeks . . . they published on the net a false news that I have been removed from my position, [although I was] in the United States giving lectures about the pyramids in some American universities. This campaign tries to popularize the idea that the pyramids are "foreign made and the Egyptians had nothing to do with its building." Hawass added: "they accused me of conspiring to close the Great Pyramid, because [they claim] I found inside it evidence indicating that the Hebrews built the pyramids, while the decision was taken by a committee headed by Farouk Hosni, the Minister of Culture . . .

"I have written and lectured in Egypt, Europe and America so much about the claimed story of the relation between the Jews and the Giza pyramids. . . . I am writing this article in response to many great authors who wanted me to respond to the Jews' claims and lies that it was they who built the pyramid. Recently they have used the image of the three Giza pyramids [as] a symbol for one Israeli TV station."[3]

As is often the case with such inflammatory and baseless propaganda, it can sometimes backfire badly—as Hawass and Hosni were to discover to their great dismay in December 1999 on the eve of the millennium. Their image of patriotic and heroic Egyptians giving lip to the Israelis or the American Jewish lobby or the ex-colonial European powers was scuttled by the introduction of yet another fictitious enemy of the Arabs who also wanted to steal the pyramids for its own dark agenda: *the Freemasons*! But as fate would have it, this time the tables turned against Hawass and Hosni. It is a story worth telling here, for it will confirm to the reader why a proper and honest review of Egypt's modern history is essential to understand what went wrong with the Egyptian Antiquities Organization, later the Supreme Council of Antiquities (SCA), over the last twenty-five years and, more important, what needs to be done to put it right—not least the historical confusion caused by the xenophobia and hysteria promulgated by Hawass and

Hosni in the world media.[4] Let us, however, get immediately to the root of this weird matter of Masonic plots, for it needs to be carefully understood before we recount the bizarre story involving Hawass, Hosni, the alleged Jewish Masons, the Giza Pyramids, and the millennium 2000 celebrations at Giza.

MILLENNIUM FEVER AND THE MASONIC-ZIONIST CONSPIRACY AT THE PYRAMIDS

A brief quote from American historian A. Miller sets the scene for us:

> At the center of contemporary Islamism is an anti-Semitic conspiracy theory, the roots of which lead back to Europe at least a century ago. The basic theme, i.e., that the Jews control, or are attempting to control, the world's governments and media, and generally work to promote Zionism, Israel, etc. is well known . . . However, that the Jews are linked to the Freemasons in this conspiracy has gone largely unexplored by observers of Islamism.[5]

It is a curious fact that in the Arab world—or at the very least within the Islamist communities—the term *Freemason* (*Massoony* in Arabic) often implies Zionist and, as such, is vilified as one and the same thing. Indeed the word *Massoony* is also loosely used in relation to various organizations supposedly secretly colluding or working for the Zionists, the Israelis, the CIA, banks, military institutions, the media, educational bodies, foreign governments, and even the United Nations! It is a matter of fact and not of speculation that many Arabs today believe that the Muslim world, and more specifically the Middle East, is threatened by a secretive satanic force masterminded and manipulated by Freemasons and Zionists linked to the United States. This imaginary Masonic-Zionist-cum-global-banking conspiracy theory has its roots in the so-called *The Protocols of the Elders of Zion,* a short document first published in Russia (1903–1935) that purports to unmask a global Zionist-Masonic-banking plot to take over the finance systems of the world with the specific intention of controlling Arab and Muslim countries. When it first appeared, *The Protocols* was initially used for anti-Semitic propaganda in Russia, then later in Nazi Germany; but in recent years, it has served the same purpose in many Arab countries. Long believed to be a hoax, the protocols is nonetheless still widely circulated in the Middle East and regarded as factual. More worrying, as Steven Simon,* assistant director of the International Institute of Strategic Studies, pointed out in the British House of Commons, militant organizations use the text to recruit people.

> The texts . . . are very influential among al-Qaeda types and recruits to the organization, texts that can be found on the Internet or in broadsheets or in bookstores in the Middle East, already postulate a world-wide infidel conspiracy against Islam. The United States may bear the brunt of responsibility, but it is seen as part of a larger challenge, consisting of, depending on what you read, the UN, the EU, NATO and the Freemasons for that matter. As odd as that sounds, they have a prominent role in much of this conspiracy thinking.[6]

In Saudi Arabia, for example, a schoolbook for tenth-grade boys gives lessons on the Zionist movement and includes "a curious blend of wild

---

*Steven Simon is the award-winning coauthor of *The Age of Sacred Terror* and *The Next Attack*. He is the Former Director for Global Issues and Senior Director for Transnational Threats at the National Security Council, and his current work examines the consequences of the American intervention in Iraq, Muslim/non-Muslim relations, and the role of religion in U.S. foreign policy. His expertise is on U.S. security policy in the Middle East and South Asia; Middle East politics; Palestinian-Israeli relations; transatlantic approaches to Islamic activism, terrorism and counterterrorism, and intelligence reform. Simon has previously worked as a Senior Analyst, Middle East and Terrorism, Rand (2003–2006); Adjunct Professor of Middle East Security Studies, Georgetown University (2005–present); Assistant Director of the International Institute for Strategic Studies and Carol Dean Senior Fellow in U.S. Security Studies, International Institute for Strategic Studies (1999–2003), and Director for Global Issues and Senior Director for Transnational Threats, National Security Council (1994–99).

conspiracy theories about Masonic Lodges, Rotary Clubs, and Lions Clubs with anti-Semitic invective. It asserts that the *Protocols of the Elders of Zion* is an authentic document and teaches students that it reveals what Jews really believe."[7] Indeed, the Internet is rife with websites that connect Freemasonry with Zionism and how they allegedly manipulate bodies like the European Economic Community, the British parliament, and even the United Nations—there are even websites that accuse this alleged unholy Jewish-Masonic alliance of being behind the Gulf War, the Afghan invasion, the Iraq War, the oppression of Palestinians in the Gaza Strip, the turmoil in Pakistan, and the current Arab spring! In consideration of this, it can be seen how the following commentaries by Hawass and Hosni, some made as recently as 2009, have added to this dangerous false perception of history. Starting in May 1997, after the international press conference given by Hawass and Hosni calling for a public relations counterattack on the theorists, New Agers, and the Israelis who, in their minds, wanted to rob Egypt's "glorious past," Hosni, in an interview with *Rose al-Yusef* under the banner "Israel Is Robbing the Pyramids as It Is Robbing Palestine," claimed that

> the Israelis do not stop claiming that they built the pyramids, and this is why we need to stand firmly and respond courageously . . . even if it leads to a crisis because those pirates are committing a robbery . . . The Israelis want everything . . . This is the way the Israelis took Palestine . . . Now they use [this method] regarding the big pyramid. These are continuous projects—people come, steal your history and civilization. This proves that Israel has no history or civilization, since those who have history of their own do not need to rob the history of others . . . Israel has many political goals . . . First of all, they steal your civilization and history. Second, they do not have any civilization . . . they do not have a country, and do not deserve a country. This is why they create a country by force.[8]

To which Hawass added the following:

A group of people are making an organized campaign. There are some people pushing them [the Israelis]. . . . These people are waging a big attack against us. I swore two years ago that I would not reveal their names, but I found out that I must mention them because it is becoming a threat . . . Robert Bauval, Graham Hancock and John West . . .[9]

In a television appearance in February 2009, Hawass went well beyond the ethos of his position and, from the wording he used, may as well have been quoting directly from *The Protocols of the Elders of Zion* when he told the interviewer that "for eighteen centuries they [the Jews] were dispersed throughout the world . . . they went to America and took control of its economy . . . they have a plan: Although they are few in number, they control the entire world . . . look at the control they have over America and the media!"[10]

The *Al-Ahram* newspaper is dubbed the *New York Times* of the Arabic world, and is distributed in nearly every major city of the world. It also can be read on the Internet. On April 11, 2012, an article appeared on the front page of *Al-Ahram* regarding the present book with the title "American Book Accuses Hawass and Farouk (Hosni) of Conspiring against Egyptian Antiquities" written by the journalist Ahmed Shahawy. The next day, April 12, also on the front page appeared an article titled "Farouk and Hawass: American Book attributes Egyptian Civilization to the Jews." In that article Hawass also accused Robert Bauval of having parents that were "Belgian Jews" from Alexandria—a claim clearly intended by Hawass and Farouk Hosni to be derogatory. (See: www.ahram.org.eg/The-First/News/142885.aspx)

One would have thought that it would have been very easy for two senior ministers of the Mubarak cabinet to verify the facts before making such rash accusations. Bauval and his parents were baptized

Christians in the churches of Alexandria. And certainly our book, as the reader can clearly attest, does not "attribute Egyptian civilization to the Jews." Indeed we oppose this (in any case defunct) theory on pages 59–61 where we label it in no uncertain terms as a "nonsensical theory." (See: http://myblog.robertbauval.co.uk/2012/04/13/zahi-hawass-and -farouk-hosni-ex-ministers-of-disinformation)

Such a bizarre outburst evoking the Jews, of course, is not the first that Zahi Hawass and Farouk Hosni have made, as we show elsewhere in this book. The irony, however, is that such outbursts may be smoke screens to Hawass's own—and very real—involvement with American Jews—something that in today's Egypt would definitely not go down too well for him. It is well known in academic circles, for example, that Hawass obtained his Ph.D. in America (at the University of Pennsylvania) and that his tutor and one of the "readers" of his Ph.D. thesis was David Silverman who is Jewish (the other two readers were David O'Connor and William Kelly Simpson). Indeed, after Hawass returned to Egypt and became a senior official in the Supreme Council of Antiquities, he was instrumental in getting Silverman and his university archaeological concessions in Egypt. Hawass also coauthored a book with Silverman and collaborated with him on many other book projects. (See: www.passportmagazine.com/businessclass/DrDavidSilverman 1079.php)

We also have shown in this book that Hawass collaborated with the Edgar Cayce Foundation of America and helped them do archaeological research in Egypt and at the Pyramids and Sphinx, with the principal funders for these projects being Joseph Jahoda and (the late) Joseph Schor, two very prominent Jewish-American businessmen.

Although we are not of the Jewish faith (Bauval is Christian and Osman is Muslim), we nonetheless wish to make clear that we do not harbor any anti-Semitic sentiments whatsoever. On the other hand, the reader may wonder what Zahi Hawass is up to by attacking his

opponents with the (often false) claim that they are Jews. We may
also wonder about Hawass's Ph.D. thesis, and how it was written
and evaluated.

Blinded by his celebrity status and his own inflated ego, Hawass
took off the white gloves and began "fighting" (to use his own word)
the Jews and the foreigners, past and present, who "exploited" Egypt's
antiquities and "perverted" Egyptian culture and happily stirred the pot
of anti-Western and anti-Semitic sentiment in Egypt that is best left
undisturbed. Also starting in 2002, when he finally became chairman
of the SCA (Supreme Council of Antiquities), Hawass began a systematic campaign against various foreign museums, demanding the return
of Egyptian antiquities, which, he claimed, were "stolen" or "illegally"
taken out of Egypt. He was particularly aggressive toward the British
Museum and the Berlin Museum where the two most well-known icons
of ancient Egypt are displayed: the Rosetta stone and the sculpted head
of Nefertiti. The curators of these museums, needless to say, were not
amused, especially when Hawass insinuated that their museums were
"buying stolen antiquities."

THE BROTHERHOOD AND THE PYRAMID

In December 1999, amid heated accusations of an alleged Zionist-
Masonic plot, the Egyptian government cancelled part of the planned
millennium celebrations at the Giza Pyramids by Zahi Hawass and
Farouk Hosni, which entailed the placing of a golden capstone on
top of the Great Pyramid at midnight on December 31. The event
had been so hyped and publicized in the international media that its
cancellation, especially for the bizarre reasons given, caused an even
bigger media reaction and put the first dark stain on Hawass's and
Hosni's characters.

The circumstances leading to this huge fiasco, oddly enough, have

Figure 2.2. Ex-President Hosni Mubarak
(photo courtesy *Al-Ahram*)

their origins in Paris, France. On May 14, 1998, a rather curious ceremony, which on the face of it had odd Masonic-Zionist symbolism, took
place at the Place de la Concorde and entailed placing a golden capstone
on top of the ancient Egyptian obelisk of Ramses II, which has stood
since 1836 in the center of this iconic square of the French capital. The
event coincided with the official visit to Paris of Egypt's then President
Hosni Mubarak, who had been personally invited by French president
Jacques Chirac.

Present at the ceremony were many senior officials of Egypt and
France, including the minister of culture, Farouk Hosni; antiquities
chairman, Ali Gaballah; and the Egyptian ambassador to France. The

timing for this strange ceremony was peculiar indeed, to say the very least, for on May 14, 1998, huge celebrations were also taking place in Israel for the fiftieth-year jubilee of the creation of the State of Israel. Similar celebrations were also taking place in many other cities of the world where large Jewish communities exist, such as London, Paris, and New York. It was during this ceremony that Hosni announced to the media that a similar event, but on a much larger scale, would take place in Egypt on the night of the millennium on December 31, 1999—namely the placing of a golden *capstone* on the top of the Great Pyramid of Giza: "We cannot rebuild the pyramids stone by stone," said Hosni, "so we have chosen a symbolic event like the ancient Egyptians did when they used to cap obelisks like what the French did at the Place de la Concorde."

In October 1998, Hosni further announced that the famous French composer Jean Michel Jarre had been commissioned to organize this millennial event at Giza. Accordingly, the official Egyptian Tourist Authorities announced that Jarre would compose a musical opera called *The Twelve Dreams of the Sun* for the sum of $10 million and that

> [a]t midnight a helicopter will fly into the site and, hovering in a starburst of lasers and spotlights, will place a gigantic gilded capstone atop the Great Pyramid—all to the accompaniment of what is expected to be an unprecedented Jarre crescendo of electronic music. The gold cap, approximately 28 feet high (about the size of a two-story house) is being especially constructed to protect the pyramid structure. In place, it will catch the first light of the new millennium as the sun rises over Egypt. Capping pyramids with gold and timing important events to the setting and rising sun are very much part of the ancient Egyptian pharaonic tradition, making this piece of Jarre theatre particularly meaningful.[11]

Let us note in passing that in July 1989, Jean Michel Jarre had also been commissioned by Jacques Chirac to organize a similar allegedly

"Masonic" event in Paris for the bicentennial of the French Revolution. For this event, Jarre raised a huge metal-framed pyramid in front of the Grande Arche de la Fraternité (Grand Arch of the Brotherhood) at La Defense in the western end of the so-called Historical Axis, which includes the famous Champs-Élysées, and projected curious occult symbols on the adjacent building with laser lights. Let us also note that a few years later another show by Jarre took place at London's Canary Wharf where the centerpiece was the glowing glass pyramid on top of a skyscraper apparently having the same geometrical proportions as the Great Pyramid of Giza (which is also the same for the glass pyramid in the main courtyard of the Louvre Museum in Paris). As usual, Hawass claimed that the original idea for the millennium ceremony at Giza was his own and proudly announced to the Egyptian press that before the May 1998 ceremony in Paris he had unearthed two ancient limestone blocks in Abusir near Giza, which contained inscriptions and drawings depicting workers moving a capstone for a royal pyramid amid scenes of dancing and celebrations.

Apparently inspired by this, Hawass suddenly had the brainstorm that Egypt should do the same at the Great Pyramid (whose capstone is missing) to celebrate the millennium. At first, three million people were scheduled to attend the event free of charge, but the Egyptian authorities put a limit of 250,000 for security reasons. A massive international promotional campaign was launched in early 1999, and construction was started for a huge stage overlooking the Great Pyramid for VIP guests. All was apparently going according to plan until late September 1999 when senior members of the Egyptian parliament began to complain of the huge costs involved and also that the millennium celebrations would coincide with the Islamic month of Ramadan. Their collective anger was published in the English language *Al-Ahram Weekly* of June 3 to 9, 1999, under the banner "MPs Blast Millennium Party."

Shortly after this, we got involved in this affair. It so happened that during 1999, we had been busy writing a book, *Secret Chamber*, due for publication in November that same year. The opening chapter of the book reviewed the planned celebrations at Giza and raised some pertinent questions as to a possible more occult motive behind this event. As odd as it may seem there was a rather blatant "Masonic" symbolism about this whole curious affair—whether it was deliberate or not. One of the images that Jean Michel Jarre had proposed to project on the Great Pyramid using laser lights was a giant eye, thus creating "the eye in the pyramid" symbol well known to be the supreme symbol of the Freemasons. Furthermore, having a golden capstone hovering over the Great Pyramid at the same time would clearly evoke the great seal of the United States as depicted on the U.S. one dollar bill, which some claim to be of Masonic origins. We were convinced that this kind of symbolism using the Great Pyramid on the night of the millennium would surely be regarded as flaunting the Masonic vision, intentionally or not, in the most extravagant manner. Dozens of international TV networks were going to be filming the event live, which would also be the subject of front-page news in newspapers and in glossy weeklies such as *Hello!, Paris Match, Newsweek,* and the like. In other words, the Masonic supreme symbol would get massive international coverage free of charge thanks to Hawass and Hosni. We felt compelled to warn the Egyptian journalists of this potential public relations fiasco if the Egyptian authorities went ahead with it.* In November 1999, we wrote about our concerns to several newspapers and magazines, including *Asharq Al-awsat, Akhbar al-Adab, Al Shaab,* and *Al Arab.* We also faxed extracts of our book *Secret Chamber* to Sekina Fu'ad, a respected member of the Egyptian Parliament Upper House and a well-known columnist at the *Al-Ahram Daily.* Fu'ad published an article in *Al-Ahram* on December 2, 1999, under the banner "Why Are the Egyptians Angry about the Capstone?"

---

*A few months before the millennium Robert Bauval had met in Cairo, at the Nile Hilton, two Egyptian journalists, Samir Refaat and Walid Wissa, both of whom had written articles on Freemasonry in Egypt before it was banned in 1964. Oddly, both men did not agree that the symbolism used for the millennium at Giza would be seen as evoking Masonic ideas, even though it may have been unintentional.

The placing of a golden top on the Great Pyramid is against the laws of protecting antiquities and contrary to historical facts. While the golden top for the pyramid represents a Masonic symbol, the Great Pyramid never had such a top. It is clear now that the idea of placing a golden pyramidion above the Great Pyramid of Giza was an old idea that started in the thirties. At the same time they talk about discovering a secret chamber inside Khufu's pyramid which, according to their fictitious beliefs, includes secrets of Atlantis knowledge and evidence that they built Egyptian civilization. Pharaonic Egyptian beliefs are at the root of all human understanding and it is very easy to understand. During our meeting with Mr. Farouk Hosni, the minister of culture, last Tuesday (November 30, 1999) at the cultural committee of Magles El Shura [the Upper House of the Egyptian parliament] he explained why he has decided to place the golden top on the pyramid. But I am asking for this event to be reviewed again. The golden top should not be placed on the pyramid unless a specialized committee decided that. Egypt has a great history and an ancient civilization and it is not possible for one man to take a serious decision like this on his own. In Germany it took the parliament a whole year to decide on building a fence around the previous Nazi building, although it is only one century old. Yesterday it was published that Dr. Zahi Hawass has challenged his opponents who deny that the Great Pyramid originally had a golden top, into a televised discussion on the subject. I believe Egyptian Egyptologists will accept the challenge providing it is transmitted directly on the air—This way we would be able to know the truth from both sides of the argument.

The debate about the capstone escalated and eventually took a turn for the worse when accusations of a Zionist-Masonic plot began to appear on the front pages of the radical Egyptian newspaper *Al Shaab* (The People), which denounced the organizers, namely Hosni and Hawass, and claimed they were behind the scam.[12] Other newspapers joined the accusations,[13] as well as previous SCA chairmen and senior personnel, such as Abdel Halim Nur el-Din, who had been steamrolled out of office by Hawass and Hosni. The controversy reached a peak in early December 1999, and Hawass and Hosni opted for a face-saving escape route by deferring the decision and thus the responsibility to a "scientific committee." Hawass then told the press, "If we find out that putting this capstone will hurt the pyramid, then we will not do it." But as some informed observers rightly pointed out, a lightweight metal-framed and hollow capstone placed on the top of the six-million-ton pyramid would be like putting a flea on an elephant's back. Hosni was more honest: at the eleventh hour he admitted that there was no real danger to the pyramid and that public outrage over the Masonic and Zionist implications of placing the golden capstone had led to scrapping the event, but the rest of the show would go on as planned.

> The high-ranking committee, consisting of the Remote Sensing Authority, the Architectural Department of the Ministry of Defence and geologists, engineers and archaeologists, have carried out in-depth technical, scientific and archaeological research and assured us that the plan is feasible. The decision not to carry out this short but crucial episode was considered necessary in order to put an end to all the talk about the celebration by people who want to diminish the role of Egypt . . .*

It has to be said in all fairness that accusations of Masonic and/or Zionist and/or Jewish manipulations backed by America are not uncom-

---

*Ironically on the night of December 31, a thick fog settled over the Great Pyramid, which would have made it impossible for the helicopter to lower the capstone on its summit. There was an almighty mess at the entrance of the site, as hundreds of cars, taxis, and coaches made their way to the show. Not being able to cope with the huge influx of vehicles and pedestrians, the police simply opened the ticket gates, and the people literally stampeded inside! Jean Michel Jarre did, however, manage to project his images on the Giza Pyramids including "eyes" until they, too, were engulfed by the fog and the thick smoke caused by the smoke of the huge firework display.

mon in the Arab world. In 1978, the Islamic Jurisdictional College (IJC)—the most influential body of Islamic affairs, laws, and ideologies (located at Al Azhar University in Cairo)—condemned Freemasonry as an evil organization. In 1995, the *Saudi Gazette* of January 13, 1995, under the banner "The Curse of Freemasonry," reprinted the official text issued in 1978 by the IJC, parts of which stated that Freemasonry

> . . . is a Jewish Organization in its roots. Its secret higher international administrative board are Jews and it promotes Zionist activities. Its primary objectives are the distraction of all religions and it distracts Muslims from Islam. . . . It has branches under different names as a camouflage so people cannot trace its activities, especially if the name of Freemasonry has opposition. These hidden branches are known as Lions, Rotary and others. They have wicked principles that completely contradict the rules of Islam. There is a clear relationship between Freemasonry, Judaism, and International Zionism. It has controlled the activities of high Arab Officials in the Palestinian Problem. It has limited their duties, obligations and activities for the benefit of Judaism and International Zionism. Given that Freemasonry involves itself in dangerous activities, it is a great hazard, with wicked objectives, the Jurisdictional Synod determines that Freemasonry is a dangerous, destructive organization. Any Muslims who affiliates with it, knowing the truth of its objectives, is an infidel to Islam.

Professor of Modern European and Jewish History at the Hebrew University in Jerusalem, Robert S. Wistrich, in an article titled "The New Islamic Fascism," published in November 2001 in *The Jerusalem Post,* wrote that "This Middle Eastern radicalism is a distinctly modern movement, though it also has indigenous Islamic roots. The conspiracy theory at its heart, which links plutocratic capitalism, international freemasonry, Zionism, and Marxist Communism, is almost identical with the mythical structure of Nazi anti-Semitism. For contemporary jihadists, a 'Judaized' America and Israel, together with heretical, secular Muslim regimes are the godless spearhead of these dark occult forces that seek to destroy Islam and undermine the cultural identity of Muslim believers."

Were Hawass and Hosni victims of a widespread xenophobia of Freemasons or naive in their choice and timing for an extravaganza show for the millennium at Giza? Or were they the victims of something else—something more covert and much more sinister? Perhaps we will never know.

Meanwhile, we hope the point has been made in this chapter that Hawass, during his long years of acting as principal spokesman for Egypt's history and civilization, has, to put it mildly, delivered and confused and blurred the vision of what has happened at the Giza Pyramids and in Egyptian antiquities in general. He also has distorted the truth, as we shall see, of foreign involvement in Egypt over the last two centuries or so, namely since the rediscovery of ancient Egypt with the arrival of Napoleon in 1798. We fervently believe that this unfortunate and misleading negative perception about the role of foreign archaeological missions, which Hawass has disseminated through his aggressive media campaign, needs to be put right. This is vitally important not only for historical reasons but, more important, for the future of the antiquities in a new and free democratic Egypt; for the truth is that even though it is commendable that the Egyptians themselves are in control and fully responsible for their antiquities, the participation of foreign missions, both practically and financially, is not only necessary but crucial. A historical spring cleanup is thus necessary.

This is, therefore, the task that we have set ourselves to accomplish in the remaining pages of this chapter.

PREEMINENCE BEFORE THE DEEP SLEEP

In the ancient world, Egypt always held a place of preeminence. Shrouded in mystery and veiled by a hoary past, the land of the pharaohs was regarded as the birthplace of occult knowledge, science, and magic. With its giant pyramids, its plethora of temples, its sacred mystical Nile, and, above all, its strange and impenetrable mummification rituals, which promised rebirth and eternal life among the gods in heaven, Egypt has ignited the imagination of all those who have come into contact with it. Pythagoras, Plato, Solon, Euclid, Eudoxus, and many more of the great Greek scholars came to Egypt to learn its secrets and its sciences.

Alexander the Great, inspired perhaps by his tutor Aristotle, chose Egypt among all other countries to build the world's first universal city, Alexandria, to serve as a beacon and a bridge between East and West and to become the greatest center of learning and enlightenment and the repository of all the knowledge of the known world. The symbol and manifestation of Alexander's dream was, of course, the great library of Alexandria. Here, from the fourth century BCE, a massive collection of books and papyri from the temple archives of the pharaohs and also from foreign ships entering Alexandria's Eastern Harbor were appropriated by the Macedonian new rulers of Egypt and deposited in the great library, the latter acting as an intellectual repository, a sort of Hall of Records, of the accumulated knowledge of the ancients. And although it is true to say that long before the coming of Alexander in 332 BCE Egypt had an advanced and learned civilization that stretched back as far as 3000 BCE and even beyond, it is equally true that it had already suffered much pillage and destruction at the hands of its own people through these millennia.

Today, we read how ancient Egypt was ruled under a divine system of order, a sort of pharaonic ten commandments, known as "Maat," which loosely translates as "justice, law, and order." Yet, part of human nature always being what it is, such order was sneered at by those solely motivated by greed and the lust for riches. We refer to those people by the general label of "tomb robbers." Although this despicable practice had probably been going on since the early dynasties, records exist dating from the Twentieth Dynasty (ca. 1200 BCE) that tell us of various trials of men accused of robbing royal tombs in the Valley of the Kings;

some also accuse the governor of Thebes and other officials of being in collusion with the robbers. An excellent scholarly work on this subject is Brian M. Fagan's *The Rape of the Nile* in which he bluntly writes:

> Most of the royal tombs of the Valley of the Kings had probably been opened illegally by professional thieves by the end of the 20th Dynasty. The depredations of these robbers were so severe that most of the royal treasures vanished forever. . . . The tombs and great monuments of ancient Egypt have been under siege ever since they were built. The Egyptians themselves used them for building stone. Theban tomb robbers were followed by religious zealots and quarrymen who eradicated inscriptions and removed great temples stone by stone . . .[14]

When Alexander the Great came into Egypt with his Macedonian army in 332 BCE, the country had just been liberated from nearly a century of Persian rule. The Macedonians were far more considerate, indeed they even adopted the pharaonic customs and religion and restored many temples as well as building quite a few of their own, such as the temple of Isis at Philae, the temple of Sobek at Kom Ombo, and the great temple of Hathor at Dendera. The Macedonian (Ptolemaic) dynasties lasted until 30 BCE, when Augustus Caesar defeated Cleopatra and Mark Antony and turned Egypt into a Roman province. It is not clear what damage took place during the purely Roman occupation before Egypt was made part of Christendom under the Byzantine emperors. There are no records of trade in antiquities by the Romans, although it is well known that they carted away many ancient Egyptian obelisks, as well as statues, to decorate their palaces and villas in Rome.

The first real systematic damage that Egyptian temples suffered was at the hands of the Church of Rome, especially after the so-called Edict of the Byzantine emperor Theodosius I in 391 CE, which called for closing all the so-called pagan temples and abolishing the practice of the ancient Egyptian religion. The Christian mob in Alexandria took this as an open license to go on a rampage and destroy the great temple of Serapis and the Serapeum and its library, where thousands of papyrus rolls and parchments, inscribed in Greek with ancient knowledge, were taken off the shelves, torn to pieces, and burned. As a result, the history of ancient Egypt and its wisdom seemed to be lost forever. An Egyptian dark age of bigotry, oppression, and religious intolerance befell this once vibrant, joyful, and exotic land. Egypt fell into a deep sleep, a sort of protracted intellectual hibernation that would last more than a dozen centuries. As strange as it may seem, such a calamity was actually predicted in writings dating from the first century CE, the so-called Hermetic texts, which, as fate would also have it, would much later be the very stimulus that would reawaken ancient Egypt, yet not in its land of origin but—irony of ironies—in that old Rome, which had caused its demise in 391 CE.

Let us then quote the relevant passage from the Hermetic texts:

Do you know, Asclepius, that Egypt is an image of Heaven, or to speak more exactly, in Egypt all the operations of the powers which rule and work in Heaven are present in the Earth below? In fact it should be said that the whole Cosmos dwells in this our land as in a sanctuary. And yet, since it is fitting that wise men should have knowledge of all events before they come to pass, you must not be left in ignorance of what I will now tell you. There will come a time when it will have been in vain that Egyptians have honored the Godhead with heartfelt piety and service; and all our holy worship will be fruitless and ineffectual. The gods will return from earth to heaven; Egypt will be forsaken, and the land which was once the home of religion will be left desolate, bereft of the presence of its deities. O Egypt, Egypt, of thy religion nothing will remain but an empty tale, which thine own children in time to come will not believe; nothing will be left but graven words, and only the stones will tell of thy piety. And in that day men will be weary of life, and they will cease to think the universe worthy of reverent wonder and worship. They will no longer love this world around us, this incomparable work of God, this glorious structure which he has built, this sum of good made up of many diverse forms, this instrument whereby the will of God operates in that which he has made, ungrudgingly favoring man's welfare; this combination and accumulation of all the manifold things that call forth the veneration, praise, and love of the beholder. Darkness will be preferred to light, and death will be thought more profitable than life; no one will raise his eyes to heaven; the pious will be deemed insane, the impious wise; the madman will be thought a brave man, and the wicked will be esteemed as good. As for the soul, and the belief that it is immortal by nature, or may hope to attain to immortality, as I have taught you—all this they will mock, and even persuade themselves that it is false. No word of reverence or piety, no utterance worthy of heaven, will be heard or believed. And so the gods will depart from mankind—a grievous thing!—and only evil angels will remain, who will mingle with men, and drive the poor wretches into all manner of reckless crime, into wars, and robberies, and frauds, and all things hostile to the nature of the soul. Then will the earth tremble, and the sea bear no ships; heaven will not support the stars in their orbits, all voices of the gods will be forced into silence; the fruits of the Earth will rot; the soil will turn barren, and the very air will sicken with sullen stagnation; all things will be disordered and awry, all good will disappear. But when all this has befallen, Asclepius, then God the Creator of all things will look on that which has come to pass, and will stop the disorder by the counterforce of his will, which is the good. He will call back to the right path those who have gone astray; he will cleanse the world of evil, washing it away with floods, burning it out with the fiercest fire, and expelling it with war and pestilence. And thus he will bring back his world to its former aspect, so that the Cosmos will once more be deemed worthy of worship and wondering reverence, and God, the maker and maintainer of the Mighty Fabric, will be adored by the men of that day with continuous songs of praise and blessing. Such is the new birth of the Cosmos; it is a making again of all things good, a holy and awe-inspiring restoration of all nature; and it is wrought inside the process of Time by the eternal Will of the Creator.[15]

Considering that the above text was composed sometime between the first and third centuries CE, it is most uncanny to say that it not only predicted the destruction of the old religion and its sanctuaries and how the Egyptian people would eventually forget their ancient origins, but it also predicted, even more uncannily, that Egypt would, in the distant future, be reawakened into "its former aspect."

AWAKENING

The fall of the Roman Empire in 476 CE ushered in a long period of intellectual and spiritual darkness in Europe known as the Middle Ages. For nearly a thousand years, from the mid-fifth to the early fifteenth centuries, the Roman Catholic Church became the only unifying force in Europe, which was regarded as one large religious state called Christendom. In the mid-fifteenth century, however, suddenly and unexpectedly, Europe began to emerge from its deep slumber and experienced a renaissance, a rebirth that first occurred in the city of Florence. The Renaissance, as many scholars have often pointed out, was largely brought about by the revival of ancient Egyptian knowledge with the discovery of the "lost books of Hermes Trismegistus" known to academics as the Hermetic texts. Composed of fourteen "books" and several addenda, the mysterious texts were thought to be from the hand of ancient Egypt's god of wisdom and science, Thoth, whom the Greeks called Hermes Trismegistus, or Hermes-Thrice-Great. Written in Greek in the city of Alexandria, probably in the first century CE, their contents were almost certainly culled from much older genuine ancient Egyptian temple literature, which the pharaohs referred to as the Sacred Books of Thoth.[16] At any rate, the Hermetic texts, after the systematic persecution of so-called pagans and heretics, which began in Egypt in the fifth century CE, mysteriously disappeared from circulation.

They were not to emerge again until the year 1460, when an Italian monk, under the payroll of Cosimo de Medici, the liberal and enlightened (and immensely wealthy) doge of Florence, found a full set of the Hermetica in a forlorn monastery in Macedonia, bought them at a derisory price, and carted them to Florence on the back of a donkey. Cosimo, now on his deathbed, immediately gave the order to his personal scholar, the brilliant linguist Marsilio Ficino, to drop everything else he was doing and translate the Hermetica forthwith into Latin. An intellectual bombshell was about to explode in Europe, which would clear the way for the emergence of all branches of scientific knowledge and the arts and lead Europe's stagnant civilization toward the Age of Enlightenment and, as some even claim, the industrial revolution and the emergence of the modern Western world.

Another factor, too, had acted as a catalyst for the Renaissance, this being the arrival in Florence of many Byzantine scholars and intellectuals fleeing Turkey when the Ottoman Sultan Mehmed II sacked Constantinople on May 29, 1453. Florence was the perfect haven for such scholars, as they were welcome with open arms into the recently founded Medici Academy under the patronage and financial sponsorship of Cosimo de Medici. As soon as the Hermetic texts were translated into Latin, hordes of intellectuals in Italy and the rest of Europe rushed to get copies. No fewer than eight editions of Ficino's translations appeared before the end of the fifteenth century and twenty-two other editions between 1471 and 1641. The philosophical message of the Hermetica, as the Hermetic texts were popularly called, even though they did not actually contain practical scientific knowledge per se, acted as a powerful stimulus in learned circles, unshackling minds from the hold and repression of the Church and prompting individuals such as Giordano Bruno and Giovanni Pico della Mirandola to engage in a new, more liberated quest for knowledge—a knowledge they fervently believed had existed in the distant past during a golden age in

Egypt. "We Greeks (and Latin scholars) owe Egypt, the grand monar-chy of letters and nobility," declared Bruno, "to be the parent of our fables, metaphors and doctrines."[17]

In about 1484, Marsilio Ficino also began translating the work of the Egyptian Greek philosopher Plotinus (205–270 CE), regarded as one of the most influential philosophers of antiquity. A native of Lycopolis (modern Asyut in Middle Egypt), Plotinus studied philoso-phy for twelve years in Alexandria, after which he went to Rome to set up his own school of philosophy. There in Rome, he taught philoso-phy for the next twenty years to the city's elite; ranking high among his students was none other than the emperor Gallienus himself and his wife Salonina. Let us note in passing that Plotinus is considered by many scholars to be the founder of Neoplatonism (a term invented in the nineteenth century to describe a type of religious and mystical phi-losophy that began in the third century CE).*

The revival of the philosophy of Plotinus and the contents of the Hermetica were the inspirations that European scholars desperately needed after ten centuries of repression by the Catholic Church. It prompted them to see the infinite potential they had within them and acknowledge the dignity of man and his unique role in the universal scheme. European scholars—long kept ignorant of the ancient pagan past—now became aware of how many of the Greek geniuses, among them Pythagoras, Archimedes, and even the great Plato had gone to

---

*Plotinus was an original profound thinker who, although appealed to the authority of Plato, he criticized him at times (*Ennead* IV.8.1). Plotinus developed a complex spiritual cosmology involving three fundamental elements: the One, the Intelligence, and the Soul. He also developed a unique theory of sense-perception and knowledge, based on the idea that the mind plays an active role in shaping or ordering the objects of its perception, rather than passively receiving the data of sense experience. According to Plotinus's doc-trine, the soul is composed of a higher divine part and a lower part, which is the seat of the personality. During the last fifteen years of his life, Plotinus wrote fifty-four treatises, which were collected by his pupil and biographer, Porphyry, who organized them into six books of nine treatises, each called *Enneads,* and published it after his death. They were first printed in a Latin translation by Marsilio Ficino in Florence in 1492.

Egypt to learn from the Egyptian priestly masters and returned to Greece enriched by their experiences and learning in the deep and advanced knowledge of the Egyptians. Important books on ancient Egypt now became available to them, such as Plutarch's book *De Iside et Osiride* (Isis and Osiris) and Iamblichus's works, which generated a deep interest in the mysteries of Egypt.

It should come as no big surprise, therefore, to learn that soon after the introduction of the Hermetica in Europe, the Polish astronomer Nicolaus Copernicus (1473–1543), inspired by the contents of these sacred books from Egypt's golden age, formulated a comprehensive heliocentric cosmology, which situated the sun, not Earth as claimed by the Church, in the center of the planetary system, and published his celebrated thesis *On the Revolutions of the Celestial Spheres*, widely regarded as the most defining moment in scientific research. Before Copernicus, it was widely held that Earth was flat and was at the center of the universe—the so-called geocentric model accepted and dogmatized by the Catholic Church. Copernicus, however, was the first scientist to challenge this erroneous view—an act that in those days was considered heresy and punishable by death. And although Copenicus's knowledge of mathematics was largely derived from Arabic sources, the now legendary heliocentric model that he proposed was almost certainly inspired by the ancient Egyptian notion of a divine sun being at the center of all things. Indeed, in some passages of the Hermetica, the sun is presented as the demiurge, the "second God," a term implying that it governed all things on Earth as well as the stars (the constellations and planets)—a poetic and albeit roundabout way of saying that the sun, not Earth, is the focus of the visible universe.

[Hermes says] "The sun illuminates the other stars not so much by the power of its light, as by its divinity and holiness, and you should hold him, O Asclepius, to be the Second God, governing all things and spreading his light on all the living beings of the world, both those which have a soul and those which have not."

NEWTONIAN SCIENCE AND HERMES

Moving forward a century, we find another scholar who revolutionized science forever (the term *revolution* to imply upheaval apparently comes from Copernicus's *On the Revolutions of the Celestial Spheres*), the celebrated Isaac Newton (1643–1727), who, according to some of his biographers, is also believed to have been indirectly influenced by alchemy and the Hermetica. For example, according to Michael White,

> Like all European alchemists from the Dark Ages to the beginning of the scientific era and beyond, Newton was motivated by a deep-rooted commitment to the notion that alchemical wisdom extended back to ancient times. The Hermetic tradition—the body of alchemical knowledge—was believed to have originated in the mists of time and to have been given to humanity through supernatural agents.[18]

We do recognize and accept, of course, that the influence of the Hermetica on European scholars from the Renaissance to the Age of Enlightenment is, to say the very least, a complicated issue fraught with misunderstanding and confusion. Perhaps the best published work on this intricate although most intriguing subject is Frances Yates's *Giordano Bruno and the Hermetic Tradition* (1974) in which this brilliant Warburg scholar traces the occult sciences to the Hermetica and shows how it acted as the bridge on which magic, alchemy, and astrology crossed into the sciences of physics, chemistry, and astronomy. Readers interested in pursuing this topic further are thus recommended to consult this work.[19] Our objective here, however, is to show how ancient Egypt was not only reawakened by the discovery of the Hermetica in the fifteenth century but also how it was the catalyst, the subtle driving force even, that put Europe on the track toward enlightenment and scientific progress. In other words, Egypt's ancient pagan pedigree is worthy of much reverence instead of the indifference (and in some cases even shame) displayed by the average modern Egyptian. And even though we are pleased to note that a positive shift in perception and pride about the ancient past is seen among the younger generation of today, this, sadly enough, was not the case after the Arab conquest until Napoleon's arrival in the country and the emergence of modern Egypt. It is therefore important that we now take a look at these events with unbiased eyes if we are to understand the mismanagement, corruption, and carelessness that took root in the EAO and, more importantly, prevent their perpetuation in the future.

The history of modern Egypt can be said to have started with the arrival of the Napoleonic expedition on the shores of Alexandria in 1798. The country had been an Ottoman (Turkish) province for nearly three centuries, and before that it had been ruled by the dreaded Mamluks, originally young men bought as slaves by the Arab rulers of Egypt from various parts of the Ottoman Empire and Eastern Europe to be trained in military schools to serve as professional soldiers. Inevitably, the Mamluks soon became a powerful military elite and wrenched power from their owners, and then ruled until 1517 when the Ottoman Turks annexed Egypt into their vast empire. The former Mamluk elite, however, cleverly collaborated with the Ottomans and were thus able to reassert their hold in the Egyptian provinces. The Mamluk emirs (princes) secured high-ranking military posts and, by doing so, maintained their powerful influence throughout Ottoman rule in Egypt. They were still very much a force to be reckoned with when the French set foot in Egypt in 1798. Indeed, Napoleon proclaimed that the reason he was occupying Egypt was to liberate the Egyptian people from the Mamluks—a half truth that the Egyptians did not for one minute believe!

Napoleon Bonaparte arrived in Alexandria on July 1, 1798, from Toulon, with a massive fleet transporting 54,000 troops and an impressive assortment of light and heavy artillery and cavalry and even a hand-selected assembly of top scientists (the *savants*). Then only twenty-nine years old, Napoleon was already seen as a national hero in France for his spectacular victories in Italy and the swift capture of the stronghold island of Malta. Now in charge of the so-called *Armée d'Angleterre* earmarked for an eventual invasion of England, Napoleon chose to first strike a massive blow to Britain's world trade by taking Egypt and thus blocking England's principal route to India, the latter the cornerstone of its empire. Napoleon wanted also to bring European enlightenment and the ideals of the French Revolution to Egypt, the cradle of civilization—a dream that took a long time to materialize.

It is said that upon seeing what precious little was left of the once magnificent city of Alexandria, some of the French savants openly wept. Gone were the magnificent palaces and temples, gone were the villas and wide paved avenues of the Ptolemies and the Romans, and gone was the famed lighthouse, the Pharos, one of the seven wonders of the ancient world. All that was left was a pathetic population (estimated at six thousand inhabitants) living in what was little more than a fishing village. Would they find the same devastation further inland and up the Nile, where, according to Herodotus, were to be found ancient wonders beyond the wildest imagination? Had not the father of history written that "There is no country that possesses so many wonders, nor any that has such a number of works that defy description . . ."[20]

What had happened to this once opulent and magnificent city of Alexandria of classical times? What, or who, could have caused such destruction? And why?

NEW RULERS AND A NEW RELIGION

In the year 641 CE, a small army from Arabia led by the soldier-poet Amr ibn el-A'ss laid siege to the weakened and corrupt Roman Byzantine garrison stationed at the southern gates of Old Cairo, at the fortress of Babylon (now part of the Greek Orthodox Church of Mari Girgis). While the bemused Roman soldiers looked down at this strange and exotic band of Bedouins on horseback, their spokesman, wearing a flowing robe and a turban, proudly announced in broken Latin that they had come to demand that all Egypt submit to the true faith of Islam: There is no god but Allah, and Mohammad is his Prophet.

Then the unthinkable happened: the religiously inspired Arabs stormed the fortress and, by this act of bravado, took possession of Memphis and Heliopolis, later to be renamed El Kahira (the Victorious) from which the modern name of Cairo is derived. Within a few weeks, the Arabs were at the gates of Alexandria. The Egyptian Christians, the Copts, seeing this as an opportunity to rid themselves of the hated Romans, negotiated favorable terms with the Arab general el-A'ss and peacefully handed him the keys of the city. As they rode into the city, the Arabs, who had never seen anything as remotely sophisticated as Alexandria, reported that so bright was the sunlight reflected by the white marble that lines the pavements and streets that they had to shield their eyes from the glare. El-A'ss himself, awed by the wonders he saw, wrote to the caliph at Makkah that he had captured a city that "contains 4,000 palaces, 4,000 baths, 400 theatres, 1,200 shops, and 40,000 Jews." Still, even with all these marvels, the city was but a shadow of its former Ptolemaic grandeur.

The Arabs, being iconoclasts and abhorring anything pagan, were totally disinterested in the legacy of the pharaonic antiquities that had survived the Roman and Christian eras. Indeed, not only were they disinterested, they were happy to make use of the temples and pyramids, using them as quarries to build their own palaces, villas, and mosques. It is even said that Sultan El Aziz attempted to actually destroy the Giza Pyramids in 1193 CE. Apparently, he gathered a large labor force, and for eight months, they hacked at the monuments, but finally gave up when they realized the enormity of the task the sultan had set for them.* There were many other deliberate

---

*On July 23, 1993, Chris Edges reported in the *New York Times* (*Luxor Journal*) that "Islamic militants have mounted a campaign to tear down the pharaohs' pyramids and their avenue of Sphinxes and slender obelisks . . ." "The Sphinx and the pyramids are statues," said Sheikh Ali Yehya, a militant cleric, "and so are all the other pharaonic monuments. The Prophet, peace be upon him, destroyed statues, and we are commanded to do the same . . ."

Figure 2.3. The French army attacking the city of Alexandria, July 3, 1798. In the far distance of the Eastern Harbor is the Qaitbay Fortress, which still stands today and is now an open-air museum.

acts of vandalism, such as when in 1378 CE a Sufi Muslim fanatic by the name of Mohammed Sa'im al-Dahr broke off the nose of the Great Sphinx of Giza. It is impossible to know the real extent of vandalism and destruction that was done during those long years before Napoleon's invasion. If the total obliteration of the classical city of Alexandria can be taken as a typical example, then we can but imagine what other destructions to ancient monuments may have happened elsewhere in more remote regions of Middle and Upper Egypt when there were no laws that protected them.

Let us, however, return to the arrival of Napoleon in Egypt.

The badly armed and undermanned Ottoman garrison of Alexandria was easily subdued by the far superior French force, and within a few days, Napoleon led his army up the Nile toward Cairo, the stronghold of the Mamluks. The brave but outdated Mamluks were easy prey for the highly efficient and heavily armed French army. On July 21, at the so-called Battle of the Pyramids near Cairo, the Mamluks were nearly all decimated as they foolhardily repeatedly charged on horseback at the French soldiers, who calmly awaited them with modern rifles and bayonets in well-formed divisions.

It was all over within hours, and the French army then entered the city of Cairo totally unopposed. Napoleon, to his dismay, found no authority to talk to. He quickly established a council of *ulema* (religious leaders). The city's population at the time was only 250,000—a far cry from the 20-million-strong metropolis that it is today. Nonetheless, it was dotted with many luxurious palaces and fine villas, which the French generals and the savants sequestered and moved into. Napoleon took up residence in the palace of Muhammad Bey al-Alfi, a Mamluk leader, in the Azbekiya section of Cairo.

A week later, news came that the British fleet under Lord Horatio Nelson had completely destroyed the French fleet anchored in the Abu Qir Bay east of Alexandria. This was the beginning of the end for the romantic French military expedition in Egypt. Encouraged and incited by the news of the British victory at Abu Qir, the Arab

Figure 2.4. Napoleon Bonaparte at the Battle of the Pyramids, July 21, 1798

population of Cairo revolted against the French, only to be ruthlessly crushed by the latter. It was, however, all very futile for the French, now totally cut off from Europe with the loss of their fleet. After a valiant but foiled attempt to find an escape route overland for his army through Syria, and after only twelve months in the land of the pharaohs, Napoleon abandoned his army in Egypt and managed to escape with a few of his trusted advisers back to France on August 18, 1799. The French army in Egypt, now disillusioned and on the verge of mutiny, was under the charge of the able General Jean-Baptiste Kléber, an architect by profession and, among other things, a prominent Freemason who is reputed to have founded the very first Masonic lodge in Egypt, La Loge Isis.[21]

Kléber wisely entered into negotiations with the Ottomans to arrange an evacuation of Egypt for his army. The British, however, intervened and demanded that the French surrender to them. Kléber was brutally assassinated on June 14, 1800, by an Arab, and was succeeded by Jacques Menou, an incompetent French officer who, among other strange decisions, converted to Islam. In July 1801, Menou surrendered to the British who, under the terms of the surrender, allowed the French army to leave Egypt for France.

Now Egypt was about to have a new ruler, but not a British one nor a native Egyptian but a near-illiterate and very common Albanian whose desire to gain control over Egypt persuaded him to rid the country of both the Ottomans and the Mamluks and to make Egypt an independent state after eighteen centuries of foreign domination. But more on this historical aberration in the next chapter . . .

Meanwhile, the humiliating military defeat and political fiasco of the French in Egypt was amazingly converted into a huge cultural victory for Napoleon—one that would have immense repercussions not only on the universities and learning centers of Europe but also, as we shall see, on the yet unborn science of Egyptology.

3
The Pasha

Central to Napoleon's dream was to be the creation of an Institute of Egypt in Cairo. This was to be modelled on the Institute of France in Paris . . . what these intellectuals discovered in Egypt would transform our knowledge of Western Civilization and form the basis of Egyptology.

PAUL STRATHERN,
NAPOLEON IN EGYPT

Je tiens l'affaire!

JEAN-FRANÇOIS CHAMPOLLION TO
HIS BROTHER JACQUES-JOSEPH AT THE
MOMENT WHEN HE DECIPHERED THE
EGYPTIAN HIEROGLYPHS IN 1822.

A horde of "collectors" . . . [aided by] the French Consul Drovetti, the British Consul Salt . . . and travellers . . . tear down piece by piece fragments of Egypt's culture: stele, statues, sarcophagi and soon obelisks are shipped to . . . museums of Europe . . . A scandalous piracy . . . which enriched important men in Egypt . . .

JEAN LACOUTURE,
CHAMPOLLION: UNE VIE DE LUMIERES

Once things had more or less settled in Cairo after Napoleon made his triumphant entry into the city, he issued a decree for an Institut d'Égypte to be immediately set up and modeled on the Institut de France in Paris. Napoleon, who was an honorary member of the Institut de France, fancied himself a scholar and a dilettante scientist, and one of his great ambitions for Egypt—if it was not even *the* main ambition—was to bring modern civilization to this ancient land and to revive ancient Egyptian wisdom and its art. It is perhaps noteworthy that Josephine, his wife, was the grand mistress of a Masonic lodge in France and that many of Napoleon's family—his father, several of his brothers, and maybe even himself—had been initiated into the Masonic Brotherhood. Indeed, many of his generals and officers of the Egypt expedition were Freemasons.[1] This Masonic connection may indeed be at the root—or at the very least was an important factor—of Napoleon's keen interest in Egypt, for it is well known that many rituals and symbolism of Freemasonry, especially the type of Freemasonry practiced in France at that time, were culled from pseudo-ancient Egyptian beliefs, systems of initiation, and mysteries.

Although the modern Freemasonry movement started in Europe in the early eighteenth century, it could be regarded as a revival of the Gnostic movement, which developed in Alexandria during the early history of Christianity. The Gnostics, who were looking for salvation through spiritual knowledge of the Supreme Being, disappeared during the fourth century, when they were persecuted by the Church of Rome, which regarded them as heretics. They opposed the power of the Church and believed in the freedom and fraternity of humanity.

In modern times, the Freemasons were believed to have been behind the Western revolutionary movement that led to the separation between church and state. However, some critics have in the last decades accused the Masons of becoming a secret society that aims to accomplish universal power on both political and financial establishments. The French Revolution of 1789 and the American Revolution of 1776 were very much influenced by Masonic ideals. The concept of freedom, brotherhood, and equality (*liberté, fraternité, egalité*) comes from the virtues that were taught and practiced in the Masonic lodges. Indeed, many Masonic historians claim with good reason that the American Constitution and the Universal Declaration of Human Rights drew their clauses from the Masonic constitution and Masonic ideals.

But in France, unlike the United States, the revolution entailed not just the toppling and eradication of the monarchical system but also the "dechristianization" of the country to be replaced by a republican cult based on reason (see *The Master Game* by Robert Bauval and Graham Hancock). For many centuries, starting in the fourth century, Europe had been plagued by religious conflicts and wars that turned into terrible genocide during the Crusades of the twelfth and thirteenth centuries and the Protestant wars of the sixteenth and seventeenth centuries. The only real long-term solution, it seemed, was to provide humanity with one world order where everyone could believe in a Supreme Being and live according to a set of common high virtues. Whereas the three Semite religions—Judaism, Christianity, and Islam—advocated separatism, which inevitably always led to conflict, Freemasonry advocated unity, which could lead to a universal brotherhood. Seen in this light, we can perhaps begin to understand the loftier motives of Napoleon's invasion of Egypt and the establishment of Masonic lodges in that ancient country. It would seem also evident that the British had somewhat the same idea, although with a much less radical approach. In the late nineteenth century, there was a rather flawed attempt by the British lodges to create a form of Freemasonry for the Arab world, and more specifically Egypt.

NAPOLEON'S SAVANTS

Napoleon appointed as president of the Institut d'Égypte the mathematician Gaspard Monge, a staunch Freemason who had been a senior member of the most elite Nine Sisters Lodge in Paris, which boasted illustrious members such as Benjamin Franklin, Jérôme Lalande, Court de Gébelin (the inventor of the Egyptian tarot), and Voltaire. Napoleon then appointed himself as vice president.

Figure 3.1. The Institut d'Egypte in Cairo, ca. 1801

From that point on began the very first systematic and scientific studies of ancient Egypt, with the dedicated savants, now all members of the Institut d'Égypte, meticulously recording everything from local fauna to cotton weaving, agricultural techniques, and the hydraulic cycles of the Nile—and, of course, the ancient temples and pyramids. Scientific articles were regularly published in the institute's journal and read during the weekly meeting, often attended by Napoleon himself. The recording and data collection that took place during those three short years of the French occupation were so voluminous and detailed that it bordered on the boring and tedious—but such is the very nature, some would say, of scientific research until the occasional thrill and exhilaration of a major discovery comes along. As it turned out, the first of such discoveries was not to come from any of Napoleon's savants but a few years later, as we shall soon see, from a young and frail boy who was only eight years old when Napoleon invaded Egypt.

Among the 167 savants—botanists, physicists, mathematicians, chemists, surveyors, engineers, and artists—all of whom had been personally selected from the Institut de France by Napoleon and Monge, one of them, an outsider to boot, would stand out and make an impact on world culture that still reverberates today. His name was Vivant Denon, a very gifted artist, who, unlike the other savants, was not a member of the Institut de France. Denon, however, had gained an immense reputation in France among art lovers and had come to the attention of Napoleon because he had been personally recommended by none other than Josephine, Napoleon's beautiful and beloved wife. As always, Napoleon yielded to Josephine's wishes and agreed to let Denon come to Egypt. He was not to regret it.

In his early fifties—an age considered rather passé in those days—Denon nonetheless bravely sailed with the troops in Egypt and marched with them, sometimes even ahead of them, up the Nile and diligently (almost religiously some may say) recorded everything of interest he saw in amazingly precise and detailed drawings. He also took extensive notes that later would be used for a book. When Napoleon, in August 1799, decided to abandon his army and return to France, he took along Denon and Monge, as well as other trusted friends. Both Denon's *Travels in Lower and Upper Egypt,* published in 1802, and the famous *Description of Egypt,* published a few years later in 1809, became huge bestsellers, translated throughout Europe, and transformed "our knowledge of the origins of Western civilization, and even the age of the world itself."[2] More important, these publications turned attention away from Napoleon's military fiasco in Egypt and converted it into a cultural triumph. This intellectual success would result in two major situations that would affect Egypt forever: the first was scientific, in that it created a wave of enthusiasm among scholars in Egypt all keen to participate and even join the new study of Egyptology, and the other was commercial, in that it created a huge interest in all things Egyptian among the educated classes, all keen to possess exotic memorabilia, whether genuine ancient artifacts or imitations. In a more frivolous manner, it also brought about the fad of Egyptomania, which was promoted by Napoleon's ever-innovative social-ite wife, Josephine. At Malmaison, their private residence, Josephine dec-orated many of the rooms in a pseudo-Egyptian style and even planted roses from Damietta (an Egyptian coastal town) in the garden and kept Egyptian gazelles in the park.

There had been, however, one particular artifact—a large granite stele with three parallel inscriptions: ancient hieroglyphs, demotic text, and ancient Greek—that the French soldiers in Egypt had unearthed while repairing the walls of fortress Julien near the small coastal town of Rosetta (Rashid). The story goes that on July 15, 1799, Lieutenant Pierre-François Bouchard found the inscribed stone where the soldiers had been repairing the exposed wall of the fortress. The discovery was reported to the Institut d'Égypte in Cairo, where one of the savants, Michel Ange Lancret, correctly pointed out that the three inscriptions could be versions of the same text. The stone was then brought to Cairo where Napoleon himself inspected it, referring to it as la *pierre de Rosette* (the Rosetta stone). Prints of the inscriptions were made and taken to Paris, where copies were sent to various scholars around Europe. Before the Rosetta stone itself could be shipped to France, however, the French army surrendered to the British, and the stone was instead shipped to England as a spoil of war (it has since been on display at the British Museum, being the artifact most visited by tourists today).

EGYPT'S ANTIQUITIES

A Story of Vandalism, Looting, and Exploitation

We now must make a short digression from narrating the amazing story of how the Rosetta stone was deciphered and how this single break-through gave birth to the modern science of Egyptology to a brief recounting of the fate of many of Egypt's treasures. Let us say from the outset that, even though on the one hand we fully endorse the sovereignty of Egyptians over their pharaonic legacy, we do not, on the other hand, condone Hawass's demands to have the Rosetta stone, or indeed other ancient Egyptian artifacts in foreign museums, brought back to Egypt[3]—at least not until things in Egypt are settled and its future known after the turbulence and uncertainties brought about by the January 25, 2011 Revolution.*

Figure 3.2. The Rosetta stone

---

*During the last meeting of the Intergovernmental Committee for Promoting the Return of Cultural Property to its Countries of Origin, held at the UNESCO premises in Paris last September, Hawass called for the return of five particular ancient Egyptian objects on display abroad. In his speech, Hawass pointed out that "Egypt had been deprived of the five artifacts, and as they are regarded as key items of Egyptian cultural heritage they should therefore be handed back." These objects are the Rosetta stone, the bust of Queen Nefertiti at the Egyptian Museum in Berlin, the statue of the great pyramid architect Hemiunnu at the Roemer-Pelizaeus Museum in Hilesheim, the Zodiac of Dendera Temple in the Louvre, and the bust of the Khafre Pyramid–builder Ankhhaf in the Museum of Fine Arts in Boston.

The author and historian Brian M. Fagan, in *The Rape of the Nile*, perhaps explains the reason more cogently, even though he was referring to the early days of Egyptology.

> In a sense one cannot blame the museum curators and collectors of a century and a half ago . . . everywhere [in Egypt] they looked they saw statuary and temples being broken up and tombs being looted for jewelry. In Egypt nothing was safe. But a papyrus carefully unrolled in the secluded comfort of the British Museum was safe from destruction, cushioned with the awesome security in the greatest museum in the world. No-one could desecrate a British Museum mummy or tear it apart . . . certainly [this was] the only practical way to save ancient Egypt from extinction . . . after all the Pasha's government was destroying and giving it away all the time. And the Fellahin [Egyptian peasants] seemed to have no respect for tomb or temple or any identity with the ancient Egyptians themselves, only in the value of their corpses . . . the ancient Egyptians themselves had helped themselves to the content of royal tombs. They had violated their most sacred places and the royal sepulchers for gold and guaranteed source of wealth that would enable them to meet life's day-to-day needs. The ancient had treated the past with casual cynicism that had been inherited by their successors . . . It is a miracle that it all has survived . . .[4]

Although the above quote from Fagan alludes to the late 1800s and early 1900s, it is a sad fact that much of what he says still applies to this day. Indeed, as recently as 2008, thus well into the directorship of Hawass, we can personally report, with pictorial evidence, the terrible vandalism and desecration of temples, pyramids, and tombs. We can also report the almost complete destruction of Nabta Playa, an important prehistoric site west of Abu Simbel, only to be ignored by Hawass.[5]

The truth, however painful and shameful it may be to Egyptians as well as Europeans of today, is that the vandalism, looting, and exploitation of pharaonic antiquities has been going on for many centuries and, as we saw after the Tahrir Revolution, is still rampant today. The list of such abuse to the legacy of ancient Egypt is far too long to report it in full. But the following few examples will reveal the scale of the matter. Quoting from Max Rodenbeck's excellent book *Cairo: The City Victorious,* we read that

> Muslim masons of the eleventh century found that decorative blocks from Heliopolis* slotted nicely into the inner ramparts of the Cairo city walls . . . nearly every column in all the hundreds of medieval mosques in the city were recycled from some pagan temple. Other ancient columns were sliced like loaves of bread into discs and inserted into the stone marquetry of pavings and walls. Mosque thresholds too, were often choice pharaonic plunder, placed so that the faithful could trample on the beliefs of idol-worshippers . . .
>
> . . . no less a personage than a son of the great sultan Saladin . . . [was] engaged in quarrying ancient sites. Courtiers had convinced the prince to tear down the smallest of the three main pyramids of Giza . . . and sell the stones to contractors.[6]

Apparently, the attempt to demolish the Menkaure Pyramid, the Third Pyramid at Giza, lasted eight months, with laborers hammering the ancient monument with pickaxes. Luckily, they gave up out of exhaustion. The horrid gash they made can still be seen on the south face of the pyramid. The Giza Sphinx also did not escape depradations. The medieval chronicler Taqi al-Din al Maqrizi reported in 1378 CE that a Sufi sheikh known as Mohammed Sa'im al-Dahr (the Perpetual Faster) attacked the face, ears, and nose of the Sphinx in a fit of iconoclastic zeal.

---

*Nothing of ancient Heliopolis, the "On" of the Bible, remains—nothing, that is, other than that lonely obelisk, a small part of a temple's foundation, and a few pitiful broken statues and stele. When the city of Fustat (medieval Cairo) was built by the Arabs starting in the late seventh century, the remains of temples and buildings of heliopolis were systematically ransacked and used as a quarry for building material.

But to be fair to the medieval Arabs, it is true that long before them the Assyrians, the Persians, and the Romans had their go at bashing ancient pharaonic monuments. The Assyrians sacked Memphis in the seventh century BCE and destroyed much of its palaces and temples. The Persian emperor Cambyses, who conquered Egypt in the sixth century BCE, demolished the great Temple of the Sun at Heliopolis right down to the foundation stones. The Romans in the early centuries of our era were no better. An enraged mob led by Theophilus, the fanatical bishop of Alexandria, tore down the great Serapeum of Alexandria stone by stone and destroyed to cinders the splendid statue of Serapis. Ancient temples survived this fanatical early Christian era only because they were "exorcised" and "converted" into churches. The evidence of this can still be seen on numerous temples such as the temples at Philae, Edfu, and Dendera.

In more modern times, the curious belief that "mummy powder" (*mumia*) has medicinal properties created a huge illegal trade. Local Egyptians plundered tombs for mummies, which they sold to Europeans. Shiploads were exported across the Mediterranean from the seventeenth century to the late nineteenth century. Rodenbeck reports the story of the seventeenth-century Italian, Pietro Della Valle, who paid a mere six piastres (the price of a good meal in those days) for two superbly decorated and fully intact coffins with their mummies of the Ptolemaic and Roman periods. The local merchants eventually ran out of genuine ancient mummies, but were not at all ready to give up this very lucrative business. "They bought the corpses of unclaimed criminals and the indigent, as well as sometimes even exhuming bodies from modern cemeteries, to create 'mummies,'[7] which they sold to credulous foreigners. . . . (Following Napoleon's invasion of Egypt), wealthy Europeans, led by the consuls of Britain and France at Cairo, competed now in extracting the richest prizes from ancient sites. Their unrestricted scavenging formed the basis of the great collections of Paris, London, Leiden, and Turin. Egypt's own nineteenth-century rulers proved equally keen for spoils. . . . It was not until 1857, with the founding of the antiquities museum at Cairo by the pioneering archaeologist Mariette Pasha that the wholesale plunder diminished. . . . Even so, in 1880 a hundred camel loads of stones per day were being carried into the capital from the pyramid of Cheop's son Djedefre . . . only public outcry (mostly from Europeans and educated Egyptians) prevented the great Giza pyramids themselves from being quarried to build the first dams on the Nile . . ."[8]

Today, there are many young Egyptians who are graduates in Egyptology and archaeology and who, unlike their nineteenth-century counterparts, are very conscientious and quite capable of protecting the ancient sites. Yet their display of anger during and after January 25, 2011, against the corruption and mismanagement of the Supreme Council of Antiquities (SCA) highlights the ongoing problems and their own frustration of not having been given jobs and thus not having the opportunity to participate in the preservation of their own ancient past.* We shall review this sensitive issue in chapter 7.

Meanwhile, let us return to the Rosetta stone story.

JE TIENS L'AFFAIRE! (I HOLD THE DEAL!)

Living in Grenoble with his older brother Jacques-Joseph, Jean-François Champollion came from a large but modest family who could not afford to pay for his schooling. Taught to read and write by Jacques-Joseph, Champollion soon demonstrated an unusual talent for languages. As fate would have it, one of Napoleon's savants, the brilliant mathematician Joseph Fourier, happened to also live in Grenoble. When Champollion was only eleven years old, Fourier, noticing the amazing linguistic abilities of the boy, showed him his small collection of Egyptian artifacts and his notes on the mystifying Egyptian hieroglyphs he had brought back from the Egyptian expedition. This fateful

---

*Protests by graduate Egyptologists and archaeologists against Hawass took place in February, May, and July 2011. He was eventually deposed on July 20, 2011, and was mobbed as he left the SCA building.

encounter with Fourier fired up the young Champollion, who apparently decided then and there to try and decipher this mysterious sign language of the pharaohs.

Egyptologists had already determined in 1799, when the Rosetta stone was discovered, that the stone had three versions of the same texts: hieroglyphics, demotic text, and ancient Greek. Since most classical linguists and scholars knew ancient Greek, many believed that the Rosetta stone could be the key to decode the Egyptian hieroglyphs. People also realized early on that both the hieroglyphic text and the demotic text—a sort of shorthand form of hieroglyphs—used phonetic characters to spell foreign names. Then in 1814, Thomas Young, a British linguist, noted that the hieroglyphic signs had pervasive similarities to the demotic writing. The race to decipher the hieroglyphs was on. Well ahead, like a furious black stallion galloping toward this glorious finish line, was Champollion. But it was not before September 1822 that a major breakthrough was made.

By that time, Champollion was thirty-two years old and an accomplished linguist specializing in ancient Coptic, Greek, and Arabic. After years of wracking his brain over the hieroglyphics, working all day and sometimes even all night by candlelight, the rather frail Frenchman was very close to the end of his quest. In the early morning of September 14, 1822, Champollion started work on his notes, trembling with excitement. In a great moment of enlightenment and epiphany, he understood and could see clearly what others had not: that the hieroglyphic sign language was made up of three systems, namely phonetics and ideas, themselves either to be seen as they are or figuratively. That was it, Champollion broke the ancient code! Ancient Egypt was about to speak again to the world after two millennia of brooding silence. It was close to midday, and the young man could not contain his excitement. He took his notes, rushed to the library where his brother, Jacques-Joseph, worked, barged into the room, and shouted his now famous phrase *"Je tiens l'affaire!"* (I hold the deal!), and then collapsed on the floor unconscious. Then came the moment of glory on September 27, when

Champollion calmly read out with a low voice his thesis—oddly titled *Lettre a M. Dacier* (the name of Champollion's mentor and permanent secretary of the academy)—to the eminent scholars and members of the Academie Royal Des Inscriptions et Belles-Lettres. It was a triumph. The scholars honored Champollion with a standing ovation. On this September day in Paris, hardly twenty-four years after Napoleon set foot in Egypt, scientific Egyptology was born.

Figure 3.3. Jean-François Champollion,
the decipherer of the Egyptian hieroglyphs

THE LONG ROAD FROM INDISCRIMINATE
LOOTING TO EGYPTOLOGY

It can be said with much certitude that Napoleon's Egypt expedition and, more specifically, Denon's publications was the intellectual stimulus that led, some sixty years later, to the formation of the Egyptian Antiquities Department (the forefather of the Egyptian Antiquities Organization [EAO] and the SCA). It also led eventually to the ongoing and hugely profitable influx of visitors (the term *tourist* was coined later in the 1940s) leading to the formation of the Egyptian Ministry of Tourism and Ministry of Culture. However, before such state-run institutions could take shape and become able to control and safeguard Egyptian antiquities, there was a protracted phase lasting from 1801 to 1858 of indiscriminate plundering and extensive black-market racketeering of antiquities. This chaotic phase witnessed a massive illegal and semilegal exportation of ancient artifacts, ranging from mummies, jewelery, papyrus texts, sarcophagi, statues, and even parts of pyramids and temples that supplied foreign museums, the shelves of private collectors, and the homes of rich dilettantes and dabblers in exotic art. To understand how and why this happened, we must briefly review the formation of modern Egypt and the rise and fall of perhaps history's biggest despot, who ruled Egypt from 1805 to 1849.

Muhammad Ali was born sometime in 1769 in Kavala, a small port in East Macedonia and Thrace, about 330 kilometers north of Athens. In those days, Kavala was part of the Ottoman Empire, stretching from Algiers through Egypt in the west, the Persian Gulf in the south, and as far north as Vienna on the Danube. Not much is known of Muhammad Ali's youth in Kavala other that he was from a poor and simple family, he himself being illiterate, and that he traded in tobacco (his father's business). Being an Albanian, he was a Muslim and bore a Muslim name made up from that of the Prophet combined with that of the first imam of the Shia. Rather short and stocky with a thick beard and a broad moustache in the traditional Turkish style, no one could have guessed— least of all himself—that in this man was the making of the future viceroy of Egypt and one of the most powerful men of his time. The year of his birth 1769 (although contested by many historians who favor 1770 to 1771) coincided with that of Napoleon Bonaparte, his hero, a curious connection that may have inspired Muhammad Ali throughout much of his life. Muhammad Ali had married at the age of nineteen an older woman, a widow named Amina Hatem, with whom he had had (so far) five children: three boys (Ibrahim, Ahmed Toussoun, and Ismail) and two girls (Tawhida and Nazli). Amina Hatem is said to have been related to the governor of Kavala.

In 1800, the Ottomans joined forces with the British to fight Napoleon in Egypt. Being a Turkish-Ottoman province, Kavala had to supply a quota of three hundred men, all Albanians, to join the allied British-Turkish army in Egypt. Muhammad Ali was one of them. In December of that year, he sailed to Marmara, leaving behind his family. There he joined the British fleet that sailed to Alexandria. Due perhaps to his marriage to a relative of the governor of Kavala or due to his bravery and ability in battle against the French at Abukir, or both, Muhammad Ali was eventually put in charge of a Turkish battalion.

After the defeat of the French at Alexandria, the British made ready to evacuate Egypt.

It is now March 1803. With the French and English out of Egypt, and with the Mamluks almost out of the way (some still held strong in Upper Egypt), the reins of Egypt were loose and there for the taking. By 1805, Muhammad Ali had risen to become one of the most prominent and powerful men in Egypt—and the one most likely to control Egypt on behalf of the Ottomans. The Ottoman sultan of Turkey, Selim III, was practically forced to appoint the "man of Kavala" as viceroy (pasha) in the land of the pharaohs, under pressure from the notables of Egypt. Muhammad Ali, within five short years, had risen from being an unknown tobacco trader in Kavala to the status of "The last pharaoh," an epiphet allocated to Muhammad Ali by one of his modern biographers, the French author Gilbert Sinoué.[9] Ruthless to the core (he masterminded the cold-blooded massacre of the last of the Mamluk beys during a feast at the Citadel in old Cairo), ambitious and courageous as few others and endowed with an oxymoronic nature of authority, generosity, and charm, Muhammad Ali indeed ruled Egypt like a pharaoh—with that unchallenged and unquestioned supreme power worthy of the great pyramid builders of old. Feared, respected, and even admired by foreign rulers and their consular representatives, Muhammad Ali was to embark on a massive program to modernize Egypt and turn it into a true world power within twenty years.

MUHAMMAD ALI'S RISE AFTER THE FRENCH OCCUPATION

The French occupation of Egypt, which lasted only three years, was to be extremely significant for the country in many ways. Egypt, which had been controlled for five centuries by the Mamluks and the Ottoman sultanates, had become an object of the contending policies of France and Britain as part of the so-called Eastern question. The impact of the French army accompanied by scholars and scientists in Egypt, even though brief, was to be increasingly felt for the next century and a half. Indeed, even after the departure of the French army, the savants continued the work of the Institut d'Égypte in Cairo. This was the first step, and indeed the bastion, from which Egypt would regain the memory of its ancient past.

A period of political turmoil followed the departure of the French. Three groups vied for power: the Mamluks who, although much weakened by French, were still strong enough and eager to reestablish their supremacy; the Ottoman army led by the sultan's primary agent Khurshid Pasha, which remained in Egypt to reestablish Ottoman rule; and the Albanian contingent, which acted as an independent party and had installed in May 1803, their own leader as acting viceroy. When the Albanian leader was assassinated shortly afterward, the command of the Albanian contingent passed to his first lieutenant, Muhammad Ali. Muhammad Ali cleverly and shrewdly strengthened his own position at the expense of both the Mamluks and the Ottomans and gradually gained the respect and trust of the Egyptians.

Muhammad Ali must have observed the way the French had wooed the Egyptian notables and scholars (*ulema*), and thus used the same strategy, making it appear to leading figures in Egyptian society that he, not his Ottoman viceroy, Khurshid Pasha, was the man who had their true interests at heart. His policy proved right when, in May 1805, a revolt broke out in Cairo against Khurshid Pasha, and the ulema invested Muhammad Ali as viceroy. Two months later, Sultan Selim III had to recognize Muhammad Ali as the new ruler in Egypt but insisted that Egypt remain a province of the Ottoman Empire and continued making annual tribute. Meanwhile, the Mamluks had retreated to Upper Egypt, waiting for the opportunity to reacquire power. And although Muhammad Ali ruled Egypt from Cairo, his authority was disputed everywhere outside the city by the Mamluk beys. However, in 1811 his chance to get rid of the Mamluks came when Mecca and Medina, the two holy cities of Islam, fell under the attacks of the puritanical Wahhabi Muslims—a serious blow and embarrassment to the Ottoman sultan, Mahmud II, who was regarded by all Muslims as the ruler and custodian of the holy shrines in Arabia. The sultan gave orders to Muhammad Ali to attack the Wahhabis.

While preparing to send troops to Arabia under the command of his son, Ahmed Toussoun, Muhammad Ali shrewdly invited the Mamluks to attend a ceremony at the Cairo Citadel. When they arrived on March 1, they were courteously received by Muhammad Ali. After the Mamluks finished the traditional coffee drinking they formed a procession and descended the steep and narrow street to the great gate of the citadel, followed by Muhammad Ali's troops. As soon as they arrived at the gate, it was closed suddenly, and the Albanian soldiers started to shoot and kill the Mamluks who were locked in like rats in the narrow street between the gates and the Albanian troops. A bloodbath ensued. Only one of the four hundred and seventy Mamluks was able to escape, leaving Muhammad Ali in the supreme and dominant position in the country.

The slaughter of the Mamluks was followed by Muhammad Ali's victory over the Wahhabis; he drove them out of the holy cities and restored the annual pilgrimages to Mecca by bringing Arabia under the control and safety of Egyptian rule. A few years later, Muhammad Ali was to send another expedition, this time up the Nile to conquer and annex northern Sudan. By so doing, he made himself master of one of the principal channels of the slave trade and began an African empire that was to be expanded under his successors.

The first thing he did was to form a new regular army, which could eventually become the dominant force in the eastern Mediterranean. Muhammad Ali, now known to all as the Pasha, first attempted to form this army with slaves from the Sudan. Thousands of black African young men were taken as slaves in military raids in the Sudan and brought into Upper Egypt at Aswan. However, this attempt failed, as the slaves, who were kept in cramped and neglected conditions, died of disease and malnutrition in large numbers. The Pasha then turned to the poor Egyptian peasants who were conscribed by force into his new model army under the authority of Turkish-speaking officers (the Pasha himself always spoke Turkish and not the language of the Egyptians, which is Arabic). To train and run his army, the Pasha invited Joseph Anthelme Sève, a Frenchman who had been an officer in Napoleon's army. Sève, who changed his name to Suleiman Pasha (al-Fransawi), converted to Islam and married an Egyptian woman. Within a few years, Suleiman Pasha created for Muhammad Ali, the Pasha, the most powerful military force in the region, as well as modern naval force at the port of Alexandria.

From the outset of his reign the Pasha was in constant conflict with his masters in Istanbul. The sultan of Turkey wanted to wrest Egypt from the Pasha's hold, while the latter had expansionist aspirations that even encroached on the Ottoman Empire. For the first twenty-five years of his reign, the Pasha used his army at the service of the Ottoman Sultan. However, in 1830, the Pasha turned against his master and sent his troops to challenge Ottoman authority in the Levant so that he could take control of the raw materials of Syria and the Lebanon, especially timber, as well as secure strategic military passageways. Two campaigns were carried out by the Pasha's new Egyptian forces, and in both, the Ottoman armies were defeated.

Muhammad Ali's army was able to cross the Taurus Mountains into the very heart of Anatolia, and thus within 150 kilometers from the Ottoman capital in Istanbul. It was only because the European powers, the Great Powers, intervened that Muhammad Ali had to back off and give up much of his territorial acquisitions. When Sultan Mahmud II died in July 1839, the Ottoman Empire was on the verge of collapse but, as always, was saved in the nick of time by the Great Powers. Fearing that the dissolution of the Ottoman Empire would be replaced by the emergence of Egypt as the new strong power in the eastern Mediterranean, the European allies forced Muhammad Ali to withdraw his troops from Anatolia, but not before the new sultan of Turkey, Abdul Mejid I (1839–1861), conferred on the Pasha hereditary rule of Egypt, although formally remaining a province of the Ottoman Empire. At the same time, negotiations between the Great Powers and the Ottomans in 1840 to 1841 limited the size of the Egyptian army and compelled the Pasha to end his internal monopolistic buying practices in Egypt by also allowing Europe's merchants to buy and sell freely in all internal Egyptian markets. Under such pressure, Muhammad Ali's Arabian domain, which now extended as far as the Yemen, crumbled, and his ambitions to build a great Eastern empire with Egypt as its center came to an end.

THE MODERNIZATION OF EGYPT

Before we close with the story of Muhammad Ali, it is important that we also place not just his militaristic achievements (and downfall) but also his civic and commercial achievements in the context of modern Egypt, for these, too, have much bearing on the main issue of our project, namely the state of affairs regarding the antiquities of this country.

In spite of not being himself of Egyptian blood, and in spite of his cruel and autocratic attitude toward the people, paradoxically the Pasha truly loved Egypt—but, sadly, not *ancient* Egypt. As the author Fagan noted:

> Muhammad Ali had no cause to legislate against the removal of antiquities, for Egypt had no national museum to keep them in. The Turkish rulers of Egypt had no interest in or identity with the ancient past. To them the antiquities of the Nile were a significant political tool, useful for gratifying eccentric but powerful visitors or diplomats with curious collection habits. The tangible monuments of ancient Egypt were merely a source of building stone . . .[10]

In many ways, the Pasha was an oriental version of his hero Napoleon; for Napoleon, too, had loved Egypt, even though he came to conquer it and control it. And like Napoleon, the Pasha wanted to bring Egypt on par with modern Europe. Yet, there was an important difference: Napoleon was a very cultured and educated man; the Pasha was illiterate and uncultured. Indeed, it was something that the Pasha himself readily admitted. The Pasha, unlike Napoleon, was indifferent to Egypt's ancient past and its legacy—which, unfortunately, left the way open to profiteers, smugglers, and black marketers to exploit this legacy. But more on this later on.

Meanwhile, let us return to the Pasha and his modernization plans. Although he was completely illiterate, Muhammad Ali was commercially shrewd and streetwise and smart enough to fully understand that a modern army had to be supported by a modern country with infrastructure, factories, and a modern elite society to run it. The first thing he did—very much like the oil-rich gulf states of the twentieth century—was to contract help and know-how from the Western world. A horde of European engineers, mostly French and Italian, poured into the country and were given special privileges and virtual free-for-all licenses to exploit the country.

The Pasha also sent educational missions to Italy (as early as 1809),

Austria, and France—the larger number (including his own sons) going to Paris. Cleverly, the Pasha demanded that all the Egyptian, Turkish, and Albanian students chosen to go to Europe translate their European textbooks, lectures, notes, and other reading assignments into Arabic. In Egypt itself, and using mostly members of his own family and close entourage, he began to build a new and modern administrative structure and government that were modeled on those of Europe and, especially, France. The Pasha created a whole range of educational institutions alongside the traditional Muslim schools of the *ulema* (Islamic scholars). Naturally, he also founded a school for infantry, cavalry, and artillery, which promoted the organization of the Egyptian army on French lines, as well as a school of medicine. Muhammad Ali also created Egypt's first local press and, very wisely, required that the new schools in Egypt be equipped with libraries stocked with modern European works and their Arabic translations.

Following the advice of Raf'i el-Tahtawi, his most brilliant student, he set up a School of Translation for the purpose of training students in European languages. Muhammad Ali sent el-Tahtawi to Paris as chaplain of a group of students, where he studied Greek philosophy, history, mythology, mathematics, engineering, geography, logic, and other subjects in the humanities. For sixteen years, el-Tahtawi remained the head of the School of Translation. He facilitated many translations of important European works, including the works of leading French enlightenment thinkers such as Rousseau and Voltaire. It is said by many that it was thanks to el-Tahtawi that the new field of Egyptology was formally introduced in Egypt, even though it was completely dominated by European scholarship. He wrote a history of ancient Egypt and urged his Egyptian students to study the ancient history of their country, which he rightly deemed vitally important for their national identity. As a direct result of el-Tahtawi's effort, two of the greatest Egyptian pioneers in Egyptology emerged: Ahmed Kamal Pasha (who was trained under the German professor Heinrich Brugsch and who eventually became a curator at the Egyptian Museum) and Marcus

Simaika Pasha (who eventually founded the Coptic Museum in Cairo).

Muhammad Ali, being from a merchant family himself, quickly recognized that a modern country and its army cannot be sustained without an equally modern and strong economy. Thus, with the help of his foreign advisers and consultants, the Pasha developed Egypt's agriculture by introducing new crops, the most important being long-staple cotton, which in time would become Egypt's most lucrative export. He had old canals cleaned and new canals constructed and built new dams and weirs along the Nile to improve land irrigation during the low Nile season (September to July). The most important of such works was the Mahmoudeya Canal from the Nile to Alexandria, which acted as a vital lifeline to that once-celebrated city of the Ptolemies and which now quickly brought it back to its thriving past glory.

MONUMENTS FOR FACTORIES

There were, however, serious downturns to the Pasha's ambitious modernization programs. Although he abolished the old tax systems that the Ottomans had employed and that crippled the *fellahin* (farmers), the Pasha imposed state control over most of Egypt's agricultural land, expropriated the landholders, and effectively became the sole landholder, with a monopoly over the agricultural trade. Egypt became the Pasha's private property and its people were put into his servitude (although later he made considerable grants of land to his family and dependents). His system of state monopolies for almost all the agricultural commodities traded domestically and internationally resulted in a huge increase in so-called government (which really meant private) revenues, which paid for the Pasha's modern army, the foreign educational missions, the hydraulic improvements, the land development, and now, more significantly, the vast industrialization programs, which included textile, paper, indigo, and munitions factories; sugar refineries; rice milling; and tanning. All of these used a local workforce—more of a slave-force some would say—and machinery and expertise imported from Europe.

Figure 3.4. Muhammad Ali Pasha, first ruler of modern Egypt, whose dynasty ended in 1952 with the deposing of King Farouk I

Ironically, the last two of these ambitious modernization programs, namely the hydraulic works along the Nile with dams and canals, as well as the factories and mills, nearly caused the total destruction of the ancient legacy of temples, pyramids, and cities of the pharaohs, for Muhammad Ali, although endowed with a natural sense of commerce and militaristic acumen, nonetheless had no interest in preserving the ancient monuments along the Nile. Everything to him had a commercial value to be exploited either for economic or political gain. In the words of his latest biographer:

> Muhammad Ali would have sacrificed a pyramid in order to build his dams on the Nile . . . like his predecessors the monuments scattered in the country have no interest for him. The orders of the Pasha are simple: construction [of dams and factories] must proceed without delay. Naturally the most available "quarries" were used, namely the temples and all other monuments.[11]

Whole ancient temples, indeed whole *cities*—Ashmunein (the Hermopolis Magna), Rakotis on the Mediterranean, Antinoe, Antoepolis, and Elephantine—were demolished, the stones used to build the modern port of Alexandria, saltpeter factories, and sugar refineries. Even the whole city of Luxor, which contained the many magnificent temples of the New Kingdom, was sold to a saltpeter factory owner![12] So extensive was the destruction of the ancient sites that Charles Lenormant, the famous French archaeologist who witnessed this shameful desecration, was to cry out that

> the monuments of Egypt never had a worse enemy than the mercantile Mohammad Ali . . . it is highly likely that if the European Powers do not intervene, within twenty years there will not be one single monument left in Egypt! It is something that must be shouted on the rooftops![13]

As late as 1859 the Frenchman Louis Vivien de Saint-Martin was moved to lament that

> Elephantine has been stripped of its lovely temples. . . . Armant has yielded to a sugar refinery the most beautiful part of its portal. The small temples of Esna, el Kab, the Typhonium of Edfu, the great tomb of Onnofre at Saqqara, half the Hypogeum of Lycopolis are lost forever![14]

In vain did the foreign archaeologists and other scholars in Egypt at the time plead with the Pasha. To be fair, the "man from Kavala" who now ruled Egypt with an iron fist had many other serious matters to sort out, not least the raising of money to pay his army and build his "modern Egypt." It also must be emphasized that he was illiterate, and, although he seemed to have a refined nature (he was always courteous and generous to foreigners), he was *completely incapable of the slightest cultural perception*.[15] On one occasion in 1824, the French consul, Jean-François Mimaut, reported that

[b]arbarous workers sent by some Bey or other or some ignorant maamour [foreman], had begun the demolition of the temple of Dendera, which is one of the most beautiful temples of Upper Egypt. Having been told of this by an indignant traveler, I begged Mohammad Ali to put an end to this horrible vandalism, and to repeat again to him the promise he had made to M. Champollion and myself that no ancient monuments should be touched . . .[16]

Lenormant, as well as other French and Italian archaeologists, also pleaded with Muhammad Ali to save the monuments from such pillage and vandalism; it was all to no avail. And even though the Pasha did issue various *firmans* (decrees) to that effect, his orders were largely ignored. It was quite obvious that the Pasha played "good cop, bad cop" with the European archaeologists—on the one hand agreeing with them, on the other hand turning a blind eye to the destruction as it suited his modernization ambitions. In his memoirs Lenormant was to write:

I had told the vice-roy [Muhammad Ali] that in spite of the orders that he had issued, the degradation of the ancient monuments went on every day and that the inscribed stones and the precious marble were removed to make chalk, and that destruction was taking place at such a rapid pace that fourteen of the main monuments described in the great publication of Egypt [*Descriptions de L'Egypte*] had disappeared.[17]

Charles Lenormant (1802–1859) was a graduate of the Lycée Charlemagne and the Lycée Napoléon where he studied law. After a visit to Italy and Greece from 1822 to 1823, however, he decided to become an archaeologist. He was named assistant inspector of fine arts in 1825 and in that same year married Amelia Syvoct, the daughter of the famous Madame de Récamier. Lenormant accompanied Champollion to Egypt in 1828, where he studied ancient Egyptian monuments. On his return to Europe, he traveled throughout Greece as assistant director of archaeology of the Morea scientific commission. In France, he was made curator of works of art in the Royal Library, where he lectured in ancient history. In 1840, he became the curator of the Cabinet des Medailles (Cabinet of Medals). He also lectured at the Sorbonne, especially on Christian civilization. In 1848, Lenormant was appointed director of the commission of historical monuments, and in 1849, the French Academy gave him the chair of archaeology at the Collège de France, where he devoted all his teachings in Egyptian archaeology. He died in Athens in November 1859, where he is also buried.

The Pasha, in reply to Lenormant's indignation and pleading, rudely told the celebrated French archaeologist that he would be very surprised that his orders had been ignored and that in any case it was not the Egyptians or Turks who were destroying the ancient monuments but rather the "Europeans . . . who are degrading the monuments which they want to sell or take away."[18] There was some truth in this, of course, but ironically it was Muhammad Ali himself who gave a free hand to these Europeans and allowed them to exploit the ancient monuments; indeed, the Pasha gave many of Egypt's most precious antiquities to European governments he was eager to please. Among those precious items were the two obelisks known as Cleopatra's Needles (one on the Victoria Embankment in London, the other in New York's Central Park); the wonderful obelisk of Ramses II, one of a pair that stood outside the temple of Luxor (now in Place de la Concorde in Paris); and, sacrilege of sacrilege, the sarcophagus of King Menkaure, which was discovered inside the Third Pyramid at Giza. It sank, along with the ship transporting it, to the bottom of the Mediterranean Sea off the coast of Spain.

By the end of 1829, this deplorable situation had deteriorated so much that even the normally timid Champollion, who was in Egypt on a mission, plucked enough courage to send a report to the Pasha in which he pointed out that

> [i]t is a matter of urgency and of the greatest importance that your agents follow your orders to the letter. The whole of Europe will be grateful to Your Highness of the active measures that you will take to ensure the conservation of temples, palaces, tombs and all other types of monuments that attest to the grandeur of ancient Egypt . . . It is high time to put an end to these barbarous devastations which deprives at all instances the science of monuments [i.e., Egyptology] of matters of great importance . . .
>
> This is the main objective of missions [to Egypt] that are undertaken by many Europeans who belong to the most distinguished classes of society. Their regrets join with all of scholarly Europe which bitterly deplores the complete destruction of many ancient monuments, totally demolished in recent years such that no traces of these remain . . .[19]

Again, Champollion's words fell on deaf ears. The destruction and vandalism went on unabated for many years—indeed until 1858, thus more than half a century from the time the Pasha became ruler of Egypt. But we are perhaps moving too fast here. Notwithstanding the deliberate removal of ancient columns, arches, and walls to satisfy the urgent commercial, industrial, and economic ambitions of the Pasha, we must now ask who were indeed these Europeans that, according to Muhammad Ali, were plundering the ancient monuments for personal profit?

BRITISH SALT AND A LITTLE FRENCH PEPPER

There is no question that among the plethora of Europeans helping themselves to the legacy of ancient Egypt as if it was theirs to exploit, the most active by far were the British and French consuls, namely

Henry Salt and Bernardino Drovetti. These two men were the principal causes behind the huge quantity of ancient artifacts that were taken
out of Egypt to literally fill the hallways of European museums and the
salons of private collectors.

Henry Salt was born in Lichfield, England, in 1870. Although the
son of an English physician, Salt was trained as a painter in London
and, in 1802, became private secretary and draftman to Viscount
Valentia, a rich dilettante in archaeology who enjoyed travels in exotic
places. They traveled to India, and during this journey, Salt explored
the Red Sea and visited Ethiopia. In 1809, three years after their return
to England, Valentia published a book, *Voyages and Travels to India*,
in which the paintings and drawings of Salt were included. That same
year, Salt returned to Ethiopia on a mission for the British government.
On his return, he, too, published a book, *A Voyage to Abyssinia, and
Travels into the Interior of That Country, Executed under the Orders
of the British Government in the Years 1809 & 1810*, which contained
many of his paintings. In 1814, hearing that the post of British consul
general for Egypt was vacant, Salt lobbied for the post with the help
of his influential friends in the foreign office. A cushy job even by
nineteenth-century standards, Salt had plenty of time to devote to the
"collecting" (to use a polite word) of ancient Egyptian artifacts, which
he sold to various interested foreign parties, mostly (although not exclusively) to the British Museum. Being the representative of Britain, one
of the most powerful nations in the world at the time, and also being
a close friend of Muhammad Ali, Salt was able to obtain any firman
he wished from the Pasha who was happy (indeed eager) to please the
British.

An amazing number of ancient artifacts were thus exported out of
Egypt by Salt, even huge items such as the giant 20-ton bust of Ramses
II taken from the Ramesseum in Western Thebes, as well as the sar-
cophagus of Ramses III, which he sold to the Louvre Museum in Paris.
Salt had virtually a free hand in appropriating ancient antiquities and
would have "collected" far more had it not been that he was rivaled

by the much more unscrupulous, although equally profiteering, French consul general, Bernardino Drovetti. A legendary rivalry between the two men, matched only by the ongoing rivalry between Britain and France, was to witness a massive exploitation of ancient Egyptian artifacts for the benefit of European museums and collectors.

Bernardino Michele Maria Drovetti was born in 1776 in Barbania in the kingdom of Piedmont-Sardenia. After his graduation in Turin, he entered Napoleon's army and joined the Hussars. In 1801, Drovetti became minister of war and chief of staff of the Piedmont division in the French army. He also became a judge in the city of Turin. In 1803, Napoleon sent Drovetti, along with Mathieu de Lesseps (father of the famous Ferdinand, the builder of the Suez Canal) to Egypt as commissioners for foreign relations. Drovetti, being the representative of Napoleon in Egypt, Muhammad Ali's hero, cultivated a close and very influential friendship with the Pasha. In 1815, Drovetti resigned from his diplomatic post to devote his time exclusively to the collection of antiquities, the most lucrative occupation one could dream of in Egypt, provided, of course, you had the blessing (and firmans) of the Pasha. (Drovetti was eventually reappointed consul general of France in Egypt in 1829.)

Drovetti not only traded in ancient Egyptian antiquities. Because of his privileged relationship with the Pasha he also amassed a huge private collection for himself. Among his best clients were the Louvre and Turin museums, but also many private rich collectors—in short the highest bidders. He had the reputation of getting exorbitant prices. It was rumored that Drovetti made a small fortune in 1824 when he sold a large number of Egyptian artifacts to King Carlo Felix of Sardinia, which was comprised of over five thousand items including more than one hundred statues, nearly two hundred papyri, dozens of mummies, stelae, jewelry, and many other objects (this collection was to serve as the foundation of the famous Museum of Turin). Drovetti employed terribly destructive methods to increase his profits. It is said that he would smash artifacts in smaller pieces to sell them individually and cut obelisks in several parts to make transport easier. Yet in spite of such deplorable methods, several statues of Drovetti himself were erected in various parts of Italy, praising him as a national hero.

Figure 3.5. Bernardino Drovetti, French Consul in Egypt, and a prolific collector of antiquities, which were sold to the museum of Turin and various other clients

To counter the success of Drovetti, Salt used the service of an Italian who lived in Egypt, the infamous ex-circus strongman Giovanni Battista Belzoni, as well as the service of a Greek "agent," Yanni d'Athanasi. Both these tough and unscrupulous men were very knowledgeable about Egyptian matters and, more important, knew how to obtain antiquities. Thanks to them, Salt was able to amass a vast collection within a few years, mostly sold to the British Museum for 2,000 pounds, a fortune in those days. A second collection also followed in 1824, which was comprised of no fewer than four thousand precious objects. But due to the very high price asked by Salt, the British Museum turned it down, and it, instead, was bought by King Charles X of France for 10,000 pounds and

Figure 3.6. Henry Salt, British Consul in Egypt, and prolific collector of antiquities, which he sold to the British Museum and other clients

donated to the Louvre. Salt's third collection of some two thousand price-less objects was auctioned by him, mostly to the British Museum. Had Salt not died prematurely in 1827 at the age of forty-seven, the British Museum would have needed another building for its Egyptian collection!

Giovanni Battista Belzoni was born in Padua, Italy, in 1778. His father was a barber who sired fourteen children. When he was sixteen, Belzoni went to Rome where, according to him, he studied hydraulic engineering. Then it seems he was going to become a priest, but in 1798, when Napoleon's army entered Italy, Belzoni dropped the idea and fled to Holland. In 1803, he made his way to England and married Sarah Bane. Very tall (well over six feet), muscular, and strong, Belzoni joined a traveling circus as a strongman. He and Bane also experimented with the "magic lantern" in their performances. To put it another way, Belzoni was a typical conman of his era.

Figure 3.7. Giovanni Battista Belzoni in Arab dress

In 1812, during a circus tour around Europe, he met a representative of Muhammad Ali, a certain Ismael Gibraltar, who told him of the Pasha's hydraulic projects along the Nile. Belzoni then went to Egypt to propose his own hydraulic machine, which he supposedly had invented. The Pasha apparently was not too impressed. Belzoni then was introduced to Henry Salt, who was in Upper Egypt trying to remove a giant statue of Ramses II from the Rameseum temple, which he was going to ship to the British Museum. Belzoni was given the task of removing the eight-ton statue, transporting it down the Nile, and shipping it to England. To get the statue out of the temple, Belzoni had to break the base of several columns. Belzoni was the first European to enter the tomb of Seti I in the Valley of the Kings and also the Second Pyramid at Giza. He also was the first European to visit the oasis of Bahariya in the Western Desert and discovered the ruins of the ancient city of Berenice in the Red Sea.

In 1819, he returned to England, published a book, *Narrative of the Operations and Recent Discoveries within the Pyramids, Temples, Tombs and Excavations in Egypt and Nubia,* and ran an exhibition of facsimiles of Seti I's tomb at the Egyptian Hall in Piccadilly in London and later in Paris (1822). Being a practicing Freemason, he created quite a sensation among the lodges keen to see how the "original Freemasons" performed rituals. In 1823, he went to West Africa, hoping to reach Timbuktu, but died of dysentery in Benin (some say he was robbed and murdered).

THE PASHA'S SON AND THE GREAT CANAL

Muhammad Ali ruled Egypt for more than four decades. But in his last years, he became senile and handed power to his eldest son, Ibrahim. As fate would have it, Ibrahim died only a few months later while Muhammad Ali was still alive. The Pasha ruled till his death in 1849, after which the reign of Egypt went to the next in line, his strange and introverted grandson Abbas, son of Tousson, who became viceroy (*wali*) of Egypt as Abbas I.

Abbas, being an intense traditionalist, did the opposite of Muhammad Ali: he ordered the *closing* of factories, abolished trade monopolies, and reduced the strength of the army to less than ten thousand men. Abbas also, very foolishly, had the various schools of languages and the translation bureau closed and sent their eminent and educated director el-Tahtawi to the Sudan. The only constructive

Figure 3.8. Khedive Abbas Hilmi I, the grandson and
successor of Muhammad Ali Pasha

action by Abbas—and that only when the British government put him
under pressure—was the construction of the railway between Cairo
and Alexandria. Luckily, Abbas's rule lasted only five years. He was
assassinated in July 1854, and the power went to his uncle Saïd Pasha,
Muhammad Ali's fourth son.

Saïd Pasha was sympathetic to his father's modernization and
Westernization policies. However, unlike his father, Saïd was lavish and

Figure 3.9. Saïd Pasha, fourth son of Muhammad Ali Pasha, and sucessor of Abbas Hilmi I

extravagant and could not resist the temptation of borrowing heavily from European financial houses. Early in his reign, the French consul general, the engineer Ferdinand de Lesseps, who was Saïd's very close friend,* managed to sweet-talk Saïd into constructing a canal that would link the Mediterranean and Red Sea across the Isthmus of Suez.

Figure 3.10. Ferdinand de Lesseps, builder of the Suez Canal

---

*De Lesseps was a sort of mentor to Saïd when he was a young boy. Apparently De Lesseps had secretly cooked for the greedy and plump Saïd his favorite meal: Spaghetti Bolognese, which his strict nanny had forbidden!

The idea for a canal across the isthmus of Suez originated with Prosper Enfantin, a senior member of a rather peculiar cult known as the Saint-Simoniens, founded by a Parisian, Claude Henri de Rouvroy, the Comte de Saint-Simon. When de Rouvroy died in 1825, his curious doctrines were taken on by a few of his disciples, the most prominent being Enfantin. The so-called doctrines are complex and not so easy to understand, but basically they involved a sort of socialist religion where industrialists and massive engineering projects (mostly canals and railways) were to be put at the service of human-kind to unite the world in a brotherly global confederation. As such, Enfantin was seen as a sort of "reincarnated Jesus" with an ambitious mission: to create a "bridge" between East and West with a canal across the Isthmus of Suez. According to Enfantin:

> The piercing of the Isthmus of Suez would not just be a technical achievement, but would fulfill a religious need. To dig on the world map this blue streak would be a symbol of peace, of concord and love between two continents.[20]

Another weird idea of the Saint-Simoniens was to fertilize the African black race, which they dubbed "female and sentimental," with the virtues of the white European race, which they dubbed "male and scientific." To this end, Enfantin and some of his followers sailed to Egypt in 1833 with two ambitions in mind: to persuade Muhammad Ali to grant them a concession to build the Suez Canal and to seek the woman or mother (quite literally) that would be fertilized with the virtues of the Saint-Simoniens. We can just imagine that the symbol of this woman or mother was eventually to inspire, a few years later, the French sculptor Auguste Bartholdi, who created the giant statue of a woman (apparently modeled on his own real mother) but which was later offered to the Freemasons of the United States in New York and is now known as the Statue of Liberty.[21]

Enfantin did meet the Pasha, but he failed to persuade him to grant a concession to the Saint-Simoniens for the canal, although apparently the Pasha did buy into the idea of a railroad to join Cairo to Alexandria. Enfantin also met Ferdinand de Lesseps, whom, he later claimed, poached the canal project from the Saint-Simoniens and got the concession from Saïd Pasha, which was largely financed by French and British banks.*

The Universal Suez Shipping Canal Company was founded and registered in 1858 with the Egyptian government holding 44 percent shares and French investors holding majority shares of 52 percent. The deal was that the company would be responsible for the construction of the canal and its operation with a lease of ninety-nine years after which the Egyptian government would take over the full control of the canal, and thus its revenue. The deal also required the Egyptian government to provide four-fifths of the labor force for the canal's construction. Work began on April 25, 1858, under the direct management and supervision of de Lesseps, who, with an army of twenty thousand Egyptian workers, began building the 163-kilometer-long canal, which would run from the Gulf of Suez to the north tip of the western branch of the Red Sea.

Saïd Pasha died in 1863 in the midst of the chaotic construction of the canal and a pronounced economic crisis in the country. He was succeeded by Ismail Pasha, the grandson of Muhammad Ali, known to the outside world simply as the khedive or Khedive Ismail.

A Francophile to the core, the khedive was even more extravagant with the country's revenue than his predecessor, in spite of the huge foreign debt that he inherited from Saïd Pasha—and the responsibility of completing

---

*When Napoleon Bonaparte led his expedition to Egypt in 1798, one of his projects was to build a canal across the Isthmus of Suez, connecting the Mediterranean Sea with the Red Sea. He believed that, in this way, the British would either have to pay dues to France or else continue sailing around the Horn of Africa. However, Napoleon's project was cancelled as a result of a *miscalculation* in measurement that showed the sea levels between the Mediterranean and the Red Sea as being too different for the canal to be constructed (in fact, the two seas have the same level, as de Lesseps eventually proved).

Figure 3.11. Ismail
Pasha, who led Egypt
to bankruptcy in
1867–1870

the work on the Suez Canal. Having spent two years in the French court
of Napoleon III in Paris, the khedive had acquired a refined taste for luxury and pomp and was rumored to have fallen deeply in love with the
French empress Eugenie (of Spanish descent and a cousin of Ferdinand de
Lesseps). So mesmerized was the khedive by the beautiful and glamorous
empress that he tried to impress her with all sorts of follies. In his eager-
ness to have Eugenie come visit Egypt, Ismail ordered the construction of
splendid palaces along the Nile and villas solely for her pleasure.

Among the khedive's many dreams was the attempt to rebuild central Cairo as a "Paris on the Nile." Amazingly, he declared to the world
that "my country [Egypt] is no longer in Africa; we are now part of
Europe. It is therefore natural for us to abandon our former ways and
to adopt a new system adapted to our social conditions." To achieve this
"Europeanization" of Egypt, the khedive ordered the complete demolition of a large part of the old city with its picturesque Turkish-style
houses in order to replace the narrow alleyways with wide Parisian-style
boulevards and avenues flanked by modern European architecture.

As for the Suez Canal, the khedive stubbornly refused to abide to his contractual obligations of supplying *corvée* laborers (forced labor) for the construction works. The matter was eventually settled by arbitration, and the khedive, who was found to be in breach of contract, was imposed a fine of 3 million pounds. Meanwhile, Khedive Ismail had to also pay for a large block of the company's share that de Lesseps had allocated to Saïd Pasha's personal account.

Luckily for Egypt, the price of long-staple cotton, the country's main export, shot up on the world markets due to the Civil War in the United States, the latter the second largest exporter of cotton at the time. Money flowed into the khedive's coffers, giving him the illusion that he could spend and spend without worry or constraint. And this he did in the most lavish ways. Other than his *folies des grandeurs* to make a good impression on the enchanting French empress Eugenie, Ismail also used the extra state revenues to launch a plethora of beautification projects for the major cities along the Nile, to extend the irrigation canal networks, to expand the number of schools, and, of course, to enlarge the size of the Egyptian army manyfold. In 1866, the khedive also managed to extort from his Ottoman rulers a sort of state independence by abandoning the "rule by succession of the oldest male" to a European system of direct male descendants; that is from eldest son to eldest son (the last of which would be the ill-fated King Farouk I).

To realize Khedive Ismail's obsession to turn old Cairo in a modern Paris, including wide boulevards, splendid plazas, and public gardens, his planners used newly reclaimed lands west of the old city leading to the banks of the Nile River as the location of these new structures. The khedive enticed Jean-Pierre Barillet-Deschamps, the designer of the Bois de Boulogne and the Champ de Mars in Paris, to lend his creative efforts to this ambitious project. The khedive also brought to Egypt the French horticulturalist Gustave Delchevalerie to fashion an elaborate set of gardens in Cairo's district of Ezbekeya.

The buildings in the city center were to have elaborate stone decorations, gargoyles, and rooftops that were as fine as the best urban buildings in the fashionable capitals of Europe. A magnificent opera was also commissioned as well as a national theater, all to attest that Cairo had indeed become the Paris along the Nile. Even today, much of downtown Cairo dates from the days of the khedive and owes its belle epoque charm to the visions of his French architects. For more on Khedive Ismail's Paris along the Nile, see *Egypt* by Robert L. Tignor and *Egypt's Belle Epoque* by Trevor Mostyn.

THE OPENING OF THE SUEZ CANAL

Six years after Khedive Ismail came to power and after nearly eleven years of frantic construction on the multimillion-dollar Suez Canal (which burgeoned the national debt from $3 million in 1863 to over

Figure 3.12. The opening of the Suez Canal on November 17, 1869

$100 million in 1869), the famous waterway that joined two continents was now ready for commercial shipping.

In spite of the huge national debt, Ismail insisted on throwing one of history's most lavish inaugural festivities, which would have made Cleopatra's triumphal entry into Imperial Rome a mere birthday party. No expense was spared by the khedive to make the event something the world would always remember.

On the early morning of November 17, 1869, a flotilla of royal yachts and luxury liners—one more grandiose than the next and flying the national flags of their respective countries—waited at the entrance of the Suez Canal in the Mediterranean near the new city of Port Saïd (named after his predecessor Saïd Pasha). As the signal to enter the canal was given, the flotilla was led, as one would now expect, by the imperial French yacht *Aigle,* carrying the lovely Empress Eugenie, the guest of honor of the khedive. Ismail had also invited many other famous people, ranging from such dignitaries as the emperor of Austria to intellectual celebrities such as the French novelist Emile Zola and the Norwegian playwright Henrik Ibsen. The khedive had even contracted the world-famous Italian composer Giuseppe Verdi to compose the opera *Aida* for the occasion (although *Aida* had to wait two more years for its premier in 1871 at the newly built Khedivial Opera House in Cairo). Verdi did, however, participate in the ceremonies for the Suez Canal and gallantly gave his permission for the performance of his other masterpiece, *Rigoletto,* to be played in Cairo. The party lasted several days with glamorous balls, entertainments, and banquets in Cairo. But when the party was over and the music stopped and all the guests returned home laden with gifts from the khedive (perhaps even with genuine ancient artifacts as souvenirs), the khedive had to face another more somber type of music: the huge financial debts. The artificially high prices of cotton on the world market (due to the American Civil War) had encouraged Ismail to borrow heavily from European financial houses until the national debt had bloated to more than ten times the annual income of Egypt. But when America's Civil War ended in

1865, cotton prices came tumbling down, forcing the khedive to turn to Europe for more funds to service the ever-increasing national debt. Ismail began to sell off state lands and even pledged Egypt's taxation revenues to Europe to service the debt. After having mortgaged or sold every thing he could, the khedive was eventually forced to sell Egypt's holdings in the Suez Canal Company to the British government in 1875 for a mere 4 million pounds.

EGYPT FOR EGYPTIANS!

Khedive Ismail, following in the footsteps of his grandfather Muhammad Ali, not only spent vast amounts of borrowed money to enlarge the Egyptian army but also engaged in several very costly military campaigns in Africa in his ambition to make Egypt the dominant power in the Red Sea region and create an Egyptian empire extending from Sudan all the way to the Horn of Africa. Although he did succeed in establishing Egyptian control on the Somali coastline, Ismail's attempts to invade Ethiopia in 1875 to 1876 were unsuccessful and marked the limits of his imperial expansion dream. An Egyptian "Napoleon" he was not—as the frivolous but very religious French empress must have early realized when she rejected several of Ismail's amorous moves.

Ismail's Europeanization program also backfired. The khedive and his family were the principal landowners in Egypt, and the royal court was surrounded by a new aristocracy that held the principal civil and military offices. But Ismail's own modernizing efforts inevitably produced a group of native-born educated Egyptians who were eager to take the modernization well beyond the limits that Ismail had actually intended. Looking at European parliamentary democracies as ideal models, these educated and rich Egyptians saw no reason why Egypt should not also have government institutions that could check the powers of the khedive.

Ismail was obliged to ask the British government to help him in fiscal reform. To this end, they sent him Steven Cave, a member of parliament, who concluded that Egypt could indeed be solvent on the basis of its natural resources, provided, of course, it was given enough time to sort out its financial crisis. European creditors, however, were in no mood to allow Ismail such time. In 1875, Britain and France negotiated new arrangements with the khedive, which included (1) the consolidation of the national debt, (2) the appointment of two financial controllers, one French and the other British, and (3) the establishment of a special "national department" to represent European creditors to ensure that Egypt serviced its huge national debt. In the years that followed, more than 60 percent of the annual revenue went to service the national department.

Such austere measures brought political and civic tension to the breaking point. In 1876, a commission of inquiry was appointed to examine all sources of revenue and expenditure and reached the decision that a new cabinet must immediately be formed that would include experienced European public servants with full ministerial powers. The khedive had no choice but to accept the commission's decision. In 1878, Ismail appointed the highly respected but weak Nubar Pasha to be Egypt's very first prime minister. The latter then formed a new government with a British minister and a French minister who would assume full control over the ministries of finance and public works. Furthermore, Ismail had to delegate governmental responsibility to an Assembly of Delegates.

Not unexpectedly, the newly appointed Assembly of Delegates, which was made up of Egyptians, as well as the Egyptian army, vehemently opposed such direct European involvement in their country's internal affairs. In 1879, the Assembly of Delegates demanded more control over financial matters and accountability of the European ministers. At the same time, a group of disgruntled Egyptian officers, angered by Ismail's proposal to reduce the size of the army from 93,000 to 37,000, occupied the Ministry of Finance. The situation was further inflamed when the khedive attempted to dissolve the Assembly of Delegates and also when the European ministers demanded that Egypt declare itself bankrupt. The Assembly of Delegates, not only refused to accept the khedive's as well as the European ministers' orders, but its leader, Sharif Pasha, proposed constitutional reform to increase the power of the assembly. Ismail caved, dismissed the Prime Minister Nubar Pasha and his whole cabinet (including the two European ministers), and asked Sharif Pasha to form a new government.

While these actions made the khedive popular at home, Britain and France decided that it was high time for him to go. Ismail refused to abdicate, but the European Great Powers eventually forced his Ottoman superior, Sultan Abdulhamind II, to depose Ismail in favor of his son, Tewfik. Ismail was nonetheless allowed to reside in exile in a palace he owned in Constantinople, and there he lived more or less as a prisoner until his death in 1895. True to his lavish ways, Khedive Ismail apparently choked to death while trying to guzzle two bottles of champagne in one draft. But perhaps it was the many women he kept in his harem (at one point three thousand)[22] that eventually but slowly wore out the lovesick khedive.

ENTER THE BRITISH "SAVIORS"

Let us pause to imagine what must have been the pitiful state of the pharaonic antiquities in this climate of financial and social chaos that Egypt found itself in. No records, at least none that we have come across, report their condition, but if we consider the disinterest that the khedive had had for such matters and his pathetic obsession with French culture, not to mention the heavy financial burden he brought upon his fellow countrymen, then we can unfortunately conclude that much pillage and illegal trafficking took place.

At any rate, after Ismail was exiled in 1879, his son, Tewfik, reluctantly accepted the rulership of Egypt under such financial and political turmoil. He unwisely restored the dual European–Egyptian control of Egypt's finances and internal affairs and dissolved the Assembly of Delegates. The country's annual revenue was divided into two approximately equal portions, one part to service the national debt. Resentment of European influence thus continued to grow, not only among Egyptian public servants and army officers but also with intellectuals, landowners, and merchants, who championed the notion of giving more powers to the Assembly of Delegates, which Ismail had created but that now Tewfik had dissolved. A nationalist group had appeared within the Assembly of Delegates led by Sharif Pasha while Ismail Pasha had been in power. Also at about the same time, a group of Egyptian officers, under the leadership of Colonel Ahmed Orabi, loudly and angrily expressed their objections to European intervention in Egypt's affairs. This new indigenous Egyptian elite, as well as Muslim reformers, soon started to challenge the privileges and financial liberties that the Turkish-Albanian-Circassian ruling dynasty, with its European modernization obsessions, had so lavishly enjoyed (and squandered) since the reign of its founder Muhammad Ali Pasha.

In 1881, hardly two short years into Tewfik's reign, the army officers led by Orabi started a mutiny against the khedive. To appease matters, Tewfik was forced to form a new government and made Orabi undersecretary for war in January 1882. Foolishly, Britain and France then issued a joint statement declaring their political and military support to Khedive Tewfik. The fact that Tewfik was, according to several reports, installed as grand master of the Masonic United Grand Lodge of Egypt in 1881 may or may not have played a part in this matter.* In any case, such a blatant declaration of support from the two European Great Powers produced an upsurge in anti-European feeling, and soon after, Orabi openly demanded the overthrow of Khedive Tewfik.

Fearing for his life, Tewfik fled to Alexandria and sought military intervention from Britain and France, who responded by sending a joint naval force to Alexandria and demanding the resignation of the new government and the exile of Orabi. Rioting in Alexandria and

---

*Freemasonry in Egypt was legal from 1798 to 1964. But many records have been destroyed and it is very difficult to be sure of the many reports in articles and on the Internet about Tewfiq Pasha's Masonic affiliations.

Cairo ensued in June 1882. A month later, British warships bombarded Alexandria and then landed to protect Tewfik in Raselteen Palace. The khedive, along with the British, declared Orabi a rebel—while Orabi himself declared war on Britain. In August 1882, a British force of twenty thousand soldiers invaded the Suez Canal Zone and marched toward Cairo. They confronted Orabi on September 13, defeated Orabi's Egyptian army in a short decisive battle at Tell el Kebir, and took Orabi prisoner. Upon arriving in Cairo, the British restored the authority of Tewfik, banished Orabi to Ceylon, and started their occupation of Egypt and the canal zone—which was to last for the next seventy-four years.

L'ÉGYPTE RECONNAISSANTE (GRATEFUL EGYPT)

There was, however, a ray of hope amid all the calamities that befell the ancient temples and other antiquities during the reigns of the khedives and pashas. This ray of hope came in the guise of a foreigner—a highly educated, highly professional, and highly responsible Frenchman in his early thirties. Finally, at long last, a huge breath of clean fresh air was about to sweep over this ancient land, this splendid land of the pharaohs, this ancient Kemet, the nurse if not the crucible of world civilization. Finally, after nearly two thousand years of sheer indifference and abandonment by its foreign rulers, after massive exploitation by greedy diplomats and adventurers, after centuries of willful or careless destruction, Egypt's antiquities were about to receive official state recognition and protection under a totally new government department: the Services des Antiquitées.

Enter Auguste Mariette.

4
Saving Ancient Egypt

À Mariette Pacha, L'Égypte Reconnaissante (To Mariette Pasha, A Grateful Egypt)

INSCRIPTION ON THE MODERN SARCOPHAGUS IN THE COURTYARD OF THE CAIRO MUSEUM OF ANTIQUITIES IN WHICH RESTS AUGUSTE MARIETTE

One finds a temple to Serapis in such a sandy place that the wind heaps up the sand dunes beneath which we saw sphinxes . . .

STRABO, *GEOGRAPHICA* (CA. 20 BCE)

What strange fate brings a person to the right place at the right time? What strange synchronicity is at play when something obvious and in plain sight is only seen by that one person? Why it is that only one person could notice a vital clue when everyone else had ignored it? We would normally think of geniuses like Copernicus, Galileo, Newton, or Einstein. Not many, however, would think of a Frenchman with the uncommon name of Auguste Mariette. Yet, the story we are about to tell will show how almost single-handedly this man changed the course of Egyptian antiquities from one of mindless destruction and desecration to one of responsible preservation and restoration. To put it in other words, the legacy of the pharaohs was saved for posterity by a Frenchman with a big heart and huge determination and grit. We fast-forward, however, to hear Mariette, on his deathbed, modestly summing up the huge service he had rendered to Egypt.

> It behooves us to preserve Egypt's monuments with care. Five hundred years hence Egypt should still be able to show to the scholars who shall visit her, the same monuments that we are now describing.[1]

The truth is that, were it not for Mariette Pasha (as he was called in Egypt), the temples, tombs, and all those wonderful artifacts that visitors to Egypt marvel at today would simply have vanished, perhaps even the pyramids. They would have been either stolen, sold, or literally pulverized into oblivion.

ROMANCING THE SERAPEUM

Mariette's story could be said to have begun, oddly enough, three millennia ago on the windy and dusty promontory known today as Saqqara. Located at the edge of the western desert some ten kilometers south of the Giza pyramids, Saqqara (the name may be a corruption from the ancient funerary god Sokar) had been the burial ground of pharaohs and nobles since the earliest dynasties. It was famed in the ancient world, however, for its huge labyrinth, the Serapeum, in which the sacred bulls of Memphis, the Apis, were buried in giant sarcophagi.

In the late first century BCE, when Cleopatra had just committed her celebrated suicide and Egypt had become a province of Rome, the Greek geographer Strabo (63 BCE–24 CE), probably in his late thirties, visited Saqqara. One has to imagine the place, without modern roads, without cars and coaches, and without postcard vendors and hustlers and lame "tourist police" soliciting baksheesh from visitors.

Probably all that Strabo encountered was a small Roman encampment or perhaps a Bedouin camp within the ruins of the great Step Pyramid Complex or, a little farther north, near a strange open air temple where statues of the Greek philosophers stood in a semicircle—for

Figure 4.1. The Greek geographer Strabo (63 BCE–24 CE)

there is no doubt that this is the place where Strabo, for reasons we shall never know, was strolling on that that fateful day. And, luckily for Mariette many centuries later, what Strabo saw strewn on the sand he diligently reported in his *Geographica* (a seventeen-volume opus that is regarded as the first-ever book of geography). In that typical delightful and eloquent archaic Greek style, the father of geography describes in volume seventeen of *Geographica* an alleyway (*dromus* in Greek) of sphinxes, some half buried in the shifting sand, others with only their heads sticking out, which led toward a temple dedicated to the god Serapis.* In Strabo's own words:

> One finds a Serapeum at Memphis [modern Saqqara] in such a sandy place that the wind heaps up the sand dunes beneath which we saw sphinxes, some half buried, some buried up to the head, from which one can suppose that the way to this temple could not be without danger if one were caught in a sudden wind storm.[2]

---

*Strabo's *Geographica* was not available to Europeans until the middle of the fifteenth century. In 1587 Isaac Casaubon published the first critical edition.

Oddly, no one took Strabo's report seriously about the Serapeum of Memphis (Saqqara) at least not until the arrival of Napoleon in Egypt in 1798, when apparently some of his savants undertook a hasty search but gave up when they found nothing.[3] Neither did the first modern Egyptologists, who were in Egypt during Muhammad Ali's reign. John Wilkinson, dubbed a "founder of British Egyptology," was in Egypt from 1821 to 1833, and although the latter discovered the labyrinth in Hawara, he somehow was not interested in Strabo's account. There was, too, Karl Richard Lepsius, dubbed a "founder of German Egyptology," who headed a mission sponsored by the king of Prussia, and although he, too, made some startling discoveries in the region, looking for the legendary Serapeum of Memphis was not on his agenda. The truth is that much of the excavation (plundering more likely) in those very early days of Egyptology focused on Upper Egypt, especially Thebes (modern Luxor), where ancient artifacts were found in abundance and easily taken away. Also as the author Brian M. Fagan pointed out: "excavation was still largely the domain of dealers and tomb robbers," while many of the serious scholars were more preoccupied in academic debates over ancient Egyptian chronology and the translation and interpretation of ancient texts.[4]

QUELQU'UN PLUS PUISSANT QUE MOI (SOMEONE MORE POWERFUL THAN I)

François Auguste Ferdinand Mariette (1821–1881) was born in the seaside town of Boulogne-sur-Mer on the northern coast of France. Mariette's interest in ancient Egypt began when he was six years old. He had a great ability for languages and taught himself Egyptian hieroglyphics, demotic script, and Coptic; when he was only twelve, he was able to read ancient Coptic texts. Mariette first worked as a teacher in a school in Douai but got indirectly involved with archaeology by writing articles for a local magazine to supplement his meager salary. His work on a catalogue of the Egyptian gallery in the

Boulogne Museum grabbed the attention of the Louvre Museum, and, in 1849, he was offered a minor job working on Coptic and other ancient manuscripts.

The amazing romantic discovery of the fabled Serapeum properly begins with the arrival of Mariette in Egypt in 1850, then a young man of twenty-nine. Mariette had been sent by the Louvre Museum to collect Coptic and other ancient manuscripts in Alexandria and Cairo, and for this mission, he had received a modest budget. When in Egypt, the whole project went pear-shaped because the Coptic monks, having been tricked before by French traders, refused to deal with Mariette. Rather than abort his mission, Mariette made the decision to use the funds of the Louvre to do some private archaeological excavations. He chose Saqqara as the most promising site.

It was a free-for-all in those early days of archaeology, with no restriction whatsoever on any foreigner who had the funds and means to undertake archaeological excavations. We have seen how Muhammad Ali himself used the stones from ancient sites to build factories and ancient artifacts and treasures as gifts for foreigners, in exchange for their know-how and expertise. His estranged grandson and successor, Abbas Hilmi Pasha, was more watchful over ancient sites—although not so much because of any love for antiquities but because he distrusted foreigners and more particularly the French: industrial equipment and other goods that his grandfather had imported from France often turned out to be of poor quality and badly maintained, which prompted Muhammad Ali to fire and expulse those French officials responsible. Indeed, Abbas Hilmy Pasha was so opposed to the French that he unwisely rejected Ferdinand de Lesseps's first attempt to build a canal across the Isthmus of Suez. And, in the case of Mariette, the intolerant and introverted Abbas placed guards at Saqqara to keep close tabs on his archaeological activities.

At any rate, and not withstanding Abbas's suspicions, Mariette hired a small team of workers, bought some basic equipment, and boldly set out to excavate at Saqqara. Unlike others before him, Mariette had a strong inkling that Strabo's narrative about the Memphis Serapeum was rooted in truth. In Mariette's own words:

> Did it not seem that Strabo had written this sentence to help us rediscover, after over eighteen centuries, the famous temple dedicated to Serapis? It was impossible to doubt it. This buried Sphinx, the companion of fifteen others I had encountered in Alexandria and Cairo, formed with them, according to the evidence, part of the avenue that led to the Memphis Serapeum. . . . It did not seem to me possible to leave to others the credit and profit of exploring this temple whose remains a fortunate chance had allowed me to discover and whose location henceforth would be known. Undoubtedly many precious fragments, many statues, many unknown texts were hidden beneath the sand upon which I stood. These considerations made all my scruples disappear. At that instant I forgot my mission [obtaining Coptic texts from the monasteries], I forgot the Patriarch, the convents, the Coptic and Syriac manuscripts . . . and it was thus, on 1 November 1850, during one of the most beautiful sunrises I had ever seen in Egypt, that a group of thirty workmen, working under my orders near that sphinx, were about to cause such total upheaval in the conditions of my stay in Egypt.[5]

Mariette was convinced that the buried avenue of sphinxes at Saqqara was the very same described by Strabo. All Mariette had to do now was to urge his workforce to expose the avenue, which led him to the entrance of the fabled Serapeum, built like a kind of huge underground maze. Upon entering the ancient labyrinth, Mariette immediately realized that he had hit the jackpot! Mariette was to write:

> [When] I penetrated into the sepulchre of the Apis, I was so overcome with astonishment that, although it is now five years ago, the feeling is still vivid in my mind. By some inexplicable accident one chamber of the Apis tombs, walled up in the thirtieth year of

Ramses II, had escaped the general plunder of the monuments, and I was so fortunate as to find it untouched. Three thousand five hundred years had had no effect in altering its primitive state. The finger mark of the Egyptian who set the last stone in the wall built up to cover the door was still visible in the mortar. Bare feet had left their traces on the sand strewn in a corner of this chamber of the dead; nothing had been disturbed in this burying-place where an embalmed ox had been resting for . . . centuries.[6]

His gamble paid off in a big way, for there, in the dimly lit corridors, were the giant sarcophagi of the Apis bulls of Memphis. The news of this stunning discovery made international headlines, and Mariette became an instant celebrity! The future now looked very bright indeed for the rather defiant young man from Boulogne-sur-Mer. And as Egypt's fate would have it, this young Frenchman was bold and full of enthusiasm; he not only exuded a genuine love for Egypt and its ancient legacy, he also would prove to be a great negotiator and visionary.

The first underground area that Auguste Mariette broke into consisted of a vast and high-roofed gallery. Into each side were cut large niches in which beautifully fashioned and inscribed single-block granite sarcophagi were inserted—twenty-four in total, some estimated to weigh more than sixty tons. They dated from the Twenty-sixth Dynasty to the Ptolemaic era. All the granite sarcophagi in this first area had been robbed and were empty. The following year, Mariette broke into other galleries, which contained burials dated from the New Kingdom. One of the burials was still intact, and in two others Mariette found two large gold-plated coffins, four large human-headed canopic jars (containing the viscera of bulls), as well as many other artifacts and statues.

Today, the Serapeum is closed for restoration. We entered it on several occasions during the 1990s. Upon entering through the gates, there is a long descending staircase leading to the first hall or gallery, partially blocked still by a large granite sarcophagus lid. The principal gallery dates to the Late and Ptolemaic eras. In it one can see several of the sixty-four giant sarcophagi. The most elaborately decorated and inscribed is located at the very end of the gallery. The other galleries are closed to the public.

After he had completed his work at the Serapeum, Mariette worked for a short while at the Giza Necropolis at the valley temple of Khafre. But his funds ran out, and he was obliged to return to France, where he became the curator of the Egyptian department of the Louvre Museum. A short while later, Mariette met Ferdinand de Lesseps, who was still trying to get the concession for the building of the Suez Canal. De Lesseps had been fascinated by Mariette's discovery of the Serapeum and his enthusiasm to save Egyptian monuments for posterity. He introduced Mariette to Saïd Pasha, who had succeeded the ultra-conservative Abbas Hilmi. Mariette lamented about the looting and vandalism by tourists and antiquity dealers, and thankfully, Saïd Pasha finally became aware of the great value of the pharaonic legacy and the risk of it being lost forever. Mariette explained that not all excavations were adequately published and stressed the importance of publication. In the following months, Saïd Pasha developed a great respect for Mariette, and the two men became good friends. Saïd Pasha offered Mariette the position of first

Figure 4.2. Auguste Mariette in his later years

conservator of Egyptian monuments. In 1858, Mariette officially became curator of Egyptian antiquities (equivalent today to the post of director general of the Supreme Council of Antiquities).

With the full approval of Saïd Pasha, Mariette began what can be termed as the first registered archaeological excavations, under the newly formed Services des Antiquitées, in many sites throughout Egypt. He employed thousands of workers (more than seven thousand at one stage) and slowly but surely organized a plethora of inspectors and wardens of archaeological sites across the whole of Egypt. This effectively brought to a halt the involvement of the foreign consuls, who appropriated antiquities for the museums of their own respective countries, and also slowed and somewhat controlled the previously unsupervised activities of private collectors and antiquity dealers. Typically, he was nonetheless criticized by the British, who accused him of "unprofessional behavior" and of "monopolizing" archaeological excavations.

Mariette urged Saïd Pasha to build a museum for antiquities to store the vast volume of artifacts that were now being found. But there were insufficient funds in the treasury. Mariette was at first allocated an old mosque (near Bab el-Gabal in the Citadel) to store the haul of artifacts. Sadly, when Duke Maximilian of Austria was shown the collection, Saïd Pasha was impressed by the duke's keen enthusiasm and ordered Mariette to give the whole lot to the duke as a gesture of goodwill. Mariette was totally dismayed but could do nothing about this. It was clear that Saïd Pasha, like his predecessors, did not really care about antiquities despite his obvious support for Mariette and the Services des Antiquitées. Fortunately, the Pasha finally approved the setting up of a museum to house the antiquities.

At first a building at Bulaq (near today's Ramses Hilton) that once belonged to a transport company was used for this purpose. Mariette had its interior stripped and redecorated to create suitable spaces. The various objects were displayed without much chronological consideration, but at least they were now relatively safe and exhibited for

Figure 4.3. King Pedro II of Brazil and Mariette Pasha (sitting at far left),
ca. 1873 at the Giza Necropolis

Figure 4.4. View of Bulaq looking east from the Nile near Cairo

the public. Mariette did his best to put labels giving details and the provenances of the objects and also wrote a museum guidebook. For the first time ever, thanks wholly to Mariette, Egypt's ancient pharaonic relics and treasures were organized and made accessible to all. To Mariette Pasha (he was conferred this title by his mentor Saïd Pasha, along with the title of *bey*) also goes the credit of clearing and beginning the restoration of the great temples at Edfu, Karnak, Deir el Bahari, Medinet Habu, Dendera, Abysos, and Esna. Mariette must also be lauded for his efforts to protect and conserve the wonderful treasures founds at Tanis, as well as protecting the pyramids and *mastabas* (meaning "flat bed" in Arabic. A type of tomb used in early dynasties) at Giza, Saqqara, and Meydum. But perhaps Mariette's most important achievement was to raise the world's sense of responsibility in saving and taking proper care of Egyptian antiquities for posterity.

A series of firmans (khedieval laws) issued by Khedive Ismail dated April 21, 1863, were addressed to inspectors of antiquities (who were at that time no more than civil servants), stipulating that all the demands of Mariette Bey to facilitate his excavations in Upper Egypt must be met; that workers on sites should be adequately paid; and that they must forbid the destruction of monuments or their demolition or use of the stones from monuments for erecting government or private buildings "because the antiquities in Egypt are the strongest means to perpetuate the history of the kingdom, and the conservation of these monuments is one of our dearest wishes." There is no doubt that in the rules of Abbas, Saïd, and Ismail, thanks to Mariette, Egyptians began to discover their country's national heritage. Ismail's law also stipulated that any antiquities chanced upon by the inhabitants of the villages should automatically become part of the Services des Antiquitées. "These relics," the firman stipulated, "should be examined on the spot if they are huge and remain where they are found, but if their size is small they must be carried to the Antiquities Service. Bearing in mind that the inhabitants of Luxor are in the habit of searching for and appropriating pieces of antiquities, using the stones for the construction of their dwellings, you are invested with the authority to stop them, making certain that such things should not take place," The Khedive, addressing the Inspectors, added, "You must give instructions to the moudirs [governors] to realize the demands of Mariette Bey, director of antiquities, supplying him with camels, horses, boats, wood [and other] material, and take any necessary steps for the conservation and transport of antiquities."[7]

In the summer of 1878, when the Bulaq Museum was damaged by a higher-than-normal annual Nile flood, the showcases with mummies and other precious objects were salvaged and placed in storage until Khedive Ismail's palace in Giza was made ready to receive them. There they stayed until the new Egyptian Antiquities Museum was built in the north end of (the now iconic) Tahrir Square and opened in 1902. The wonderful neoclassical edifice contained more than one hundred rooms set on two levels around a central atrium that, when fully equipped, could display over one hundred and fifty thousand items, ranging from sarcophagi, statues, mummies, and a plethora of ancient artifacts from the Pharaonic and Roman eras.

In January 1881, when Mariette was laid on his deathbed, he asked that his body be placed near the artifacts he had saved. He was now a very tired old man. Gaston Maspero, his successor, was at his side. Mariette had endured the pain of seeing his loyal wife, Eleonore, and all his children die before him. Yet this giant of a man had brought back to life a whole civilization for which Egypt, ancient *and* new, would forever be grateful. Mariette died on January 19; at first, his body was placed inside a sarcophagus that was in the garden of the Bulaq Museum. In 1904, however, the sarcophagus was moved to the

Figure 4.5. The tomb (sarcophagus) of Mariette Pasha in the courtyard
of the Cairo Museum of Antiquities in Tahrir Square

west side of the garden of the new Egyptian Antiquities Museum, and
a bronze statue of Mariette was raised behind it. There the great man,
the savior of Egypt's pharaonic legacy, still stands tall, arms folded confidently, with a wonderful expression of sober satisfaction and pride.
In a semicircle around the statue are the various busts of several other
great Egyptologists, forever paying respect to their peer. A small bronze
plaque simply reads, both in Arabic and French: *À Mariette Pacha,
L'Égypte Reconnaissante.*

Of Mariette Pasha, the *Al-Ahram Weekly,* Egypt's most popular
English language newspaper, recently wrote

> Mariette did more to help Egypt preserve its Pharaonic heritage and
> draw attention to the ruthless pillage of monuments than any other
> single scholar of his generation. A month before he died he managed
> to extract a cabinet resolution that, "hereafter no Egyptian monu-
> ment shall be given to any power not forming a part of the Egyptian

Figure 4.6. Statue and tomb of Mariette Pasha. In the background is the headquarters of the National Democratic Party, which was burned in January 2011.

territory." He set a tradition that continued through to the Egyptian revolution in the 1950s and the basis of which is still in operation today.[8]

However, the *Al-Ahram Weekly* continues thus

One point that needs to be mentioned is that although Khedive Ismail was anxious for Egyptians to be trained to work profession-ally alongside Europeans in the field of Egyptology, to benefit from their expertise, and eventually to take responsibility for their own monuments, both Mariette and his successor Gaston Maspero were opposed to the idea.[9]

From today's perspective, Mariette's attitude would be regarded as colonial chauvinism and terribly ungrateful to a host country. Yet seen

Figure 4.7. Gaston Maspero, successor to Mariette Pasha, inside the Pyramid of Unas. He discovered the Pyramid texts in 1881–1882.

from the context of his times, Mariette did have a point. He knew, from bitter firsthand experience, how corrupt and unprofessional many of his Egyptian counterparts were. The pashas and khedives themselves had practically sold or given away the priceless legacy of their own country. Mariette had seen the senseless vandalism of the local *fellahin,* who had pulverized ancient organic artifacts—wooden sarcophagi, papyri, and even mummies—to use as fertilizer for their crops; and the rich beys had carted away the blocks of ancient temples and cities to build their modern factories and their own villas. Sad to say, but it was true that the Egyptians in those days were far from ready to take over from the French. Saying this may embarrass national pride today, but the truth must be faced if the *new Egypt* that is emerging from the January 25 revolution is to heal itself from the deep wounds of the past. For it is not only "democracy" but also the courage and will to face up to the truth and nothing but the truth that will justly set Egypt and its people truly free from that repressive past when it was ruled by autocrats who treated the country as their own property and the people as their servants.

At any rate, Mariette would have his way: all his successors as directors of the Services des Antiquitées were Frenchmen. It would not be until 1953 that an Egyptian would at long last take the helm.

Khedive Ismail assumed all archaeological discoveries as his own. It was he who, in spite of Mariette's opposition, decided what went into his own possession and what went into the museum. In February 1859, Mariette, upon hearing that the khedive had ordered a boat to bring to him treasures discovered in the tomb of Queen Ahhotep I, Mariette risked the wrath of the omnipotent powerful monarch by diverting the boat's contents to the museum. Mariette returned temporarily to France to supervise Egypt's stand at the Exposition Universelle and was hailed as a national hero by the French press. It is said that the empress Eugenie, wife of Napoleon III, flirtingly asked the khedive for a few ancient items. Amazingly, the khedive (who was rumored to have had a romantic crush on the beautiful but elusive Eugenie) gently rebuked the request with exquisite tact and replied to her (in impeccable French) that she ought to ask "someone more powerful than I," meaning Auguste Mariette. She never did. In 1869, at the request of the khedive, Mariette wrote the libretto for Verdi's *Aida* and acted as consultant for the opera. France and other Western governments and institutes bestowed many honorary titles upon Mariette.

5

The End of an Era

On March 17, 1965, [King] Farouk took his latest girlfriend, a hairdresser named Anna Maria Gatti, to dinner . . . he started with a dozen oysters . . . followed by lobster thermidor, a double portion of roast lamb and a huge helping of trifle. He had just lit up a cigar when his face turned puple and he reached for his throat. At 45, he was dead.

ANDREW EAMES, *THE NILE*

There is no doubt that the greatest obstacle to democratization of the Egyptian regime is the nature of Nasser's own personality. It is partly that whereas he is a democrat by intellect, he is an authoritarian by temperament.

P. MANSFIELD, *NASSER*

By the early 1950s, Egypt had survived the sovereign bankruptcy caused by Ismail Pasha with the Suez Canal and his own excesses; the consequences of the national uprising of Ahmed Orabi and the British occupation; World War II and its effects; and finally an abortive war in 1948 with Israel and Yemen—and now Egypt was to see the end of Muhammad Ali's last descendant, the ill-fated King Farouk I.

The son of Fuad I, Egypt's first modern king (his predecessors were khedives) and tenth ruler after Muhammad Ali, Farouk succeeded his father in 1936 at the age of sixteen. With the ostentatious title of "King of Egypt and Sudan, Sovereign of Nubia, Kordofan, and Darfur," Farouk was at first hailed as the young prince who would rid Egypt of the hated British and restore dignity and pride to its people. Dashingly handsome and impeccably groomed in the best of both Western and Eastern manners, the young king promised to be what Egyptians desperately yearned for: a nationalistic ruler who would make them proud.

They couldn't have been more wrong.

EGYPT UNDER LORD CROMER

Under Muhammad Ali, Egypt had been able to break loose from the Ottoman Empire and become once again a separate state. During the reign of his grandson Ismail Pasha, Egypt emerged as a true nation looking forward to being a democratic state using the European parliamentary model. Thus during the first half of the twentieth century, although Egypt had fallen under British occupation since 1882, it was able to take a great step toward democracy when it became a constitutional monarchy—a situation that was to last until 1952.

The arrival of the British troops in Cairo in 1882, after they had defeated the rebel army of Ahmed Orabi, effectively secured the reins of the country to Sir Evelyn Baring (1841–1907)—later named Lord Cromer—Britain's consul general in Egypt.

We recall that the ruling khedive, Tewfik Pasha, had asked the British to intervene and quench the Orabi uprising against him, and now Tewfik had to pay the price, by being a puppet manipulated by his British masters. For Sir Evelyn was "king" of Egypt in every way but in name. The bulk of the British troops occupied a main location in Cairo and set their military barracks in the wide open space of Ismailia Square (today's iconic Tahrir Square), along the east bank of the Nile. Now Lord Cromer (the very same Sir Evelyn Baring) not only had the military backing of the occupying British troops but also the full support of the Egyptian army, which was put under British command. In Egyptian international matters, it was the British government that made all decisions while the internal affairs of Egypt were supervised and controlled by Lord Cromer himself.

Not much attention has been paid by historians to the British occupation of Egypt regarding the role of Freemasonry in Egypt during those times. We have already seen how Masonic lodges had been installed in Egypt since the arrival of Napoleon in 1798; but now with the British practically running Egypt's affairs, British lodges and Egyptian lodges (under the jurisdiction of the United Grand Lodge of England) became the fashion among the British military as well as the Egyptian elite. In those days, most, if not all, of British generals, officers, and high officials belonged to the brotherhood, and a surprisingly large number of Egyptian high officials also joined the lodges. For although Egyptians resented the British (the Engleez), they nonetheless secretly admired their discipline, expertise, and power and presumably hoped that they could learn the secrets of their successes by rubbing shoulders with them in the fraternal and congenial atmosphere of the Masonic lodges. As for the intentions of the Freemasons for Egypt's future, they may have been much more profound than hitherto assumed by conventional historians (see appendix 1).

Lord Cromer, slowly but surely, tightened the reins on Tewfik Pasha; this he did by increasing British control over the state and administrative machine of Egypt. He appointed British advisers in the various ministries, who, in reality, had more influence on decisions than the Egyptian ministers whom they supposedly "advised"! Cromer also appointed Mustafa Fahmi Pasha as prime minister, who obeyed his British master unequivocally. Although the Egyptians resented the British occupation, it is nonetheless true that Cromer was able to bring political stability to the country and even restore its battered financial state. He increased agriculture productivity by building a large dam at Aswan, which was completed in 1902. Aswan at the time was the largest dam in the world and provided much additional irrigation water for agricultural use through the Nile Valley. Also Cromer used a British-Egyptian army, under General Kitchener, to reconquer Sudan (which had been under the Mahdi's rule after the fall of Khartoum in 1885). Kitchener entered Sudan on November 18, 1896, with eleven thousand men and the most modern military equipment of the time and decisively defeated the Mahdi's force at Atbara in April 1898, putting Sudan back under Anglo-Egyptian rule. But this Anglo-Egyptian administration of Sudan became a burden for Egypt, for while Britain retained the top administrative positions, the Egyptian exchequer had to make up the considerable financial deficits of the Sudanese government.

Lord Cromer cringed at spending money on education for Egyptians and appointed Douglas Dunlop as adviser to the department of education. Dunlop was contemptuous of Egyptians, especially educated ones, whom he regarded as bad-tempered upstarts. More humiliation followed. When in 1906 a group of Egyptian intellectuals (including the famous Egyptian reformer Sheikh Muhammad Abduh) approached Cromer with plans to establish an Egyptian university, they were arrogantly told that Egyptians were not ready for university training! (However, the group defiantly went ahead and opened a private Western-style university after Cromer's death in 1907, which in 1925 became the King Fuad University and eventually today's Cairo University.) Even more arrogantly, Cromer refused to allow free elections and parliamentary government as he believed that Egypt was not yet ready for this.

The death of Tewfik in 1892 and the accession of his seventeen-year-old son Abbas Hilmi II marked the real beginning of Egyptian opposition to the British occupation. The young khedive hated the British and defiantly and openly clashed with Cromer from day one of his rule. While Abbas was not prepared to accept Cromer's tutelage, the arrogant consul general claimed that the young khedive should not have a serious role in Egyptian politics. So when in 1895 Abbas dismissed Mustafa Fahmi (Cromer's puppet prime minister), Cromer restored Fahmi to office. Abbas provoked a clash with Cromer when he publicly

Figure 5.1. Sheikh Muhammad Abduh (1849–1905), the celebrated Islamist and reformer, founder of Islamic Modernism. He became Grand Mufti of Al-Azhar. (photo courtesy *Al-Ahram*)

criticized Kitchener (now British *sirdar*, or commander in chief, of the armed forces in Egypt), but Cromer forced the young khedive to make amends.

Abbas's bold but fruitless actions nonetheless made him the symbol of opposition to British dominance in Egypt. The true active "symbol of British opposition," however, came from a young journalist, Mustafa Kamel, whom Abbas enthusiastically supported. The son of an Egyptian officer who fought in Orabi's rebel army, Kamel had studied law and dedicated himself to the national cause. A secret Masonic-style society called the Secret National Party was established by Abbas and Kamel; its aim was to assassinate senior members of the British occupying forces, as well as any Egyptians who worked with them. Kamel's brave patriotism rallied the entire nation around the khedive and against the British. This blatantly overt opposition to British rule climaxed in 1906, the last years of Lord Cromer's tenure in Egypt.

An incident occurred in the Delta between a group of British soldiers out on a hunting expedition near the village of Dinshwai and enraged the local farmers (*fellahin*) when the foolish British soldiers killed their domesticated pigeons. In the midst of the dispute that followed, a British soldier was killed. The farmers were duly arrested by the British, and after a hasty trial, six of the fellahin were hanged and another six were brutally flogged in front of the entire village to set an example. Rather than learn from this example, the negative repercussions of this senseless act of British discipline were enormous, not only in Egypt but also in Britain itself, as the parliament, the press, and the public were appalled that their countrymen could behave in such an irresponsible and high-handed manner. In Egypt, the nationalists took up the cause of the Dinshwai villagers and hotly condemned the British for what they considered a brutal act of criminal behavior.

To calm the situation down, Cromer tried to make concessions by appointing a young moderate nationalist, Saad Zaghloul, into the Council of Ministers as minister of public instruction (a not-so-surprising move by Cromer, since Saad Zaghloul was married to Safiya, a daughter of Mustafa Fahmi, the pro-British prime minister who danced to Cromer's tune). Cromer also revived the Egyptian National Assembly, which had fallen into disuse since the Orabi revolt. Although the assembly was only to have advisory powers, Egyptians saw this as the first step in creating a parliamentary system that at least shared power with the British. Not much was resolved, while the clamor of the nationalists became even louder, especially their calls for the return to the Islamic caliphate in Turkey by claiming that there was no separate national community within the Islamic state. Such a move, however, would have made the Copts (Egyptian Christians) into subjects rather than citizens in their own country.

Cromer used this situation to alarm the Coptic community and claimed that only the British occupation could give them protection. To make a show of this, Cromer decided to replace the Grand Ottoman judge in Cairo with an Egyptian judge. Abbas refused; Cromer insisted. As a result, the relationship between Muslim and Coptic Egyptians deteriorated between 1906 and 1910, with the Copts now reluctant to support the Muslims' demand for an end to British occupation. In 1908, Akhnoukh Fanous, a Coptic lawyer, established the Egyptian Party, calling for Egypt to be for the Egyptians, in response to the Nationalist Party's call for a return to the Ottomans.

Lord Cromer died in 1907, and Mustafa Kamel, the symbol of opposition, died the following year at the young age of thirty-four. Cromer was followed as consul general by Sir Eldon Gorst. A more congenial

Figure 5.2. Saad Zaghloul

and understanding man, Gorst endeavored to diminish British influence in Egypt. But he foolishly advised the khedive to appoint as prime minister a Christian Copt, Boutros Ghali Pasha—an obvious misjudgment in a predominant Muslim country and with tempers flying high at that time. The worst happened: Boutros Ghali was assassinated in 1910 by a fanatical member of the Nationalist Party, which then fueled sectarian troubles. A Coptic conference was organized in Asyout in Upper Egypt to demand Coptic national rights, which was immediately followed by a sectarian Muslim conference. When Gorst suddenly died in 1911, London appointed Lord Kitchener as consul general, a move that much infuriated the khedive and the Nationalists—especially when it became very clear that Kitchener wanted to limit the power and influence of Abbas II.

REVOLUTION AND INDEPENDENCE

In November 1914, Britain declared war on the Ottoman Empire, the latter an ally of Germany. In December of that year, it made Egypt a protectorate and deposed Abbas II, replacing him with Hussein Kamel as new ruler of Egypt with the (Turkish) title of sultan. During the war period, Sir Reginald Wingate became high commissioner of Egypt.

Figure 5.3. Sir Reginald Wingate in Egypt (photo courtesy *Al-Ahram*)

Let us note in passing that Wingate was a staunch Freemason and the right worshipful district grand master of the Grand Lodge of Egypt and the Sudan—as indeed Lord Kitchener had been before him (the first grand master when the District Grand Lodge of Egypt and the Sudan was created in 1899). Wingate also belonged to the celebrated and influential Bulwer Lodge No. 1068 and first English Masonic lodge in Cairo installed in 1865. (Prince Halim Pasha, a staunch anglophile, was initiated in that lodge in 1867 and served as grand master for Egypt).

At any rate, the British introduced military rule and a state of emergency in Egypt and placed General John Maxwell in charge of all the military in the country. At the end of 1914, Maxwell commanded a force of 82,000 British troops.

Sultan Hussein Kamel died in October 1917 and was succeeded, also as sultan, by his brother Ahmad Fuad.

Figure 5.4. Sir Reginald Wingate as guest of honor at a Masonic banquet given at the Shepheard's Hotel, Cairo, in 1913 (photo courtesy United Grand Lodge, Queen's Street Library)

There is a rather interesting and romantic story related to the wife of King Fuad I, the glamorous and beautiful Queen Nazli (Cairo, 1894– Los Angeles, 1978). She was the great-great-grandaughter of a French officer in Napoleon's Grande Armée named Joseph Anthelme Sève (1788–1860). Sève was recruited by Mohammad Ali Pasha to help him create and train an Egyptian army. Sève converted to Islam and changed his name to Suleiman Pasha el-Fransawi (the Frenchman). He married Myraim Hatem and from her had three children, one also called Nazli who became the grandmother of the future Queen Nazli. In 1919, Nazli married King Fuad I. Highly educated in French religious schools (Lycée de la Mère de Dieu in Cairo; Notre Dame de Sion in Alexandria), this vivacious and versatile woman was a peculiar match to Fuad who was ultra-concervative, shy, and reserved, and not much liked by his people. Indeed, before marrying Fuad, Nazli had had quite a turbulent life: when her mother, Tewfika Hanem, died, Nazli's father sent her to Paris for two years. When she returned to Egypt she was was forced to marry a cousin, Khalil Sabri, but less than a year later she got divorced. After her divorce she lived for one month in the house of famous feminist Safiya Zaghloul, wife of Saad Zagloul. There Nazli met Zaghloul's nephew, Said. The couple got engaged but Said broke up with her when he was sent into exile with his uncle. In 1919, King (Sultan) Fuad I proposed to her. Fuad was twenty-five years older than Nazli. The young Nazli was forced by her father, who obviously could not go against Fuad, to accept the proposal of marriage. She bore several children, one being Farouk (the ill-fated future king), and a daughter, Fathia (who in 1976 would meet a tragic death in San Francisco when her drunken husband, Riad Ghali, shot her six times). Queen Nazli's marriage to King Fuad I was not a happy one (she tried to commit suicide on at least one occasion). It is believed that after the king's death in 1936, she had a romantic affair with the dashing Ahmed Hassanein Bey, the tutor of her son Farouk and also well known for his daring desert explorations (See Robert Bauval's *Black Genesis,* chapter 2). Apprently Queen Nazli and Hassanein Bey were secretly married in 1942. After Hassanein Bey's accidental death in 1946 (he was hit by a British army truck), Queen Nazli left Egypt and went to settle in America. In 1950 her son, King Farouk I, stripped her of her royal titles, her money (although she had taken to the United States all her jewels, apprently worth a fortune). The reason for this was that King Farouk was furious that she had allowed her daughter, Fathia, to marry a commoner Copt, Riad Ghali, against the king's expressed refusal. In 1976 President Anwar el Sadat agreed to grant back to Queen Nazli her Egyptian nationality and passport. In her later years Queen Nazli had converted to Catholicism. She died in Los Angeles in 1978 and is buried there in a Christian cemetery.

A year later, on November 13, 1918, to be precise (and two days after Armistice), Sir Reginald Wingate, the British high commissioner,

Figure 5.5. Suleiman Pasha
(Joseph Anthelme Sève)

was visited by three Egyptian politicians led by Saad Zaghloul Pasha. Zaghloul demanded autonomy for Egypt and announced his intension of leading a delegation, the Wafd, to state his case in England. Not unexpectedly, the British government refused Zaghloul's demand, promptly arrested him (along with his companions) and deported him to Malta. This sparked mass demonstrations across Egypt, which eventually turned into an uprising known as the First Revolution of 1919. There was widespread violence all over Egypt against the British and foreign residents, and in the countryside, peasants tore up rail lines in an attempt to isolate themselves from Cairo and retribution from the British army.

Almost overnight, Zaghloul became the hero of the educated and politically informed. The son of a local notable, he had studied at the Islamic institution of al-Azhar, where he became a disciple of the grand mufti Mohammad Abduh before the British occupation. Unlike the Islamic reformist Mohammad Abduh, however, Zaghloul called for the total separation of state and religion. In 1907, along with Ahmed Lutfi el-Sayed, he established al Ummah (the Nation) Party. Both men believed in equality for all men and called for Egypt to be independent from both the British and the Ottomans. Zaghloul's insight became the basis for the formation of the Wafd Party as a secular political institution in which Muslims and Copts played an equally prominent role in

Figure 5.6. Queen Nazli, ca. 1940

the struggle against British occupation. Zaghloul was particularly sensitive to Coptic demands and declared that Copts have equal rights as Muslims—a move that encouraged the Coptic population to join his movement from the very start. Although from a Muslim background, Zaghloul was a hero to all Egyptians, Copts as well as Muslims, all of whom joined his Wafd Party. The most influential among the Copts who joined was Makram Obeid. Obeid came from a wealthy family and had studied law at Oxford. He became an assistant to the British adviser at the Egyptian ministry of justice, but was forced to resign when he gave his support to Zaghloul. Obeid and Zaghloul became close friends and were both exiled together by the British to the Seychelles. It was during this exile that Obeid became a close colleague and friend with Nahhas Pasha, who succeeded Zaghloul as chairman of the Wafd Party while Obeid became its secretary general.

Before long, however, Britain was forced to free Zaghloul and his companions and allow them to travel to France. The violence nonetheless continued unabated in Egypt, and as the country spun out of control, the British lost nearly all authority in the cities and had no authority at all in the countryside. To deal with this dangerous situation, Lord Allenby (the victor over the Turks in Palestine) was sent to Egypt to restore order. The revolt was brutally quenched, and a precarious calm returned.

Finally, after forty years of authoritarian rule, on February 18, 1922, Britain declared Egypt's independence. On March 15 of that year, Sultan Fuad became King Fuad I of Egypt (after having received formal recognition of his kingship by many European monarchs). The new Egyptian kingdom was to be a constitutional monarchy, and Allenby asked King Fuad to draw up a new constitution for governing the country (apparently based on the Belgium model), which, inter alia, defined the king's executive powers. But no sooner was this done when it spurred a political struggle between the king, the Wafd Party, and the British—all vying for political control—directly or otherwise. Elections were set for 1924, and the Wafd won. To the dismay of the British (and Fuad I), Zaghloul was installed as prime minister. His tenure, however, was short-lived—for the assassination of Lee Stack, the new commander general of the Egyptian army caused the British to dismiss Zaghloul from office and to deny him the prospect of ever returning to power.

Fuad I of Egypt was the youngest son of Ismail Pasha. He had accompanied his father during his early exile to Italy, where he received his early education. Fuad had returned to Egypt at the time of Abbas II, when his father was then exiled to Istanbul. When Egypt became a constitutional monarchy in 1922, the constitution vested considerable powers in the king. Fuad could (and did!) initiate legislation, convene and dissolve the parliament, and also actively interfere in the affairs of the state. His tendency toward autocratic control, however, led to clashes with nationalist forces in the country spearheaded by the popular Wafd Party. Fuad's only son, the ill-fated Farouk, was destined to become the last of Muhammad Ali's lineage to rule Egypt. Fuad also had four daughters, one of whom, Fawzeya, became the first wife of the shah of Iran. As an aside, we, the authors of this book, were born in Egypt during the Farouk era and witnessed his demise in 1952 (see appendix 5).

King Fuad was never really popular among the Egyptians, and his insecurities prompted him to mingle with the British to secure his position and powers. The Wafd, however, with its massive following and elaborate organization, was the only true national party in Egypt—for it genuinely stood for national independence against British domination and also for a constitutional government against that royal autocracy that never seemed to go away. Meanwhile, the primary aim of the British government, represented by its high commissioner until 1936 when the latter became an ambassador, was to secure imperial interests, especially the control of the Suez Canal.

AFTER THE "FIRST" REVOLUTION OF 1919

The so-called First Revolution of 1919 produced significant political changes, including a new constitution, Egypt's independence from Britain, and a newly elected government: the Wafd. It also resulted in a number of significant economic and social changes. The Egyptian elite had realized that political independence without economic strength counted for little. A group of leading Egyptian businessmen—some native Egyptians and some foreign residents—formed a commission to study Egypt's commerce and industry.

Notable among them were Talaat Harb, Egypt's most prominent entrepreneur; Ismail Sidqi, who would become prime minister in this era; Henri Naus, head of the Egyptian Sugar Company; and Yussef Aslan Qattawi, a Jewish businessman with international contacts in commerce, finance, and business. The commission concluded that Egypt's agricultural expansion and prosperity were coming to an end, as the amount of new land that could be brought for cultivation through dam construction and irrigation improvements was limited, while at the same time the population of the country was growing at a fast rate (less than ten million at the start of the twentieth century to more than eighty million today). The commission thus agreed that if Egypt were to further develop economically, it would have to promote local industries and stimulate a more diversified economy less dependent on the export of the single crop of cotton. Oddly, tourism was not yet foreseen as viable revenue for Egypt.

After World War I, the brilliant Egyptian entrepreneur Talaat Harb, whose statue today graces one of the main squares in Cairo (and whose name is given to one of the main avenues leading to Tahrir Square) led the way. The son of a minor railway employee, Harb received his higher education at the Egyptian School of Law. He then worked in various government ministries where his special skill in financial matters was brought to the attention of Egypt's wealthy landlords.

Harb was acutely aware that Egypt's economy—96 percent of the stock-market investments, the majority of business firms, factories, hotels, and banks—was predominantly in the hands of non-Egyptian residents, that is the *khawagas*. Indeed, during one of his early trips to Europe before the war showed to Harb that banks with large capital at their disposal, especially those in Germany, had used their clout to stimulate the impressive industrialization of the Western world. Harb became convinced that such a powerful bank in Egypt—one not run by foreigners but purely by Egyptians—could play a similar dynamic role in diversifying and industrializing the Egyptian economy. In 1920, Harb made this happen when he persuaded 124 wealthy Egyptians to contribute 80,000 Egyptian pounds to start the new bank, with all shareholders and directors to be Egyptians. And so was born the Bank Misr (Bank of Egypt), which was to play a vital role in Egypt's economy.

The 1919 revolution was also the starting point for the feminist movement in Egypt. At that time, women's education and literacy lagged significantly, and women were hardly seen—if at all—in commerce or political life. Indeed, they were hardly seen at all, since the veil was a very dominant aspect of their lives. The leading spokesman for women's reform was Qasim Amin, who, in a rare moment of concord with the British, was in complete agreement with Lord Cromer, who had written several treaties on the matter—*The Emancipation of Women* in 1899 and *The New Woman* in 1900—demanding radical reform in women's education and even calling for an end to the veil.

In the early part of the twentieth century most Egyptian women were confined to their houses and could not go out without covering their hair and faces with the veil. But during the 1919 revolution against British rule, veiled women surprised everyone (including themselves) by parading in the streets of Cairo and other cities, shouting slogans for independence and freedom. The educated and well-to-do minority of Egyptian female society went out en masse in the streets of Cairo for the first time in support of Egypt's men, who had demonstrated against the British, demanding Saad Zaghloul's return from exile. (In a similar vein, women today were one of the main driving forces in the January 25, 2011, revolution in Tahrir Square.)

Hoda Shaarawi, the wife of Ali Shaarawi who was Zaghloul's companion in the Wafd, organized lectures for women in order to bring them out of their homes and invited them to actively participate in Egypt's social and political reform. Shaarawi also opened a school for girls, which taught useful academic subjects, rather than the hitherto very limited home economics. Legend has it that in 1923, when Shaarawi stepped out of the train in Cairo's Central Station (upon returning from a women's conference in Rome), she defiantly pulled off her veil in front of the hundreds of Egyptian veiled women who had gathered to greet her. At first shocked by this bravado, the women then broke into a loud applause! This was the beginning of the end of the veil in Egypt (ironically, only to return with a vengeance today). Shaarawi became the leader of the Women's Committee in the progressive Wafd Party and created the first Egyptian feminist movement, demanding better education, better social welfare, and full equality for women. Shaarawi went even further by calling for the abolition of polygamy.

Another of Egypt's most admired women of the period was Safiya Zaghloul (the wife of Saad Zaghloul), who was known to many as mother of the (modern) nation (*om el umma*). Alexandria's main downtown avenue, the fashionable Boulevard Safiya Zaghloul (dubbed Egypt's Champs-Élysées) was named after this great feminist, yet one cannot help wondering if the black-veiled women who stroll up and down this avenue today (which puzzlingly has stores with window displays of outrageously erotic types of women lingerie) are aware of Safiya's bold efforts to abolish this ancient tradition of the veil, which has been revived in Egypt.

Other well-known feminists were Aisha El-Taimuriya, Nabawiya Moussa, Duriya Shafiq, Malak Hifni Nasif, and Aisha Ratib. One of today's most outspoken feminists in Egypt is Nawal El Saadawi. According to Khalil Al-Anani, an expert on modern Islamism, "The basic difference between the current movement and the one preceding it lies in capabilities and interests. It is the difference between liberal Egypt, which experienced cultural and political emancipation during the first half of the twentieth century, and totalitarian Egypt which has been suffering from political repression and cultural dogma since the 1952 Revolution." (See "Towards an Egyptian Feminism" in *Daily Star Egypt,* September 9, 2008.)

EGYPTIAN ANTIQUITIES AFTER THE REVOLUTION

As for the situation with antiquities, 1922 marked the most extraordinary event in the history of archaeology: After working in the Valley of the Kings for five years, on November 4, 1922, British archaeologist Howard Carter found the intact and unviolated tomb of the boy king Tutankhamun, a pharaoh of the golden Eighteenth Dynasty in the Valley of the Kings at Thebes (modern Luxor). So stunning and so mind-boggling was this single discovery that it changed the direction of the affairs of the Services des Antiquitées forever.

Winter Solstice sunrise at the Great
Sun-Temple of Amun-Ra, Karnak

The Giza Necropolis, eastern entrance

From left to right: Robert Schoch, Robert Bauval,
Jean-Paul Bauval, and John Anthony West (sitting)

The Great Sphinx

Robert Bauval at the site of the Pharos,
Qaitbay Fortress, Alexandria

Summer Solstice sunset at Giza

The pyramid
allocated to king
Huni at Meydum

View from the garden of the Mena House
Oberoi, once a palace to Ismail Pasha

The Temple of Isis on the Island of Philae

The Temple of Luxor (the second "missing obelisk" is in Paris, Place de la Concorde)

The Solar Boat of King Khufu, south of the Great Pyramid

Left and Right: Old Cairo ca. 1800

Tomb of the Caliphs,
Old Cairo ca. 1870

The eastern entrance of the Step Pyramid
Complex of King Djoser, Third Dynasty

The Step Pyramid of Djoser, Saqqara

Model of the Pharos of Alexandria
(photo courtesy of Jean Yves Empereur)

The Corniche (sea front) of Alexandria

The Bibliotheca Alexandrina, Alexandria in 2010

The Egyptian Antiquities Museum, Tahrir Square, Cairo

From left to right: Zahi Hawass, Graham Hancock, Robert Bauval, and John Anthony West in 1998 during the FOX TV filming

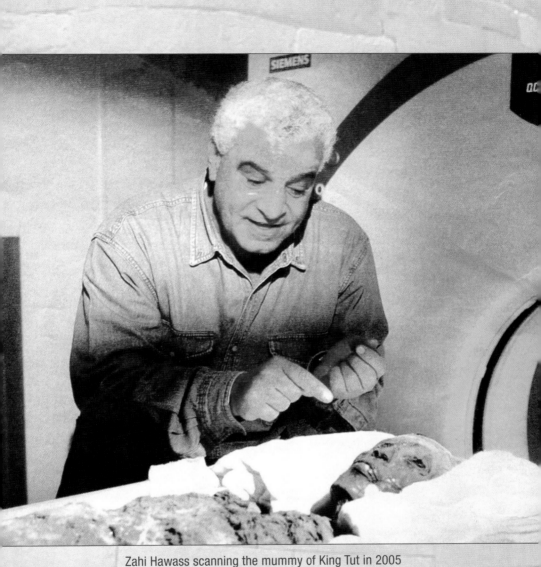

Zahi Hawass scanning the mummy of King Tut in 2005
(photo courtesy of *The Sunday Times*)

Robert Bauval with elders at the Oasis of Siwa

Robert Bauval and his Egyptian godchild, Sabra

From left to right: Prof. Yuri Stoyanov, Robert Bauval, Ahmed Osman, and John Gordon at the British Museum, Egyptian section

Robert Bauval with his daughter, Candice, in front of the Great Sphinx

Graham Hancock and Robert Bauval on top of the Great Pyramid, 1995

Iside-Pharia, Isis of the Pharos,
the tutelary goddess of ancient Alexandria

More important, however, this discovery managed, at last, to draw the attention of the whole world to the legacy of ancient Egypt, prompting many governments to start taking an active interest in the protection, restoration, and preservation of the pharaonic legacy. With this event, which made headlines all over the world, modern Egyptians began to be conscious of their valuable ancient history and, at long last, felt a sense of pride and even admiration for their pharaonic past.

The author and historian Max Rodenbeck describes the mood in Cairo in the 1920 to 1930s.

> In the 1920s and 30s Cairo emerged as the forward-looking capital of a young nation, a confident city graced with institutions of democratic government, of learning and of the arts. In these days Egyptians rediscovered their ancient past. Spectacular archaeological finds—most dramatically the unearthing in 1922 of the boy pharaoh Tutankhamun's intact, gold-stuffed tomb in Luxor's Valley of the Kings—inspired a flurry of building in neopharaonic style. Saad Zaghloul was himself laid to rest under the outstretched wings of Horus in a magnificent, temple-like mausoleum. Mahmoud Mukhtar (1891–1934), a brilliant, Paris-trained sculptor, reworked ancient themes in the granite monument he designed for the entrance to Cairo's flourishing new university. The Renaissance of Egypt, as it was called, showed a peasant girl casting back her veil with one hand and rousing a sleeping sphinx with the other.[1]

There was one big hitch regarding the Tutankhamun discovery—one that, at the time, the foreign press simply ignored: the Wafd government was not happy at all with such foreign intervention in Egypt's cultural affairs. They were also very angry at the deal Lord Carnarvon (who was Carter's sponsor) had made with the *Times* of London, allowing them exclusive rights to publish the story of the discovery. Humiliatingly, Egyptian newspapers were not allowed access to the discovery and understandably protested loudly about this matter.

The Egyptians became especially furious when Carter and Carnarvon claimed legal ownership of the tomb's treasure. Before Egypt's independence, the antiquities department was governed by British rules, which allowed archaeologists to take out of the country half the antiquities that they found. The new national government refused to allow that. Under the strict terms of agreement between Lord Carnarvon and the Egyptian director general of antiquities (it was Professor Pierre Lacau at the time), if the site discovered contains an intact pharaoh's tomb, its full contents must revert to Egypt. When they refused to allow the excavators' wives to visit the tomb before the press viewing, Carter went on strike. On February 6, 1924, Carter traveled to Cairo to complain to Morkus Hanna, Egypt's new minister of public works who had ultimate responsibility for all antiquities in Egypt. The minister forbade Carter from entering the tomb and canceled the concession for clearing the tomb. If he wished for the concession to be reissued, Carter and Lady Carnarvon* (Carnarvon had died in Cairo) would have to sign a waiver stating that they would not make a claim on objects found in the tomb. After a year of negotiations, the Egyptian government agreed to pay Lady Carnarvon 36,000 pounds (a small fortune in those days) of which Carter received 8,500 pounds. Only then was Carter allowed to resume work on the excavation site. Slowly but surely, Egyptians were gaining control over their own heritage.

Hardly two years after the sensational discovery of Tutankhamun, another scandal implicated a major archaeological discovery: the

---

*The daughter of coauthor Robert Bauval, Candice Bauval, is presently employed by Lord and Lady Carnarvon (the 8th Earl and Countess of Carnarvon) as their public relations and events organizer at Highclere Castle, the ancestral home of the Carnarvons. "I had the pleasure to meet Lord and Lady Carnarvon in 2011 at Highclere and found them to be a wonderfully friendly and very kind couple. Lady Carnarvon has recently published a biography of Almina Carnarvon (*Lady Almina and the Real Downton Abbey*), the wife of the 5th Earl of Carnarvon who, with Howard Carter, discovered the Tomb of Tutankhamun in 1922."

Figure 5.7. Lord Carnarvon, the 5th Earl, in 1922

Egyptian authorities were incensed when they learned that a price-less and very unique artifact—an exquisitely preserved plaster bust of the hauntingly beautiful Queen Nefertiti, Tutankhamun's (assumed) mother—had been clandestinely taken out of the country! The story goes back to 1912, when Ludwig Borchardt, a German archaeolo-gist, was excavating at the desolate site of Tell el-Amarna, where had once stood Akhetaten (Horizon of Aten), the legendary capital of the pharaoh Akhenaten.

On December 6, 1912, Borchardt, who was employed to do exca-vations at Tell el-Amarna for the German Oriental Company, while clearing the newly discovered workshop of the pharaoh Akhenaten's sculptor, a man called Thutmose, came across something sticking out of the sand. As he cleared away the sand carefully with a brush, he couldn't quite believe his eyes—he had found the bust of an unfinished statue: it was so perfect and well preserved that it almost came alive in his hands. Borchardt was holding the head of one of history's most legendary queens: the amazingly lovely Nefertiti, wife of the heretic pharaoh Akhenaten. When Borchardt met Egyptian officials to discuss the division of the archaeological find, he concealed the Nefertiti bust in order to claim it for his company. The bust was put among the items approved for exportation, and the lot shipped to Germany. Never in the ancient sculptor's wildest of dreams could he have imagined that his masterpiece would undertake such a journey. Upon arrival in Germany, it was eventually stored in the Berlin Museum but was not displayed until 1924. When the Egyptian authorities realized what had happened, they naturally demanded its return to Egypt. The Germans refused. The matter remained unresolved until Adolf Hitler came to power a decade later. The führer had requested that a small copy of the ancient queen's now-famous bust be made to put in his office, and forthwith settled the Nefertiti controversy in his own authoritarian way: "I will never relinquish the head of the queen." And that was that. In a later chapter, we shall review the abortive attempt recently made by the Egyptian authorities to have the bust brought back to Egypt.

THE RISE OF THE MUSLIM BROTHERHOOD

Another aspect that must be reviewed here is the birth—and the recent alarming rise and success—of the Muslim Brotherhood in Egypt, for it inextricably exerts a political influence on all life in modern Egypt and, consequently, the role played by the Ministry of Culture and the antiquities department of the country. The most radical and fundamentalist of the brothers (*ikhwan*) not only advocate the limitation or even

Figure 5.8. The bust of Nefertiti, discovered in Tell el-Amarna in 1912

the end of foreign tourism in Egypt but, more dramatically still as we have already seen in chapter 2, have called for the closure (and even removal!) of ancient monuments that they consider unholy and detrimental to Islam.

The root cause that provoked the birth of the Muslim Brotherhood can be traced back to the defeat of the Ottoman Empire in World War I, and when Mustafa Kemal Atatürk, first president of the Turkish

Republic, decided to abolish the caliphate in Istanbul after thirteen centuries of being one of the main institutions that had been a vital part of Islamic life. Although the history of Egypt and Turkey (as well as other Middle East countries, such as Syria and Lebanon) goes back long before Islam (which only came in the seventh century CE), their people on the whole lost their national identity when they were subjugated into the new Islamic empire that emerged from Mecca in Saudi Arabia. In 1924 with the abolishment of the caliphate in Turkey, these Muslim peoples were again faced with another loss of identity; for to the Islamic communities the caliph was both the political and religious leader and regarded as the successor of the Prophet and the commander of the faithful. In Egypt, in order to fill this psychological vacuum, two different and opposing movements appeared in Egypt, one being the nationalistic movement vying for the independence of the country and the other a religious movement vying for the revival of the caliphate (which is the aspiration of all fundamentalist Muslims today). Regarding the latter, a caliphate congress was held in Cairo in May 1926 with the aim to restore the institution of the caliphate. However, the majority of the thirty-eight delegates from the thirteen Muslim countries that took part concluded correctly that the restoration of the caliphate was not possible at this time when the majority of the Muslim peoples were also vying for their national independence.

There were those, however, who stubbornly insisted that it was indeed possible to unite all Arabs into one Islamic state. In 1928, Al-Ikhwan Al-Muslimeen, the Muslim Brotherhood, was created in Egypt by Hassan Al-Banna. The brotherhood declared their objective as "building the Muslim national state" by establishing a unified caliphate system.

Al-Banna, who was only twenty-two years old at the time, was born into a very religious family in the Delta town of Al Mahmoudeya, some 140 kilometers northwest of Cairo. At sixteen, Al-Banna moved to Cairo to complete his religious studies. There, in the sophisticated metropolis with its sidewalk Parisian-style cafés, its gambling houses and

Broadway-style casinos run by *khawagas,* and its unveiled ladies parading in the latest European clothes, with hairdos mimicking Hollywood movie stars, Al-Banna was deeply disturbed by what he saw as degrading Western-style secularism and the breakdown of Islamic morals—and, more alarming to him, the younger generation's drift from strict Islamic values to loose Western morals. He began to believe that the only way to redress this outrage was a "battle for the hearts and minds" of Egyptians in order to restore an Islam now seemingly besieged and tainted by Western influence.

After his graduation in 1927, Al-Banna took a teaching position in an Arabic primary school at Ismailia in the Suez Canal Zone, now the epicenter of the British military occupation. In 1928, Al-Banna created the then secret Society of Muslim Brothers, better known today as the Muslim Brotherhood. Within a decade, the brotherhood had opened branches in every Egyptian province with its headquarters in Cairo. Soon after, Muslim Brotherhood branches appeared in almost all other Arab countries. As King Fuad I was hoping to be proclaimed the new Islamic caliph, he secretly encouraged Al-Banna's movement in Egypt. This was later to prove a fatal mistake.

FAROUK, THE WAFD, AND THE BRITISH

Meanwhile Farouk, who was only sixteen years old when he became king of Egypt in 1936, was given a basic education at the Woolwich Royal Academy in England but later, at his palace in Cairo, preferred to surround himself with Italian and French friends and playmates. It was already obvious—though not to all yet—that the young and dashingly handsome king was totally enamored with his glamorous Europeanized and royal lifestyle. At any rate, no sooner was Farouk on the throne than he overthrew the Wafd Party (then headed by Nahhas Pasha) and promptly assumed his full royal powers.

At the outbreak of World War II in 1939, Egypt was swamped by Allied troops, mostly British. Although Egypt provided a base and

Figure 5.9. King Farouk I, the last monarch of Egypt, ruled from 1936 to 1952. (photo courtesy *Al-Ahram*)

facilities for the British war effort, few Egyptians supported Britain, and many secretly hoped for its defeat by the Germans. Encouraged by King Farouk, some young officers secretly communicated with the German high command in the hope that they would rid Egypt of the hated British military presence. When, in February 1942, Rommel's Afrika Corp crossed the Libyan-Egyptian border and made straight for the Nile Delta, the British were getting ready to evacuate from Egypt and move to Palestine. Suspecting that Farouk might try to negotiate with the Germans, and also because the king wanted to install a pro-German prime minister in his cabinet, the British surrounded the king's palace with tanks and issued an ultimatum for him to reinstall Nahhas Pasha, the head of the Wafd, who was known to be pro-British. The king was then told in no uncertain terms by the British Ambassador Sir Miles Lampson (Lord Killearn)—who referred to Farouk as "the boy"—that "[u]nless I hear by six o'clock tomorrow (February 4) that Nahhas Pasha has been asked to form a cabinet, your majesty must accept the consequences."[2]

Figure 5.10. King Farouk I and Queen Farida at their wedding, 1938
(photo courtesy *Al-Ahram*)

Figure 5.11. Sir Miles Lampson in Egypt (photo courtesy *Al-Ahram*)

By the word *consequences* Lord Killearn clearly implied Farouk's abdication. With useless bravado, Farouk rejected this ultimatum. The king was at his desk when Lord Killearn barged into his office, pulled a document out of his pocket, and shoved it in front of the king to sign. "Isn't it rather a dirty piece of paper?" Farouk told Lord Killearn in a very tongue-in-cheek manner.

The British ambassador was not amused. With a stiff upper lip (although he couldn't avoid a nervous twitch in the eye), Lord Killearn bluntly told Farouk to read it, then sign it. The document began with these words: "We, King Farouk of Egypt, mindful as ever of the interest of our country, hereby renounce and abandon for ourselves and their heir of our body the Throne of the Kingdom of Egypt . . ."

With tears in his eyes, Farouk meekly asked Lord Killearn, "Won't you give me another chance, Sir Miles?" The ambassador smiled and pulled away the document. Nahhas was promptly re-installed as prime minister, and within days, Farouk was again in the British officers' mess, happily chatting and drinking with the very people who were about to depose him. The Egyptian officers were deeply embarrassed and humiliated by Farouk's weakness and treachery.

Nahhas and the Wafd did, in fact, back the British, whose forces, under the brilliant control of General Montgomery, were able to stop the German advance at the famous battle of al-Alamein in October 1943—a mere one hundred kilometers from the city of Alexandria. The Wafd, headed by Nahhas Pasha, remained in power until October 1944, when the war had moved far away from Egypt's borders. Only then did King Farouk have the courage to again dismiss Nahhas.

Ahmad Mahir, Nahhas's successor, was appointed prime minister. Upon assuming power, Mahir tried to suppress the growing influence of the Muslim Brotherhood, who, by then, had established a paramilitary organization. When Mahir called a general election in January 1945, many members of the Muslim Brotherhood presented themselves as candidates, but most of them were defeated. This prompted the Muslim Brotherhood to accuse the government of rigging the outcome, and so it decided to follow a more radical line of confrontation with the government. On February 24, 1945, Prime Minister Ahmad Mahir was assassinated by a member of the brotherhood.

EGYPT AND THE STATE OF ISRAEL

There was soon to be another bothersome issue that would provide the brotherhood with the fuel it needed to rouse popular support for its Islamic and political cause. When in 1936 the Palestinian Arabs in Palestine rebelled against their hated British colonial rulers, the already tense situation was made even worse with the large-scale Jewish immigration into Palestine, forcing the Egyptian government to become deeply involved in the "Palestinian problem." To deal with the problem, on March 22, 1945, the Arab League was officially formed in Cairo with six countries: Egypt, Iraq, Transjordan, Lebanon, Syria, and Saudi Arabia (today the Arab League has twenty member states). Two years later, the General Assembly of the United Nations issued a resolution calling for the withdrawal of British forces, the termination of the mandate over Palestine, and the partition of Palestine into two states, Arab and Jewish. Although the resolution was accepted by the Jewish Agency, it was rejected by the Palestinians and the Arab League.

The following year, when Britain decided to relinguish its mandate and evacuate Palestine on May 15, 1948, the Zionist-backed Israeli Provisional Government announced the creation of the State of Israel, on the very eve of the British withdrawal, with the full de facto approval of the new superpower: the United States. This, in the eyes of the Arabs, was an unacceptable act of aggression, and it was immediately followed by a declaration of war against Israel by a coalition of five Arab states (those of the Arab League excluding Saudi Arabia). Within days, twenty thousand Arab troops entered Palestine with the aim to liberate their fellow Arabs from the Zionist "squatters."

President Harry Truman's full backing for the formation of the State of Israel, given only eleven minutes after the declaration by Ben Gurion, surprised everyone and infuriated the Arab world, for it precipitated a domino effect, with other countries, Russia in particular, quickly falling in line behind the United States in its support for the Zionists. The nagging fact that Truman was a 33rd Degree Scottish Rites Freemason (the highest possible level in the Masonic brotherhood) and that his decision was heavily influenced by the Jewish-Zionist lobby in Washington convinced many Arabs, rightly or wrongly, of a conspiracy by Freemasons and Jews to control the affairs of the Middle East. (For more on this issue see *The Master Game* by Robert Bauval and Graham Hancock, 2011, chapters 20–21.)

When King Farouk issued the orders for the Egyptian army to cross into Palestine, he was only twenty-seven years old. At first, the Arab forces made progress against the Israelis, but Israel took advantage of the truce imposed by the United Nations Security Council, lasting from June 11 to July 8, 1948, to increase its troops and to import a significant amount of armament despite the UN embargo. When fighting resumed on July 8, Israelis had the upper hand. By January 1949, Israel had captured more than 20 percent of the land allocated to the Palestinian Arabs. The Egyptian army returned home in defeat.

Frustrated, humiliated, and angered by the folly of going to war with ill-trained and badly equipped troops, the officers blamed the king and the government for their treachery in giving the orders. A group of young Egyptian officers calling themselves the Free Officers began to secretly plot against the monarchy. Led by a young colonel called Gamal Abdel Nasser, this group of officers (Anwar Sadat among them) met in October 1949 and together agreed to take over the country through a military coup.

An end of an era was in the making that would change the course of Egyptian history forever.

THE FREE OFFICERS MOVEMENT AND THE RISE OF NASSER

Gamal Abdel Nasser was born in Alexandria, in the district of Bacos, on January 15, 1918. He was the eldest son of a common postal worker who had strong nationalistic feelings. From a very early age, Nasser got involved in politics and often took part in anti-British

Figure 5.12. The so-called Free Officers who instigated the "Revolution" of 1952. Gamal Abdel Nasser is seated on far left; Anwar El Sadat is seated on far right. (photo courtesy *Al-Ahram*)

demonstrations. He spent much of his time reading the history of Islam and also, not surprisingly, the history of the French Revolution. In 1937, when he was only nineteen, Nasser applied to join the military academy in Cairo but was refused, almost certainly because of his modest background (because of such humiliations Nasser, throughout his life, bore a deep resentment for those born into wealth or powerful families—a weakness in his otherwise strong character that would manifest on a nationwide scale later in his life). Nasser got his first lucky break later when he was introduced to Ibrahim Khairi Pasha, then the secretary of state, who took a liking to the young man and offered to pull a few strings on his behalf to get him enrolled in the military academy.

After graduating as an officer in 1941, Nasser served briefly in the Sudan. Back in Cairo in 1943, Nasser managed to land a good job as an instructor in the same military academy. In 1944, Nasser married Tahiya Kazim (whose father was Iranian, and whose mother was Egyptian). The couple moved into a modest house in Manshiyat el-

Bakri near Heliopolis, a suburb in Greater Cairo (where they lived for the rest of their lives).

In 1948, Nasser took part in the Arab-Israeli war, serving as an officer in the 6th Infantry Battalion. Toward the end of the war, his unit was besieged by the Israeli forces at Faluja near Beersheba in the Negev Desert. After a fierce resistance, during which Nasser demonstrated great courage, his unit was allowed to return to Egypt safely after negotiations between the Israeli and Egyptian high commands. In 1949 (and after he had established the secret Free Officers), Nasser became part of the Egyptian delegation that negotiated a ceasefire with Israel at Rhodes Island. He then returned to his job at the military academy and, along with his fellow Free Officers, started preparing for the coup to oust the king and take control of the government. To this purpose, Nasser also secretly established contact with various underground movements, such as radical Marxist groups and the Muslim Brotherhood.

By the spring of 1952 the Free Officers were ready to make their move. On July 23, 1952, under the leadership of General Mohammad Naguib (only there as a figurehead to give credibility and status to Nasser's young Free Officers), and in what was to be an almost totally bloodless coup d'etat, the army speedily moved their tanks to occupy several strategic military posts, the Internal Ministry, the radio station, and other government installations. On that historical day, the Egyptian people woke up to hear the voice of a very young Anwar El Sadat (the ill-fated future president of Egypt) on the radio issuing the very first communique of the revolution (he called it the Blessed Movement) in the name of General Naguib.

Sadat went on to state that

Egypt has passed through a critical period in her recent history characterized by bribery, mischief, and the absence of governmental stability. All of these were factors that had a large influence on the army. Those who accepted bribes and were thus influenced caused our defeat in the Palestine War [1948]. As for the period following the

Figure 5.13. General Mohammad Naguib, first President of Egypt, 1953–1954 (photo courtesy *Al-Ahram*)

war, the mischief-making elements have been assisting one another, and traitors have been commanding the army. They appointed a commander who is either ignorant or corrupt. Egypt has reached the point, therefore, of having no army to defend it. Accordingly, we have undertaken to clean ourselves up and have appointed to command us men from within the army whom we trust in their ability, their character, and their patriotism. It is certain that all Egypt will meet this news with enthusiasm and will welcome it. As for those whose arrest we saw fit from among men formerly associated with the army, we will not deal harshly with them, but will release them at the appropriate time. I assure the Egyptian people that the entire army today has become capable of operating in the national interest and under the rule of the constitution apart from any interests of its own. I take this opportunity to request that the people never permit any traitors to take refuge in deeds of destruction or violence because these are not in the interest of Egypt. Should anyone behave in such ways, he will be dealt with forcefully in a manner such as has not been seen before and his deeds will meet immediately the reward for treason. The army will take charge with the assistance of the police. I assure our foreign brothers that their interests, their souls and their property are safe, and that the army considers itself responsible for them. May Allah grant us success . . .[3]

Now with the British support he had once enjoyed being totally neutralized, Farouk asked the United States for help, but to no avail. On July 25, the army moved to Alexandria where the king was in residence at his palace at Montazah (east of the city). Terrified, the king moved to Ras el Teen Palace on the waterfront of the western harbor where his private yacht, *al-Mahrousa,* was anchored and always readied to sail. Naguib, however, gave strict orders to the captain of *al-Mahrousa* not to sail without specific instructions from the army, while the Free Officers debated what to do with the king. Some, including Naguib and Nasser, favored exile, while others wanted to put him on trial and execute him for "crimes committed against the Egyptian people." They finally agreed that Farouk should abdicate and leave the throne to his son, the crown prince Ahmed Fuad, who would become King Fuad II, but with a regency council appointed by the army. Naguib then issued this statement (more like a warning) to Farouk.

In view of what the country has suffered in the recent past, the complete vacuity prevailing in all corners as a result of your bad behavior, your toying with the constitution, and your disdain for the wants of the people, no one rests assured of life, livelihood, and honor. Egypt's reputation among the peoples of the world has been debased as a result of your excesses in these areas to the extent that traitors and bribe-takers find protection beneath your shadow in addition to security, excessive wealth, and many extravagances at the expense of the hungry and impoverished people. You manifested this during and after the Palestine War in the corrupt arms scandals and your open interference in the courts to try to falsify the facts of the case, thus shaking faith in justice. Therefore, the army, representing the power of the people, has empowered me to demand that Your Majesty abdicate the throne to His Highness Crown Prince Ahmed Fuad, provided that this is accomplished at the fixed time of 12 o'clock noon today (Saturday, 26 July 1952, the 4th of Zul Qa'ada, 1371), and that you depart the country before 6 o'clock in the evening of the same day. The army places upon Your Majesty the burden of everything that may result from your failure to abdicate according to the wishes of the people.[4]

The Free Officers then agreed to let the king and his retinue go into exile, on the condition that they leave on that very day. The king was allowed to load the royal yacht with his personal possessions. A frantic packing and loading on the *al-Mahrousa* was ordered by Farouk. No doubt, Farouk made sure to pocket his checkbooks of the foreign currency accounts he held in European banks. At six o'clock in the evening, the king set sail for Italy under the protection of the Egyptian navy.

Upon docking at Capri, King Farouk met by chance the husband of the English actress Gracie Fields. "Boris, my friend!" cried Farouk. "I am no longer king, and I am here with only one pair of pants. Please take me to your tailor."

Farouk settled first in Monaco, then in Rome. In 1958, Nasser revoked the Egyptian citizenship of Farouk. A year later, however, Farouk was granted Monegasque citizenship by Prince Rainer of Monaco. Although Farouk had been a handsome and lean man when in his twenties, he grew into a very obese person, weighing nearly three hundred pounds at one time.

He died during a dinner at the Ile de France restaurant in Rome, apparently while enjoying a Havana cigar after a lavish meal. Some suspected poisoning by the Egyptian secret police, but no autopsy was conducted on his body. At first Nasser refused to allow Farouk to be buried in Egypt. Eventually, Nasser relented, and Farouk was buried in a vault at the Ibrahim Pasha Mosque in Old Cairo.

To explain his "frugal" style of living, Farouk was once reputed to say: "If I donate my fortune to buy food, all of Egypt eats today, eats tomorrow, and the day after that they are starving once again."

Figure 5.14. King Farouk's last salute to his palace staff as he left Egypt forever on July 26, 1952 (photo courtesy *Al-Ahram*)

Figure 5.15. Farouk in his later years in exile with his Italian mistress, Irma Capece Minutolo, an opera singer (photo courtesy *Al-Ahram*)

Figure 5.16. Irma Capece Minutolo singing in the presence of ex-king Farouk (first on left). Later in her life she claimed to have been Farouk's last wife. (photo courtesy *Al-Ahram*).

Figure 5.17. King Farouk's funeral in Rome, March 18, 1952 (photo courtesy *Al-Ahram*)

Out of the chaos that ensued from this "revolution," things began to move very fast on the political front. On January 16, 1953, the Free Officers had dissolved and banned all political parties, declaring a three-year transitional period, during which the Revolution Command Council (RCC) would rule (it was effectively going to stay until 2011). On June 18, the RCC declared Egypt a republic and abolished the monarchy.

On July 28, 1953, Mohammad Naguib, aged fifty-two, became the first president of Egypt, marking the beginning of modern Egypt's self-governance. Nasser was appointed deputy premier and also minister of the interior.

In opposition to the RCC's new constitution and its secularism was the Muslim Brotherhood. Angered at being left out of the political and economic spoils (all foreign and non-Muslim properties were seized by the RCC), the Muslim Brotherhood organized street riots, clashes, arson, and all sorts of civil unrest to undermine popular support for the RCC. In January 1954, the Muslim Brotherhood was outlawed by the RCC (and remained so until the January 25, 2011 revolution). On October 26, the Muslim Brotherhood attempted to assassinate Nasser during a rally in Alexandria. Several members of the brotherhood were caught, hastily tried, and executed. Nasser, now emerging as the true hero (and leader) of the revolution, became chairman of the RCC and then prime minister—while Naguib was quietly dismissed from office and placed under house arrest.

Meanwhile, the RCC opposed British (and to a lesser extent French) control of the Suez Canal. Despite calls from the RCC and much pressure from the Americans and the Russians (who happily supported the new Arab republic), the typically stubborn and arrogant British simply refused to transfer control of the canal to the new Egyptian regime. On June 18, 1956, Nasser raised the Egyptian flag over the Canal Zone and announced the complete evacuation of British troops. On June 23, Nasser was "elected" the second president of the Republic of Egypt.

On July 26, 1956, marking the fourth year since the abdication of the monarchy, Nasser, in a historical speech on the radio, announced the nationalization of the Suez Canal. Immediately, the British formed a coalition with France and Israel and attacked Egypt in October 1956—the so-called Suez War.

Figure 5.18. Gamal Abdel Nasser, second President of Egypt, 1956–1970. He became the symbol of Arab freedom and dignity. (photo courtesy *Al-Ahram*)

In a very foolish display of old colonial politics and intrigue, the British and French devised a secret plan with Israel for a joint military plan to return the Suez Canal Zone to the British and French and also to remove Nasser from power. Their plan entailed using "false flags" operations pretending that Israel was attacking the Canal Zone. This, according to the canal treaty, allowed the British and French to "defend" the Canal Zone. An Anglo-French force would invade the Canal Zone and then march into Cairo.

On October 29, Israeli troops invaded Gaza and advanced toward the Sinai. British and French troops then "defended" the Canal Zone by, ironically and paradoxically, attacking it on October 31 with a massive combined force of air, naval, and ground force. But the whole operation lacked speed, and soon enough the ploy was unmasked, and the Americans and Russians were livid. President Eisenhower intervened and forced the "tripartite aggressors" to retreat their forces and get out of Egypt. Within days, the British government, under Anthony Eden, collapsed. Nasser claimed a massive victory. He had, in a single brilliant coup of diplomacy, beaten and pushed away the so-called tripartite aggression—the coalition of Britain, France, and Israel—and overnight became the superhero of the whole Arab world. The Egyptian people were overjoyed. Nasser was hailed not just as a hero but almost as a sort of "god." Very soon a bizarre "Nasser cult" took hold in Egypt, with photographs of the *rais* (president) to be seen everywhere, even in primary school classrooms and at the entrances of mosques.

A new era for Egypt was beginning. But not everyone was happy about it. The historian Max Rodenbeck gives a very vivid picture of the events that followed the 1952 revolution.

For most the enchantment endured. For some—and not only for Cairo's cosmopolitan elite—it was soon cut short. Police shot dead eight striking workers within a month of the coup, putting paid notions that Egypt's new leaders were sympathetic to the powerful Communist movement. Rather than hold elections as promised, the regime abolished political parties. Hapless politicians were rounded up, tried, and imprisoned . . . [Nasser's] security forces squashed critics with unprecedented zeal, dispatching 3,000 of them by 1955 to prison camps where many endured torture. Charged with plotting Nasser's assassination, the Muslim Brotherhood was crushed. As six of its leaders were led to the scaffold, one of them cried out a curse on the Revolution. To its detractors the Revolution was a cruel joke. The old regime had been torn down only to be replaced by a regime that harked back to Mamluk rule. Trusting no one, Nasser handed out fiefdoms to his officer friends: governships of the provinces, directorships of nationalized companies, editorships of newspapers. Like a jealous sultan of old, he chiseled out the memory of his predecessors. Street names were changed: Ismailia Square, the hub of the modern city [of Cairo] became Tahrir Square. . . . With school curriculum sanitized, a whole generation grew up ignorant of its past, believing that Egypt before the Revolution had been a sorry place of oppressed peasants lorded over by imperialists lackeys and wicked feudalists. Cairo forgot itself. . . . A single soft voice [Nasser's speeches] poured from the radio, drowning the old cacophony of debate, reducing the old quandaries to idle café chatter. To the chagrin of Nasser's victims, it was a voice that touched the masses. The Rayyis was a masterly orator. Egyptians thrilled to hear a leader speak in words they could understand, proclaiming a vision they had only dreamed of. Forget democracy, forget Islam; it was Nasser who embodied the aspirations of the real people . . .[5]

But on the whole that is exactly what Nasser's words and dreams were: just words and dreams and lots of promises that not only would rarely be fulfilled but would lead Egypt into a disastrous war with Israel in 1967—a war that deeply and brutally affected the psyche of all Egyptians and should have (but did not quite) expose Nasser for the dangerous dreamer that he was. He lulled (brainwashed, some may say) his countrymen into a false sense of pride and confidence only to shatter their illusions in the Sinai Peninsula with the sight of thousands of dead Egyptian soldiers strewn on the hot sand, the survivors walking back dazed without their boots on. Worst of all, Nasser's "dreams" manifested the Islamic world's worse nightmare: the loss of their beloved and sacred Jerusalem, El Quds, to the hated Zionists.

Nasser died in bed in 1970 at the age of fifty-two. He was given a state funeral that equaled—some say even exceeded—that of the pharaohs of old. Over a million people crowded along the funerary procession, some of them in a state of frenzy, having lost their beloved hero. So brainwashed were the people that many of them believed that Nasser had actually achieved for Egypt all that he had promised. Some were so deluded that they (almost) believed that he had won the war against Egypt's traditional enemies, the *Engleez* (British) and the *Yahud* (the Jews). But the stark reality showed when gaps began to appear in the propaganda mantle that Nasser had cast over Egypt: the country's economy was in tatters; a deep corruption and excruciating red tape had infiltrated and plagued every aspect of public and private life; and poverty had grown, matched by a burgeoning population (ten million in 1900 growing to forty-five million in 1969). So bad and derisory was this situation that Egypt, with its formerly highly admired culture and entrepreneurial ways, had become the laughingstock of its rich Arabian Gulf cousins. Egypt, in a nutshell, was in a mess.

We should also not be at all surprised if the chaotic Nasser era sounds a little bit like the Hawass era vis-à-vis the antiquities of Egypt. Indeed many observers have made this uncanny comparison. Let us note that in 1954, when the Nasser era began, the main protagonist of our story, Zahi Hawass, was just a boy of seven. Hawass's growth into manhood, then, ran smoothly in parallel with the growth of the Nasserite movement. Like many young men of his age, Hawass was awed by the larger-than-life image of Nasser, his rags-to-riches story from being the son of a modest postal worker to becoming the president of Egypt. To Hawass, Nasser was the perfect role model. This is an important point as we move on to review the Hawass era (1974–2011), for it explains much about the authoritarian ways, the megalomania, the bullying, the anti-Semitism and anticolonialism, and the deep corruption that set in during his twenty-five-year reign as "king of the pyramids."

6
Secret Chambers

Can you believe it?! We are inside the Sphinx! Inside this tunnel! Even Indiana Jones will never dream to be here! This tunnel has never been opened before, no one knows, really knows, what is in this tunnel, but we are going to open it for the first time . . .

ZAHI HAWASS, *THE SECRET CHAMBER*

I will reveal the secrets behind these doors. . . . It's very important to reveal the mystery of the pyramid. Science in archaeology is very important. People all over the world are waiting to solve this mystery.

ZAHI HAWASS, *THE SECRET CHAMBER*

The Nasser era (1954–1970) was followed by the Sadat era (1970–1981), the Mubarak era (1981–2011), and the General Tantawi era (2011)—all of them holding high military ranks before becoming presidents of Egypt. In other words, from the two short years of Naguib, to the sixteen years of Nasser, the eleven years of Sadat, and the twenty-nine years of Mubarak, Egypt has been ruled for a staggering sixty years by a military junta or, to be more accurate, by military men posing as "civilians." All these presidents, especially Nasser, served as role models for impressionable and ambitious young men in

Egypt. With possibly the exception of Sadat, all governed with an iron fist and were ruthless toward anyone who opposed them or stood in their way.

In the case of Nasser, the ruthlessness came with a huge megalomaniacal ego, a gift for rhetoric, and the burning desire to be venerated as a hero defending Egypt against foreign enemies, Masons, and Jews. Indeed, Nasser played this political card so well that even four decades after his death, the mere mention of Masons and Jews can send a crowd into a xenophobic frenzy, rushing like packs of Don Quixote to fight fictitious foes who want to "pervert and control" Egyptian civilization (later we will review in chapter 7 how the riot police and the army had to be called in when enraged Islamists threatened to storm the Giza Plateau on the mere rumor propagated on the Internet that some 1,400 so-called Jews and Masons were planning to perform a pagan ritual at the Great Pyramid of Cheops on the supposedly mystical date of November 11, 2011).

FAST-FORWARD TO GIZA: THE "HOLY GRAIL" OF EGYPTOLOGY

We fast-forward now to Giza in 1974, just a few years before Sadat's assassination on October 6, 1981. In January 1974, Zahi Hawass, then a young man of twenty-seven, made his first official appearance on the Giza Plateau. He was given the important title of first inspector of the Giza Pyramids, Saqqara, and Bahariya. There normally were—and still are—a dozen or so inspectors at the Giza Pyramids, their job being to supervise the activities on the ground—either when assigned to an archaeological team doing exploration or research, or when special visits to the site are organized (groups can obtain official permits for such visits). You'll find them hanging around at the entrance gate or in the small offices northwest of the Great Pyramid. We have befriended several of these inspectors over the years, and most are affable and helpful. Their salaries tend to be low (by Western standards), but they all seem to love their work and enjoy meeting people from all walks of life—including the New Agers who, of course, this unique archaeological site also tends to draw.

In 1974 a very interesting person approached Hawass. It was the now-famous American archaeologist Mark Lehner, then a young man of about the same age as Hawass. The two men immediately took to each other, bonding into a collegial friendship that would lead to heights that neither of them—certainly then—could ever have imagined. Yet, looking at it with hindsight, it all seems to have been carefully planned or, as the case may be, *prophesied*. For Lehner was on a very special mission, and Hawass was the very man that could (and would) help Lehner (or rather his employers) fulfill this mission. In chapter 1, we reviewed how Lehner was sent to Egypt by the Edgar Cayce Foundation (ECF) to somehow find a way to search for the so-called Hall of Records at Giza—a perhaps mythical stash of knowledge left there, according to Edgar Cayce, by survivors from Atlantis in 10,500 BCE. We have also seen how both Lehner and Hawass were groomed and possibly even funded by members of the ECF to obtain Ph.D.s so that they could move up in their careers and, consequently, be in better and more influencial positions to help find the legendary Hall of Records.

Actually, the first (rather amateurish) attempt by the Edgar Cayce Foundation (ECF) to find the legendary Hall of Records happened in 1957, when a daring and amazingly whimsical expedition was undertaken by two Edgar Cayce disciples. One of them was twenty-seven-year-old Marjorie Hansen (a.k.a. Rhonda James), and the other remains unnamed. Apparently, no funds could be made available to Hansen by the ECF, so she and a woman friend financed the expedition on a shoestring budget. The idea of two young American ladies in Egypt, without credentials, licenses, introductions, or financial sponsorship, seems, on the face of it, utterly naive. A year earlier, Egypt had been at war with Britain, France, and Israel, and there was an intense antiforeigners feeling in the country. Indeed, many foreign residents had left Egypt en masse, either expulsed by the new Nasser regime or departed by their own free will. It clearly was the wrong time for any foreigners to visit this country, let alone two young American women with a secret agenda on behalf of a psychic organization. In the words of Edgar Evans Cayce, a grandson of Edgar Cayce:

> Strange as it may seem, "Rhonda" (Marjorie) eventually obtained permission to bore holes about three meters apart at the base of the Sphinx. They used hand-operated drills (augers), and after about eight feet they hit water.

It is unclear how Hansen obtained permission, let alone [to be allowed to] drill holes near the Sphinx. The Giza Necropolis was swarming with dragomen, donkey and camel riders, souvenir sellers, and all sorts of shady characters and hustlers, as well as dozens of badly paid security guards and soldiers extremely sensitive to foreigners, especially those behaving in a suspicious manner, such as Hansen and her friend must have appeared. Even Edgar Evans Cayce expressed surprise: "I don't know how they got permission, maybe their good looks . . ."

Hansen claims that the authorities charged her $300, which she apparently paid in traveler's checks. The director of the Egyptian Antiquities Organization at that time was Moharram Kamal. It is most unlikely that he would have approved of such a project. Nonetheless, the fact that *they did drill several holes* without being stopped by the guards would suggest that the "permission" Hansen got was from a high authority. At any rate, Hansen's drilling operations produced no significant results. She nonetheless reported to the ECF that

> . . . the evidence, though slight and not conclusive, is promising. The visual evidence alone is sufficient as a basis for a thorough examination of the Sphinx . . . there is almost no contemporary information

on the Sphinx . . . foundation deposits containing such information were usually placed under most temples, so possibly some such might be found under [the Sphinx] . . .

To the ECF, Hansen's report was "a precursor to extensive later work by other individuals" backed by them or acting in their favor. Hansen's ease at getting permission encouraged Hugh Lynn Cayce, the son of Edgar Cayce and head of the ECF. This is probably how and why the idea came to Hugh Lynn of sending Mark Lehner to Egypt to search for the Hall of Records. (See A. Robert Smith and Hugh Lynn Cayce, *About My Father's Business*, chapter 19.)

The chances, however, of obtaining official permits from the Egyptian Antiquities Organization (EAO) to search for a legendary Hall of Records were almost nil. The EAO (and all Egyptologists) cringe at such far-fetched ideas by the likes of Edgar Cayce, let alone hand out permits to the ECF to do digs or experiments involving Egypt's most prestigious national monument, the Sphinx. Yet against such minimal odds, Lehner, then the ECF representative in Egypt with the specific mission to find the Hall of Records, would succeed beyond everyone's expectation.

The big chance for the ECF to have another more serious attempt to find the Hall of Records came in 1977, when Lehner was introduced to Lambert Dolphin, project director of the Stanford Research Institute (SRI) in Cairo.

In 1971, then a young man in his early twenties, Mark Lehner entered the Edgar Cayce Foundation headquarters in Virginia Beach. Lehner came from Sacramento, California, and his parents had been keen followers of Edgar Cayce:

My parents joined an ARE Study Group in Sacramento, California, when I was 15 years old. Edgar Cayce literature was always in the house, and I grew up with it. While attending an ARE conference in Asilomar I met Hugh Lynn Cayce who invited me to headquarters— that was in 1968. I became a resident of the [Virginia] Beach in 1971, when I came to stay for two years.[1]

Hugh Lynn Cayce recalls his encounter with Lehner and says,

Mark was a college student in California and was involved in a lot of student protest activity at Berkeley and around there. He was pursuing a girl at our Asilomar conference. She dragged him into a meditation class I was giving. It enabled me to look at him, and I saw somebody that I thought I recognized. So I asked him to come to Virginia Beach. He came right at the time in 1972 that Charles Thomas [Cayce, who had just joined the staff of ARE for youth activities] was taking a youth group to Egypt and Europe. Mark very much wanted to go, so I gave him the trip.

Lehner immediately took to Egypt. While at Giza, he left the group one day, spent much time alone around the pyramids and Sphinx, and meditated for a while in the King's Chamber of the Great Pyramid. It was there and then that he decided to make a career involving Giza. Lehner then devoted a year researching the Cayce readings on Egypt and published his findings in a book entitled *The Egyptian Heritage*. Lehner clearly was convinced that the Edgar Cayce story about the Hall of Records was rooted in truth. (Later he would totally repudiate the idea of a Hall of Records.)

After discussions between Lehner and Dolphin, the SRI agreed to undertake some preliminary tests in the area of the Sphinx using resistivity equipment. The results revealed that

several anomalies were observed as a result of our resistivity survey at the Sphinx . . . [the resistivity] traverses indicate an anomaly that could possibly be a tunnel aligned northwest to southwest. Another anomaly exists in the middle of the south side. . . . There are two anomalies in front of the front paws of the Sphinx. . . . One anomaly occurs on large electrode spacing, suggesting a cavity or shaft as much as 10 m deep . . .[2]

According to Lambert Dolphin:

[i]n 1978 further work using the high-frequency seismic sounder, resistivity, aerial photography was sponsored by a group of private investors from Milwaukee [these investors were, in fact, senior member of the Edgar Cayce Foundation, one of them being Joseph Jahoda]. . . . the investors gifted to the Egyptian Antiquities Organization a large 4-inch drilling rig with compressor and accessories as part of this project. . . . the drill made it possible to drill holes in bedrock in and around the pyramids using only air (instead of water) to remove cuttings. . . . Dr. Hugh Lynn Cayce [head of] the ARE [Edgar Cayce's Association of Research and Enlightenment] asked us to conduct special studies in and around the Sphinx. Some of the readings recorded by the late Edgar Cayce concerned the Sphinx . . .

Lambert Dolphin explained his connection with Hugh Lynn Cayce and Joseph Jahoda.

Hugh Lynn Cayce was a very gracious sponsor and spent considerable time with us during the time the field work was being done . . . ARE had ongoing interest in and around the Sphinx. Ongoing work has in fact continued by Dr. Joseph Jahoda . . .[3]

In 1977 Lambert Dolphin had visited executives from the ARE (Association of Research and Enlightenment) at Virginia Beach, and according to the private agreement they reached, the SRI would help the ARE search for the Hall of Records, and in return the ARE would fund the project initially with a budget of $100,000—quite a generous sum for 1977. Hugh Lynn Cayce appointed Lehner as "our man in Cairo" to represent the ARE/ECF. Work began in early 1978. Hugh Lynn came to Giza, sometimes directly supervising the project, along with Hawass, who had been assigned as a representative of the EAO. Hawass was also in charge of excavations at the northeast corner of the Sphinx and other digs in the area. The details of these events, showing Hugh Lynn, Hawass, and Lehner working and drilling around the Sphinx, were recorded on 8-mm color and sound films. It is clear from these films that the project was not just scientific research and restoration but a concerted attempt to find the Hall of Records. This, in any case, was confirmed by Hugh Lynn while the work was being carried out.

> Within a short time, perhaps, we will begin to discover just how accurate the Edgar Cayce readings may be, and if his information is established as being accurate, it is possible for us, perhaps, to make a small contribution to man's understanding of himself in a new dimension of time and for this new age. . . . Mark suggested that the SRI team explore the area immediately around the Sphinx and specifically around the right paw where Edgar Cayce had in 1923 mentioned specific anomalies, possible passageways etc. Now, in February and March 1978, this work is going on. . . . Any drilling now in relationship to the right paw [of the Sphinx] would for me possibly touch the entrance to a passageway to a chamber that would lead to distant passageways to places where the [hall of] records . . .[4]

To conform to the Cayce prophecy regarding the location of the Hall of Records, the first drilling operation took place at the right paw of the Sphinx, on the southern flank of the monument. Drilling took place also in various locations around the Sphinx, but before anything conclusive could be determined, the project ran out of funds.

Jahoda, the ARE funder of the project, however, spoke of a much more grave reason why the work was stopped.

The army came with their guns and they made us stop. . . . However I was not there. I was in the United States at this time yelling frantically over the phone "Don't stop! Keep Drilling! Let them shoot!" I was threatening everybody. I really got excited . . .[5]

It was at this point that Hugh Lynn Cayce, according to A. Robert Smith, arranged for Hawass's further education in the United States. The general idea was, as we have already seen in chapter 1, to provide Hawass with a Ph.D., which he would need if he were to advance within the EAO and open doors for Hugh Lynn Cayce to get permits for work at the Sphinx.

Meanwhile, Hugh Lynn turned to the American Research Center in Egypt (ARCE) to further Lehner's career in archaeology. It presumably wasn't very easy to get him a position there, so Hugh Lynn "gave them a little money and Mark got attached" to the ARCE.

Today Mark Lehner downplays his involvement with the Edgar Cayce Foundation (ECF) back in the 1970s and 1980s. He insists that the goal of his work at the Sphinx "was not to explore for hidden chambers but to document the monument with accurate large-scale maps, profiles, and elevations."[6] As for Hugh Lynn Cayce's claim that it was he who got Lehner to join the American Research Center in Egypt (ARCE), it was apparently Lehner who approached the ARCE with a proposal to investigate the Sphinx from a mapping viewpoint. The project was approved by the ARCE archaeological review committee, and a permit was obtained from the Egyptian Antiquities Organization (EAO). Lehner was appointed as field director under the responsibility of James Allen. The director of the ARCE at the time was Paul Walker. The Edgar Cayce Foundation (ECF) was the main sponsor for this project. Small donations came from the Chase National Bank of Egypt and the Franzhein Synergy Trust (the latter putting up some $20,000). From the details given in the ARE 1982–1983 budget breakdown for this project, it is clear that the organization had Lehner directly on its payroll, with a stipend of $1,200 per month (a very generous sum for Egypt in 1982). Lehner also received travel expenses to the United States as well as local expenses. The ARE budgets for this project were $30,000 for 1982 to 1983 and $61,950 for 1983 to 1984. The money came through the ECF from "a small number of people with particular interest in Egypt and the Edgar Cayce readings," according to the ARE News (number 12, 1982). One of the funders was again Joseph Jahoda, owner of Astron Corporation in Virginia.

After the ARCE Sphinx Mapping Project was completed in 1982 Lehner was retained as a field director for the Giza Plateau Mapping Project, also run by the ARCE. This time the main funds came from the Yale Endowment for Egyptology and from millionaires and real estate tycoons, such as Bruce Ludwig of TRW Realties in Los Angeles and David Koch (renowned, among other things, for having bought the Jacqueline Kennedy Onassis furniture collection). The ECF also made contributions. In the ARCE acknowledgment for this project, the name of Joseph Jahoda again appears alongside other contributors, including Matthew MacCauley, a musician from Los Angeles.[7]

Hugh Lynn Cayce died in 1982, and the presidency of the ARE went to his son, Charles Thomas Cayce. Sometime in 1984, Lehner detached himself from the ARE and opted to join mainstream Egyptology.*

---

*Today Lehner is regarded as one of the world's leading authority on the Sphinx and the Giza Necropolis. Lehner is currently the curator of the Harvard Semitic Museum.

In 1991, another covert attempt was made to find the Hall of Records by ECF members (Jahoda was again involved). At that time the director of the EAO was Mohammed Bakr, who, we recall, was Hawass's most hated rival. Hawass was working under Bakr and held the position of general director of antiquities for the Giza Pyramids, Saqqara, and Bahariya. In other words, Hawass was in control of all activities at the Giza Plateau, even though he was under Mohammed Bakr, who was the boss of all antiquities in Egypt. Although Hawass was meant to be under the direct orders of Bakr, this line of authority was broken because Hawass's true mentor was the minister of culture, Farouk Hosni, who not only was the boss of Bakr but bore a deep grudge against him. The reader will recall from chapter 1 the bitter feud that went on for many years between Bakr and Hawass and Hosni.

Sparks were about to fly . . .

A permit was granted by Mohammed Bakr for seismographic explorations to the Boston University, which acted as the academic front for the Cayce funders. Representing the university was Robert Schoch, a geologist who was eager to verify the "older Sphinx theory" proposed by the rogue Egyptologist and author John Anthony West (see Robert Bauval and Graham Hancock, *The Message of the Sphinx*, chapter 2). Schoch (and also John West) were not particularly interested—at least not then—in the ARE's search for the Hall of Records. Although he was open to the idea, Schoch was a man of science and as such responded only to evidence. And as far as he could make out, there was no convincing evidence that there was a Hall of Records beneath the Sphinx—either way. What was convincing to Schoch, however, was the geological evidence, namely the vertical erosion on the Sphinx and its enclosure, which indicated a much older date for the carving of this monument. Furthermore, the seismographs showed a large rectangular cavity under the left paw of the Sphinx, more or less where Edgar Cayce had said it would be found. When these two sets of evidence were considered together—older Sphinx and a possible chamber under the paws of the sculpture—it had to be admitted (albeit cautiously) that the Cayce prophecy of a Hall of Records hidden in 10,500 BCE under the paws of the Sphinx was not so far-fetched after all.

Adding to the geological evidence and the possibility of finding the Cayce Hall of Records under the Sphinx was also the astronomical analysis of the Giza Plateau that was published by us from 1994 to 1996. According to this analysis, the Sphinx was an earthly simulacra or image of the constellation of Leo as it appeared in the sky in 10,500 BCE. Furthermore, Bauval also theorized that this sky-ground scheme, if correct, showed that the ancients used the sky landscape containing Leo and Orion (and the Milky Way) as a map to pinpoint the position of a chamber underneath the Sphinx (see Robert Bauval and Graham Hancock, *The Message of the Sphinx*).

Egyptologists, too, had always claimed that the human face of the Sphinx, which seemed to represent a pharaoh, was that of King Khafre, builder of the Second Pyramid at Giza, which stands about half a kilometer west of the Sphinx. So entrenched was this view that it has been quoted as established fact in all Egyptology textbooks. The evidence presented in support of this alleged fact is a statue of King Khafre that was found in the early 1900s in the so-called Valley Temple, which lies some distance east of the Sphinx. The face of Khafre, Egyptologists affirm without hesitation, is the same face seen on the Sphinx. The trouble with this affirmation, however, is that when one looks at both faces in question, they do not look the same! The faces are clearly not depicting the same individual. The nail in the coffin was hammered by a forensic and profiler expert from the New York Police Department, Lieutenant Frank Domingo who, upon hearing of this "face of the Sphinx" debate, came to Egypt to judge for himself whether or not the Egyptologists were justified in their affirmation. Domingo did what all expert profilers do when studying a face: A series of photographs of the Sphinx were taken from all angles and compared to a similar photographs of the Khafre statue, with every feature— eye separation, angle of chin to brow, and so forth—examined in great detail using fine optical and measuring instruments. Domingo's report, with typical endearing New York bluntness, was brief and damning: "After reviewing my various drawings, schematics, and measurements, my final conclusion concurs with my initial reaction i.e. that the two works represent two separate individuals."[8]

Here, therefore, was more evidence piling up in favor of an older age for the Sphinx. Though the evidence was not conclusive by any means, it was definitely worth keeping an open mind and investigating further. One would have thought that Lehner and Hawass would have been thrilled at all this since, after all, they had themselves been part of the ARE's quest for Cayce's Hall of Records at Giza, but not so.

The negative and aggressive reaction from these two men was bizarre, to say the least. They immediately got on their high horse and verbally pounced on Schoch and West in the media, accusing them of being amateurs, liars, and (this from Hawass) Jews, trying to pervert, corrupt, and undermine Egyptian history and culture for their own fame and fortune. In his typical xenophobic manner, Hawass told the Egyptian press that

I found out that their work [includes] shooting films for all phases of the work in a propaganda . . . not scientific manner. I therefore suspended the work of this unscientific mission . . .[9]

American hallucinations! [John] West is an amateur! There is absolutely no scientific base for any of this! . . . they [the Pyramids and Sphinx] were definitely not built by men from space or Atlantis! It's nonsense, and we won't allow our monuments to be exploited for personal enrichment. The Sphinx is the soul of Egypt! This is a form of Zionism![10]

This strange volte-face reaction by Hawass reeked of a "good cop, bad cop" performance. How, after having participated in the ECF's search for the Hall of Records and having been sponsored by them at the University of Pennsylvania for his Ph.D., could he turn against them in such an aggressive way? The "them" in the case of direct funding were the two senior (and wealthy businessmen) members of the ECF, namely Joseph Jahoda and Joseph Schor. Surely, now, Hawass would never again allow them to work again at Giza, let alone conduct searches for the Hall of Records.

But he did, and not only once but on at least three other occasions . . .

In March 1996, while the Florida State University/Schor Expedition was actively searching for the Hall of Records at Giza, the Edgar Cayce Foundation (ECF) announced a conference at its headquarters in Virginia Beach where Ahmed Fayed (the ARE official Egypt guide) was to give a talk titled "Searching for the Hall of Records: Current Excavations at Giza," clearly in anticipation of what the Florida State University/Schor Expedition might discover at Giza. After the latter, however, was cancelled—and in spite of the public accusations Hawass made against Joseph Schor's expedition, and the strong opposition he displayed regarding Edgar Cayce's Hall of Records— Zahi Hawass attended conferences at the ECF in August 1997 and August 1998, specially organized for him and Schor and specifically geared to reveal the latest research for the Hall of Records at Giza. The ARE's magazine, *Venture Inward*, announced the August 1998 conference in the July–August 1998 issue:

> At the third annual conference on Egypt, "Egypt Rises Again," ARE will host some of the world's foremost experts on Egyptology,

officials who have access to the latest news and discoveries currently coming out of Egypt. It was during the 1997 conference that Joseph Schor revealed his discoveries by radar of a "huge underground room" beneath the Sphinx . . . both (Zahi Hawass and Joseph Schor) are on the roster of speakers for the '98 conference scheduled for August 6–9 at Headquarters in Virginia Beach. . . . Joseph Schor, a longtime ARE member from New York, will share the latest results of the ongoing efforts to explore the Giza plateau and, in particular, any new information about the Queen's chamber door and the Sphinx chamber . . .

Other speakers on the roster were Mark Lehner, John West, and John Van Auken, the latter the executive director of the ARE.

Figure 6.1. Joseph Schor directing exploration between the paws of the Sphinx in 1996. Behind Schor is Joe Jahoda. The man operating the computer is Thomas Dobecki. (photo courtesy of Boris Said/Schor Foundation)

QUESTING FOR THE HALL OF RECORDS

In 1996, under the name of Florida State University (a front) and the Schor Foundation (a nonprofit organization created by business tycoon Schor, a senior and longtime member of the Edgar Cayce Foundation), the Egyptian Antiquities Organization (EAO) granted a permit for conducting repair work on faults and chasms in the Giza Plateau for the protection of visitors. The members of the team provided by the Florida State University were Daniel Pullen (associate professor of the Department of Classics), Alan Zidler (chair of geology), Leroy Odom (professor of geology), and James Tull (professor of geology). The behind-the-scenes motive—and certainly unknown to the general director of the EAO, Abdul Halim Nureldin—was, as it always had been with Schor, to search for the Hall of Records. This time the American team (which included filmmaker Boris Said, scientist Thomas Dobecki, and Joseph Jahoda) was directed by Schor himself. In April 1996, we encountered Jahoda, Schor, and Said at the Movenpick Hotel near the pyramids.

Boris Said confirmed to us that it was Hawass who had lobbied on their behalf to get the permit. When Nureldin realized that he had been duped, he asked Hawass to get rid of the Florida State University/Schor Expedition team. This order Hawass was obliged to obey, and consequently told the press that he stopped the expedition "because they were not following the correct steps." In fact, Hawass had collaborated a few months before with Schor and Said in the making of a promotional video titled *Secret Chamber,* in which Hawass is seen entering a tunnel under the Sphinx while a narrator proclaimed:

Edgar Cayce, America's famous Sleeping Prophet, predicted that a chamber would be discovered beneath the Sphinx, a chamber containing the recorded history of human civilization. For the first time we'll show you what lies beneath this great statue . . . a chamber that will be opened tonight, live, for our television cameras.

This promotional video, Boris Said claimed, was to be presented to Fox TV and other main U.S. channels in order to hook a big budget documentary deal.

When Hawass was confronted about this matter, he denied all knowledge about what the promotional video was for and claimed that he had been tricked by the producers. As for Joseph Schor, he too denied that the purpose for the promotional video was for big commercial purposes and claimed it was merely a "trial shoot." Florida State University also claimed that the promo film, which named the university in the credits, "was circulated without our authorization." In any case, they all categorically denied that the expedition had anything to do with finding a secret chamber, let alone promote the prophecies of Edgar Cayce about Atlantis. Regarding the latter, Schor issued legal warnings that he would sue for damages anyone trying to expose these "false accusations" in the media.

The truth, however, was told by the producer of the promo video, Boris Said, just before he passed away (from liver cancer).

> I was over there [Giza] working in conjunction with a group called the Schor Foundation. It was about the search for Atlantis. There are a lot of published reports as to what the real purpose of the expedition was, but we were to find access to a room which we believed we had identified under the front paw of the Sphinx. That room was identified by the exploration by geophysicist and seismologist Thomas Dobecki in 1991, and it was later confirmed by ground penetration radar in 1996 [by Florida State University/Schor Expedition] . . .[11]

EXPLORING THE GREAT PYRAMID

Since time immemorial, people who saw the Great Pyramid of Giza have inevitably wondered what it might really be concealing within its huge mass of stone. Imaginations, in some cases, have run wild with visions of secret chambers filled with magnificent treasures and, in the more extreme fantasies, with records of Atlantis or even with evidence of extraterrestrial visitation. Starting in the ninth century, with Caliph el Ma'amun, who was the first to break into the internal system of the monument (made up of corridors, grand galleries, and three empty burial chambers), many attempts have been made, both officially and covertly, to explore the pyramid in the hope of finding a secret chamber. It would, unquestionably, be the supreme jackpot of archaeological discoveries—and, consequently, of enormous commercial value if cleverly exploited.

The first organized modern exploration of the Great Pyramid occurred, as far as we can make out, in 1836 to 1837, when the infamous British colonel Howard-Vyse used gunpowder indiscriminately to blast his way through the masonry of the monument. It was Howard-Vyse who discovered the five so-called relief chambers—in reality, more like low-roofed attics made of granite—that are above the so-called King's Chamber in the very heart of the monument. These chambers, like the ones entered by Al Ma'amun in the ninth century, were totally bare, with absolutely no trace of any treasures that might have been stored in them.

Howard-Vyse was followed a few decades later by Wayman Dixon, a British engineer sponsored by (of all people) the Astronomer Royal of Scotland, Professor Charles Piazzi Smyth. Dixon is the person who, in 1972, discovered the openings of the mysterious narrow shafts that emanate from the so-called Queen's Chamber. The strong urge to find out what might be at the end of these shafts had to be stifled until the right technology could be developed to explore them.

In 1986, however, two French architects, Gilles Dormion and Jean-Patrice Goidin, somehow managed to obtain a permit from the EAO to conduct an exploration inside the Great Pyramid. Dormion and Goidin had persuaded certain senior officials at the EAO that a hidden chamber could lie behind the west wall of the horizontal corridor leading to the Queen's Chamber. In a rare move, the EAO gave official permission for the drilling of a series of small holes to test the theory. Apparently, some evidence was found of a large cavity that was filled with unusually fine sand—nothing more—but this was enough to send the world press into a frenzy and turn Dormion and Goidin into a hot media property for a while. Egyptologists quietly fumed—especially Zahi Hawass, who presumably resented the Frenchmen stealing what he saw as his thunder. The project was abruptly stopped before the Frenchmen could explore any further. Dormion and Goidin made several official requests to Hawass to allow them to return and complete their exploration. But all fell on deaf ears; Hawass would not budge.

The same thing happened in 1988 when a Japanese scientific team from Waseda University, led by professor Sakuji Yoshimura, took up the challenge. This time the Japanese used nondestructive techniques based on a high-tech system of electromagnetic waves and radar equipment. They, too, detected the existence of a cavity off the Queen's Chamber passageway three meters under the floor and very close to where the two Frenchmen had drilled two years earlier. (Yoshimura also detected a large cavity behind the northwest wall of the Queen's Chamber itself and a tunnel outside and to the south of the pyramid, which appeared to run underneath the monument.) Before any further exploration or drilling could be done, Hawass intervened and halted the project. Yoshimura and his team were never to return to complete their work in the Queen's Chamber.

Oddly enough, and despite all the excitement about possible secret chambers in the vicinity of the Queen's Chamber, nobody thought of taking a closer look into the Queen's Chamber's mysterious and hitherto unexplored shafts. Considering that they shot deep into the unknown bowels of the pyramid, one would have thought that the temptation to explore them would have been irresistible. But apparently not so for Egyptologists. Yet even in the 1980s, the technology was available to investigate them using in a nonintrusive method with simple video-camera reconnaissance—instead of all the unsatisfactory and inconclusive drillings and radar scanning probes. One of the problems, however, was that the consensus among Egyptologists was that the shafts (like the Queen's Chamber itself, they also believed) were abandoned by the builders in favor of the King's Chamber higher up the monument. So, according to them, there would not be much point exploring those shafts.

GANTENBRINK
AND THE QUEEN'S CHAMBER

Rudolf Gantenbrink, however, did not share this consensus. In 1991 he submitted a proposal for the videoscopic examination of the shafts to Rainer Stadelmann, the director of the German Archaeological Institute in Cairo. It so happened that Stadelmann had been asked by the EAO to install a ventilation system inside the King's Chamber of the Great Pyramid (which, unlike those in the Queen's Chamber, emerged on the outside faces of the pyramid). The task involved cleaning rubble from these shafts and then installing powerful electric fans in their mouths to boost the air flow within the pyramid. A deal was struck between Gantenbrink and Stadelmann: if the former took over the ventilation project then Stadelmann would obtain for Gantenbrink the required permits from the EAO to explore the shafts of the Queen's Chamber with a high-tech robot (this project was officially called *Videoscopische Untersuchung der sog. Luftkanale der Cheopspyramide*). Gantenbrink informed Stadelmann that he also planned to make a documentary of the exploration for television.

However, when he arrived in Cairo with his television team on March 6, 1993, to start exploration and filming, Stadelmann had not yet obtained the necessary permits from the EAO. Gantenbrink approached Hawass, who told him to go ahead regardless of permits (Hawass even assigned an inspector, Muhammad Sheeha, to work with Gantenbrink). Exploration of the southern shaft of the Queen's Chamber started on March 7, 1993. Early morning on March 22, 1993, however, Gantenbrink learned that Hawass had been suspended from his post on account of a scandal concerning the missing statue during

Muammar Gaddafi's visit (see chapter 1). Gantenbrink kept a cool head and decided to push on with the exploration. With him, on that fateful day, were the filmmaker Jochen Breitenstein, Dirk Brakebusch, and the EAO inspector Muhammad Sheeha. By 10 a.m., Gantenbrink had maneuvered his robot (called Upuaut II) a distance of 170 feet up the shaft. Then at 11:05 a.m. and now 200 feet into the shaft, the floor and walls became smooth and polished, and the robot reached the end of its journey—its way was blocked by a small door with peculiar metal handles. The urge to see what was beyond it was unbearable, but at this stage Gantenbrink decided not to push his luck. The team packed their gear and returned to the makeshift laboratory they had set up at the Movenpick Hotel. Gantenbrink then called Stadelmann to report the discovery. Stadelmann told him not to speak to anyone until he and Hawass arrived at the hotel. What happened when they arrived is not clear, but whatever occurred, Gantenbrink returned to his home in Munich a few days later, carrying with him the videotapes of the discovery. Realizing that something wasn't quite right in the way Hawass had handled the affair, Gantenbrink decided to break the news of his discovery in the international media.

The first major story appeared on the front page of *The Independent* of April 16, 1993, with the banner "Secret Chamber Found in Great Pyramid." Not surprisingly, this caused a sensation throughout the world media. A media bonanza or, better still, a sort of journalistic "tsunami" flooded newspaper stalls around the world with banners like "Pyramid May Hold Pharaoh's Secret" (*The Age,* Australia); "Secret Chamber May Solve Pyramid Riddle," (the London *Times*); "Nouveau Mystere dans la Pyramide" (*Le Monde,* France); "Pyramid Mystery" (*Los Angeles Times*); "Vive la Technique: Porte pour Kheops!" (*Le Matin,* Switzerland)—to name but a few. Literally everyone, even those with the only tiniest bit of curiosity, desperately wanted to know what was on the other side of this door! Speculation ran wild: the tomb of Cheops, manuscripts, or tablets revealing the secret of the pyramids, a golden effigy of the god Osiris or the goddess Isis, evidence of Atlantis, evidence of aliens, a hall of records, even the body of Jesus! This was not just a mysterious unopened door in an ancient tomb; it was, no less, a mysterious unopened door in the most mysterious (only surviving) wonder of the ancient world! It was a mystery that touched and titillated the collective soul of the whole human race. With such media and public excitement, it was obvious to anyone with any marketing savvy that a TV documentary of this discovery aired on a major channel followed by another live documentary of the "opening of the door" would be of huge commercial value—especially if a TV channel could garner exclusive rights to the story. One would have thought that the Egyptian authorities, or Hawass or Stadelmann, would have embraced this opportunity with open arms.

Oddly, they didn't. In fact, they did the opposite: they tried to kill this exemplary "golden goose" at birth. Stadelmann opened the campaign by fuming angrily at Gantenbrink and lamented to the bemused journalists at a press conference in Cairo (who were all eager to know more about the discovery) that "I don't know how this story happened but I can tell you this is very annoying. [T]here is no room behind the "stone". . . [the report of a possible hidden chamber] . . . is very annoying. There is surely no other chamber!"[12] Far worse negativity came from the EAO and the *Egyptian Gazette* in an article titled "German Scientist's Claim a Hoax" (April 20, 1993).

> In a statement to the press, Dr. Mohammed Ibrahim Bakr, Chairman of the Egyptian Antiquities Organization (EAO) . . . ruled out allegations that the German scientist had successfully done his experiment because "EAO never granted the approval to this German."

However, at a press conference nine months earlier, on June 8, 1992, Bakr, Hawass, and Stadelmann jointly had issued this official statement, clearly showing that they were very aware of what Gantenbrink was doing at the pyramids:

Figure 6.2. (From left) Rudolf Gantenbrink, Robert Bauval, Sir I. E. S. Edwards, and Mrs. Edwards, Paris 1993

> Following an appeal by the EAO . . . the German Archaeological Institute contacted a specialized engineer, Mr. Rudolf Gantenbrink of Munich. . . . Mr. Gantenbrink constructed a small device fitted with a video camera that could walk up the airshafts . . .

As for Hawass, he told the press: "I do not think this is a 'door' and there is nothing behind it!"

Gantenbrink, not getting any joy from the Egyptian authorities or Hawass, and shunning the big TV channels that ran after him offering millions of dollars for exclusivity to film the opening of the door, Gantenbrink decided to make his own TV documentary using the footage he had shot during his exploration at the Great Pyramid.

But although the story of the discovery itself could have easily fetched a nice sum of money, the real prize would be, of course, the *live opening* of the door—any fool could see that. So here was the drill: Gantenbrink's discovery of the unopened door in the Great Pyramid generated huge media hype for a follow-up live show of the opening of the door. But he *must* have the all the necessary permits from the Egyptian authorities for such an event to take place. However, the heated feuds that were now going on between the various parties involved made matters very difficult, to put it mildly. The inevitable happened, or, to put it another way: *nothing happened*. The whole affair got lost in the politics and verbiage that took place in the months and years that followed. Finally the media and the public got tired of asking when the door in the pyramid would be opened, for all they got from Hawass were vague statements such as "very soon," "at the end of the year," "in a few months," and so forth. It became a cruel joke. So after nearly ten years of this cat-and-mouse game with the media and the public, no one seemed to be interested anymore in the mysterious door in the Great Pyramid.

NINE YEARS LATER
Secret Chambers Revealed

Then in May 2002, the whole mood changed. Hawass was appointed chairman of the Supreme Council of Antiquities—which in effect meant being in control of *all antiquities in Egypt*. At the same time, another appointment came his way, one that would dovetail perfectly with his new role as supreme keeper and authority of antiquities in Egypt: The National Geographic Society (whose TV station, the National Geographic Channel [NGC], is owned by Rupert Murdoch's Fox TV) appointed Zahi Hawass as "explorer-in-residence." This very prestigious (and very lucrative) appointment came with a generous "stipend" of $200,000 per year and other privileges. It made Hawass a recognized National Geographic–accredited explorer in league with only a handful of other explorers in the world.

No sooner were all these new honors bestowed on Hawass, then the NGC revived the "door" and "secret chambers in the Great Pyramid" hype with the support and full force of the worldwide media that NGC had through its connection to the Murdoch media empire to which Hawass now was part.

On August 5, 2002, an important notice appeared on the main website of the NGC. This notice proclaimed that on September 17, 2002, a secret chamber inside the Great Pyramid of Egypt would be revealed to the world and that the opening of this chamber would be televised live around the world. The notice ran the following text:

WE UNLOCK EGYPT'S SECRET CHAMBERS TO REVEAL CENTURIES-OLD MYSTERIES AND MAGIC. EGYPT: SECRET CHAMBERS REVEALED. TUESDAY 17TH SEPTEMBER LIVE AT 1 A.M. AND RE-BROADCASTED AT 9 P.M.

National Geographic Channel and two of the world's pre-eminent archaeologists take viewers inside the heart of the Great Pyramid in a global, live television event. This is history in the making. Take part in a modern exploration in our Live Two-Hour Special from Egypt. Be there as the Experts try to unravel more mysteries from the site of the ancient pyramids in Giza. National Geographic's explorer-in-residence is searching for answers to how the pyramids were really built. . . . Dr. Hawass and fellow archaeologist Mark Lehner are working to solve one of the great riddles of our time: in "Egypt: Secret Chambers Revealed" they hope to find the answers. And deep inside the Great Pyramid—the largest pyramid ever built—Dr. Hawass has also found a narrow shaft. Why is it there? And why is there a blocking stone lodged some 200 feet up preventing anyone from discovering what is on the other side? Could the stone conceal a secret chamber containing the elusive body or treasures of King Khufu? Come with us as we send a custom-built robot, fully fitted with the latest imagery and sensory technology, to get a first glimpse of what lies beyond this stone. Watch history in the making as the future and the past are set to collide. Modern technology may unlock the secrets of one of the world's most ancient constructions, rewriting the history of the Great Pyramid forever.

After nearly ten years of excruciating delays and with Gantenbrink himself out of the picture, Hawass had taken over the project and had finally given the green light to a new joint-venture team formed between Egypt's Supreme Council of Antiquities (SCA) and the National Geographic Society of America. This high-powered new team was to be headed, of course, by Hawass. It was also announced that a state-of-the-art high-tech robot named Pyramid Rover, costing over $250,000, had been specially designed by i-Robot (an offshoot of MIT Laboratories at Boston). A pertinent point was made by National Geographic that i-Robot had previously supplied robots that had been used to search for victims of the September 11 attack in New York. It was also announced that Fox TV had bought the broadcast rights for live transmission in the United States. The provocative title of the program was "Secret Chambers Revealed" and this, when coupled with the high-profile team, was seen as a guarantee of wonderful things to come. Huge expectations of a hidden chamber with pharaoh's treasures and golden mummies stimulated the public's imagination. Fox TV put into motion an aggressive promotional campaign, and the public was teased into a frenzy with headlines like: "Egypt: Secret Chambers Revealed: 4500 years ago, a door was sealed for eternity. On September 17, we open it LIVE."

Since 1993, there had been much speculation whether the door led to a secret chamber, and thus it was not surprising that the millions of potential viewers expected that National Geographic would, indeed, open this door and reveal a secret chamber live on September 17, as they so boldly advertised. After all, this was a prestigious and highly respected institution with a reputation for credibility and scientific sobriety. Although normally shy to speculate on a potential archaeological discovery of this kind, National Geographic allowed their promotional departments a wide margin of license to hype this show. The same was done by Hawass and Lehner, the latter also a grantee of National Geographic and a main participant in the show. Both men went on promotional tours in Asia, Australia, and Europe. In an interview given to the British *Daily Mail,* Lehner exclaimed:

What do I think is in there? I think it might be a serdab. A serdab
is a sealed room for a Ka-statue, a statue of the dead king which
embodied his Ka or life spirit. The oldest pyramid of the hundred
major pyramids of Egypt is the step-pyramid of Djoser at Saqqara;
and that has a serdab. . . . Because his stone box is tilted, he [the
statue of Djoser] is looking straight at the sky. It is almost as if he
is sealed in a stone capsule, about to be launched towards Orion.[13]

And Hawass told the same newspaper that

[t]here might be a papyrus of Khufu's sacred book, which has never
been found. We know it once existed. The Egyptian priest who first
wrote out the list of the pharaohs of Egypt gave potted histories [*sic*]
against each name. And one entry is: "Khufu also wrote the Sacred
Book." As Khufu was the man who built the biggest pyramid, his
Sacred Book might reasonably be expected to explain how, and more
importantly, why.[14]

Such bold speculation was most uncharacteristic of these two
men. Indeed, in 1993, when Gantenbrink found the supposed door,
Hawass was quick to downplay the find and insisted it was just a stone
block. The same went for Lehner in the subsequent years. So what had
changed the view of these scholars to the point of making a complete
180-degree turn? Was it because they were now part of a global promotional campaign for a big bucks, live, worldwide broadcast? The game,
of course, was to hook sponsors and advertisers with a dazzling array
of on-air and off-air possibilities to stamp their products and logos on
ancient Egypt and, more excitingly, on the Great Pyramid and its potential secret chamber. The off-air opportunities entailed organizing road
shows of lectures, interviews, and exhibitions, with Hawass and Lehner
presented as real-life Indiana Joneses. Lehner would have a lecture series
to complement this global programming event, while exhibitions were
organized in the Far East for Hawass. According to NGC marketing

manager Jacinta Lenehan, these events were designed to promote pro-gramming, which in turn offered substantial leverage for advertisers and sponsors.

> World-renowned Egyptologist Dr. Mark Lehner will deliver, for the first time on Australian soil, his lecture "Who Built the Pyramids?" to audiences in Sydney and Melbourne. In addition to the educational publicity road show that surrounds his visit, these events will be free to the public and offer advertisers and other partners an additional forum for involvement with National Geographic. The channel is striving for greater interactivity with viewers and its advertisers so these events are not simply about sponsors stringing up banners and plastering logos. At such events, sponsors have the opportunity to showcase and align their products with the National Geographic brand and be involved in comprehensive marketing and communi-cations initiatives targeting the many demographics. It is all about participation and integration between the channel and the brands.

The "Secret Chambers Revealed" media stunt was not the first time that Fox TV had involved Zahi Hawass. In March 1999, Fox TV had bought the exclusive rights for a two-hour live special, *Opening the Lost Tombs: Live from Egypt*. To assist Hawass in the show were Fox's presenters Maury Povich and Suzy Kolber. According to Mahmoud Kassem of the *Cairo Times* (Vol. 4, Issue 13, June 1–7, 2000), "for over a month a legion of American television producers, aided and abet-ted by Video Cairo and Israeli freelance cameramen, have bewildered residents of the town of Bawiti with their Indiana Jones costumes, convoy of busses and vast satellites." The lost tombs that were wait-ing to be opened live were that of Queen Khamerernebty II, whose small crumbled pyramid lies south of the third Pyramid at Giza, and that of an unknown person. In addition, the mummy of a nobleman called Nefer at Saqqara was to be examined in front of the cameras.

This, apparently, was the first time that an ancient Egyptian tomb was to be excavated live on television, and naturally Fox TV made a big media deal of this. The whole promotion campaign turned out to be pure Hollywood schmaltz.

Seemingly not discouraged by such criticism from his peers, a year later Hawass again participated with Fox TV on yet another live extravaganza titled "Opening the Tombs of the Golden Mummies Live!" with Hollywood superstar Bill Pullman and presenter Lisa Guerrero. This show proved to be a great embarrassment to both the Egyptians and the scholarly community. The most damning scene was when Hawass kicked open a sarcophagus during the live broadcast. The *Al-Ahram Weekly,* a popular English language newspaper in Egypt, summed up the public outrage:

"Opening the Tombs of the Golden Mummies: Live!" was "the second time in recent years that Fox has mined ancient Egyptian history for compelling subject matter. . ." says the website. Mined it for money is more like it . . .

Gradually, however, the interest of the major U.S. channel documentaries for Hawass's "real Indiana Jones" act and his "discoveries" began to wane. Having milked dry the big "archaeological cows" live on air (the secret chambers in the pyramids, the Bahariya golden mummies, the opening of the tomb, and so on), they had taken the public's appetite to dangerous heights and expectations. Typical of such Hollywood extravaganzas, having now exhausted the portfolio of great "discoveries" allegedly made by Hawass (many of which, incidentally, were not really his discoveries), somehow new and bigger sensational "discoveries" had to be found to interest the discovery-fatigued public. NGC and FOX-TV having gobbled down the lion's share, Hawass turned to other satellite channels such as Discovery Channel and History Channel, who, it is supposed, were less aggressive in their demands but nonetheless commanded subtantial budgets.

Meanwhile in 2009, an annoying technicality came up that risked putting an end to his career as director general of the Supreme Council of Antiquities (SCA) (the name had been changed from Egyptian Antiquities Organization [EAO] in 1996): Hawass had reached the age of retirement fixed at sixty-three for government officials; only ministers and vice ministers were exempt from this rule. Many who had opposed Hawass through the years were hoping that finally they were going to see the back of him. They were, however, to be disappointed. Somehow a legal way was wrangled at the very last minute for him to remain in charge of antiquities by no less than the president of Egypt, Hosni Mubarak. This is what happened in Hawass's own words:

> There is a rule in Egypt that when a government official reaches a certain age, they retire. Therefore I was planning to retire next May. . . . But then President Mubarak called me on the phone to ask me when I am really retiring. He said he would appoint me as Deputy Minister of Culture, which would mean that I would not have to retire next year, as Ministers and Deputy Ministers in Egypt have no set age for retirement. . . . I would also like to say how grateful I am to President Mubarak. He is a unique man, who has given a lot to his country. He has been in public service for years and I have not once seen him make a decision just for himself. Everything he does, he does for Egypt. His wife, Mrs. Suzanne Mubarak, I feel deserves a Nobel Prize for the work she has done for peace . . .[15]

Apparently the new post of deputy minister of culture, especially created for Hawass by President Mubarak, was *for life*—a very unusual honor, indeed, ratified by presidential decree. Hawass, to say the very least, was clearly in Mubarak's good books. In this way, Mubarak (or was it really the first lady, Suzanne Mubarak?) made doubly sure that Hawass would remain for the duration of his lifetime directly or indirectly in charge of Egypt's antiquities.

All was going extremely well for Zahi Hawass. A bright and

lucrative future lay ahead of him. He was, in his own words, very powerful and famous. The U.S. media had turned him into a real Indiana Jones, a bright star in the Hollywood pantheon, and it seemed that the American public lapped it all up and just could not get enough of him. He was booked months ahead on prestigious lecture tours, and journalists queued patiently outside his office for interviews. Had he not served as a private host at the pyramids for mega-celebrities, rubbing shoulders with Princess Diana, Tony Blair, Naomi Cambell, Shakira, Roger Moore, Bill Clinton, and President Barak Obama, to name but a few? Had not Laura Bush, America's former first lady, introduced him as a "friend" at a lecture in Dallas, her words almost drowned by the enthusiastic applause of 4,500 adoring fans, as Hawass walked onstage?

Yes, all was going very well indeed for the "world's most famous archaeologist" (Laura Bush's own words). Until something rather strange and wonderful happened on a cold day in late January 2011 in Cairo's main quadrangle called Tahrir Square.

7
Revolution!

No to Zahi Hawass! . . . Shut Up Zahi Hawass! . . . The
People Want Zahi Hawass to Go on Trial! . . . Hawass Is
a Thief! . . . A Spy for America!

SLOGANS BY PROTESTERS IN
TAHRIR SQUARE, MAY 27, 2011

I have had to spend a great deal of my time dealing with
false accusations that have been made against me. . . . I do
not use my private car; I take taxis and walk on the street,
enjoying the crowds of Cairo. Every day I am blessed to see
first-hand how so many Egyptians respect and love me.

ZAHI HAWASS ON HIS WEBSITE,
AUGUST 15, 2011

ENOUGH IS ENOUGH

Tunisia: On December 17, 2010, at 11.30 a.m., Mohamed Bouazizi
(Bassboussa to his friends), a twenty-six-year-old street vendor, calmly
dowsed gasoline on his body in front of the governor's office at Sidi
Bouzid (a small town in rural Tunisia) and set himself on fire. He
died several weeks later, on January 4, 2011, after suffering the most
excruciating agony imaginable. His amazing, although gruesome, act

of courage was to protest the confiscation of his small cart and wares by municipal officials and the brutal harassment and humiliation that was inflicted on him by these cruel and corrupt public servants. One of them, a woman, apparently had slapped Bouazizi across the face—a gesture of total humiliation for an Arab man. For young Bouazizi, this was the last straw. Living in a town where more than 30 percent of the people are unemployed, having a large family to support and feed, with mounting debts he could not repay, and, to boot, with corrupt officials on his back demanding exorbitant bribes, young Bouazizi had had enough—enough of living under a corrupt and heartless government whose officials filled their own pockets with bribe money and made shady deals while he and the majority of hardworking Tunisians were living on the most meager of earnings and were trampled on like dirt. Bouazizi, sadly, did not live to know that his exemplary act of courage sparked the Tunisian Revolution and, on January 14, 2011, brought down President Zine el Abidine Ben Ali and brought an end to his twenty-three years of cruel and corrupt oppression.

Egypt: On January 25, 2011, a huge crowd, mostly students and young people from the many poor suburbs, gathered in Tahrir Square in central Cairo. They, too, had had more than enough living under the oppressive and corrupt regime of President Hosni Mubarak. "Enough is enough! Mubarak get out! The people want the old regime out!" chanted the crowd. And this time, unlike the many thwarted protests in previous years, the people also said that they were ready to die here and now, just like young Mohamed Bouazizi, and to everyone's great surprise—even their own—they actually meant it. More than eight hundred of them (apparently many more according to unofficial sources) did, in fact, die in Tahrir Square—brutally killed by the riot police and the National Security officers disguised as thugs. But the protestors held their ground and refused to balk.

Day after day, night after night, they remained in Tahrir Square, thwarting assault after assault thrown against them by the riot police and pro-Mubarak supporters, while the rest of the world watched these incredible events unfold live on television; all the major channels were there—CNN, BBC, TV5, Al Jazeera, Al Arebeya, Fox News, to name but a few—on a twenty-four-hour basis. Anderson Cooper, a high-profile presenter at CNN, was both stunned and awed by the amazing courage and resistance shown by the Egyptian protesters. Cooper's ten-minute clip shown on CNN prime time (February 8, 2011) titled "Fear Has Been Defeated, There's No Turning Back" almost certainly helped tip the international pressure in favor of the protesters.

> Eleven days and counting; it's hard to believe so much has changed in so short a time. In Tahrir Square the anti-Mubarak protesters will tell you "fear has been defeated, there's no turning back." When morning comes you see the makeshift barricades, the hand-forged weapons, dug up rocks, bandaged bodies—they are still standing their ground. "Fear has been defeated," they'll tell you, "there's no turning back." They bought this square with blood, paid for in pain, bruised they're not broken, battered they're not bowed. . . . Raised to be silent, not criticize the state, beaten by cops, gassed and abused, turned on, attacked by fire-throwing thugs, they stayed in this square and today more kept on coming, peacefully protesting. There are lives on the line. Fear has been defeated, there's no turning back . . .

Just a few days before Anderson Cooper's inspiring piece, President Mubarak in a desperate bid to stay in power announced the reshuffling of his cabinet on January 30. Many ministers were replaced, including the much-hated minster of interior, Habib el-Adly, and the corrupt minister of finance. But to everyone's surprise Mubarak also created a new ministry, the Ministry of State for Antiquities Affairs, and Zahi Hawass was made its first minister. After thirty-seven years of climbing up the ranks in the antiquities department with the help of powerful friends, Hawass was now an integral part of the Mubarak new cabinet.

Hawass was over the moon and proudly (and perhaps foolishly) spouted his full support for President Mubarak in a bombastic way in a live interview on the BBC.

> The president is fine, the president would like to stay and all of us would like him to stay . . . the people elected President Mubarak as the president, no one can forget what he did for Egypt, he did for peace, he did the war in 73 [?], he made the whole world respect Egypt, and he was a kind man and a good man. And I myself always respected this man, and I would like this man to stay . . . the army is completely supporting the people and the president, because the president was elected by the people! . . . *We are not a religious country! No way the Muslim Brotherhood will come to power!*[1]

Let us recall how Mubarak had on a previous occasion in 2009 created a new ministerial post just so that Hawass, who was due for retirement at sixty-three, could remain head of Egypt's antiquities. And now again, hardly two years later, Mubarak was creating yet another ministerial position—this time a whole brand-new ministry—to keep Zahi Hawass in power! Such special favoritism and cronyism was unheard of before.

But then everything changed very quickly. On February 10, the army declared that they would "not shoot at protesters" even if they marched toward the presidential palace. With this announcement, even Hawass must have realized with dismay that he had backed the wrong horse. On February 11, Mubarak stepped down, and a Supreme Council of the Armed Forces (SCAF) headed by Field Marshal Mohammad Tantawi assumed power. A new prime minister was appointed, Essam Sharaf, who quickly reshuffled the cabinet. Hawass's days were numbered—or were they?

What happened next was to confuse everyone and will remain the topic of several conspiracy theories.

MUSICAL CHAIRS AT THE ANTIQUITIES!

Prime Minister Essam Sharaf suddenly announced that he had appointed a new minister of culture *and* antiquities, Emad Abu Ghazi. The latter, in turn, announced that the newly created Ministry of State for Antiquities would be dissolved and would revert to being again the Supreme Council of Antiquities (SCA), under the authority of the Ministry of Culture. But no sooner was this decision announced by Abu Ghazi, that Prime Minister Essam Sharaf revoked it and, to everyone's bafflement, *re-created* the Ministry of State for Antiquities Affairs! So did this mean Hawass was still minister of antiquities? Apparently not! For Sharaf quickly appointed Alaa Shaheen, a professor of Egyptology at Cairo University, as the new minister of antiquities! Then, on April 1, in a dramatic twist of events worthy of a Hollywood B-rated political thriller, and even before the "new minister" Alaa Shaheen could be sworn in by General "President" Tantawi of SCAF (the head of the Supreme Council of the Armed Forces who had replaced Mubarak), it was announced that Zahi Hawass was *re-reappointed* minister of antiquities! Was this SCAF's idea of a national April's Fool joke? Apparently not! So again, and one might say against all logic and all odds, Hawass was back as the head of all Egyptian antiquities . . . and at the very same time, amazingly, the local media was actually printing *damning accusations* against Hawass that included misappropriation of funds, corruption, theft of antiquities, mismanagement, and profiteering! Indeed, at the very moment Hawass was being sworn in again by SCAF, the new Wafd TV channel was airing an interview with an Egyptian archaeologist at the Cairo Museum, Nur el din Abdel Samad, who angrily accused Hawass of all these crimes as well as saying that Hawass had put in danger Egypt's national security by getting involved with "Zionist organizations" and allowing them to exploit Egyptian antiquities for propaganda! And to add more confusion to this erratic situation, on April 17, barely two weeks after Hawass's re-reappointment as minister of antiquities, the Central Criminal Court of Giza convicted

Hawass to a "one year hard labor" jail sentence for "contempt of court" and the "manipulation of a public tender" involving an alleged trickery by Hawass regarding the public tender for a new gift shop at the Cairo Museum. But then Hawass appealed, and on June 7, the sentence was revoked.

More controversy was to follow. On April 18 the Internet was rife with an announcement by an American fashion company that Hawass had made a deal with them to use his name, "Zahi Hawass," as the logo for a new line of men's clothes and, sacrilege of sacrileges, to do a photo shoot in New York's Discovery Center in Times Square using the King Tutankhamun Exhibition as background! American journalist Kate Taylor, in a blog for the *New York Times* (April 18, 2011) titled "Using History to Sell Clothes? Don't Try It with the Pharaohs!" wrote this about the deal.

> Mr. Hawass has lent his name to a men's wear brand: a line of rugged khakis, denim shirts and carefully worn leather jackets that are meant, according to the catalog copy, to hark "back to Egypt's golden age of discovery in the early 20th century. . . ."
>
> "Zahi Hawass is a novel fashion line, not just for the traveling man, but the man who values self-discovery, historicism, and adventure," says the website for the company that designed the line. Some detractors have said that the Hawass clothing, which was first sold at Harrods in London this month, commercializes Egyptian history, and some object to the catalog. . . . Any profits, Mr. Hawass said, will go to the Children's Cancer Hospital in Cairo, which offers free care to children with cancer. . . .
>
> In the clothing field, Mr. Hawass already sells a line that reproduces his trademark Stetson hat, which very much resembles the Indiana Jones hat. (Mr. Hawass claims that he has made the hat more famous than Indiana Jones and that he gave one to President Obama when he visited Egypt.) . . .
>
> The clothing line was actually initiated by John Norman

and Andres Numhauser, executives of Arts and Exhibitions International, the American company that organized the King Tut show that recently appeared at the Discovery Center in Times Square.

Not unexpectedly, many Egyptologists around the world would cringe at this sort of behavior by one of their senior peers. Notwithstanding the legality of whether or not a minister of state was authorized to commercialize his name and his ministry in this blatant manner, the very idea Egyptology could be dragged to such levels would be repugnant to many academics. That the funds allegedly were meant for charity was not really the issue here, and many felt that in this particular case, the end did not justify the means. Commercializing one's public name in such a manner should not be acceptable; and, at the very least, it should be condemned as unbecoming behavior for any professional Egyptologist, let alone a state minister of antiquities. Nevertheless, again Hawass somehow managed to avert this scandal.

In the meantime, while all this was going on, widespread looting and vandalism of the antiquities was taking place at various archaeological sites and museums in Egypt. Gangs of robbers, some even armed, were taking advantage of the political and social unrest to break into the ill-protected depots and museums where precious artifacts were stored. Even the Egyptian Antiquities Museum was not spared. Hawass, however, appeared to be in total denial or, more likely perhaps, realizing how damaging to his reputation this would be, he used the media to downplay the severity of the matter. Journalists around the world were confused and bewildered at the blatant contradiction between Hawass's statements and what was being reported on the ground. We, too, reported on this unfolding drama to the *Al-Ahram Daily* (evening edition, March 11, 2011).

On the evening of January 28, the demonstrators set fire to the headquarters of the National Party overlooking the River Nile, and then, some vandals broke into the Egyptian Museum in Tahrir Square, behind the building of the National Party, through the window glass on the top floor. The following morning, Dr. Zahi Hawass, Secretary of State for Antiquities in the government of Ahmed Shafik, came to preview the museum. Confirming that no item was stolen from the museum, Hawass said that the intruders have damaged 70 pieces and the demonstrators have arrested nine people, and handed them over to the military.

When Ms. Irina Bokova, Director of UNESCO, called Dr. Hawass on February 4 . . . [and] offered establishing an international team to help to protect the museum, but Hawass refused her offer, assuring her that the Egyptian Museum was safe. Hawass also spoke to international media confirming that all rumours about stolen objects from the museum were unfounded. Hawass told CNN that the nine were not able to steal anything from the museum.

Osman went on to say that Hawass also published on his web site on the 4th of February that he has personally made sure that no item of Tutankhamun's collection was missing, and that he saw Akhenaten's small statue making offering in its position. He also confirmed that the surveillance cameras were operating in all galleries of the museum. However, sixteen days later, Dr. Hawass surprised the whole world by announcing on the 13th of February that 18 important items have been stolen from the Cairo Museum, all of which are related to King Tutankhamun and his family: two statues of Tutankhamun, a statue of his mother Nefertiti, a statue of his father Akhenaten (the same statue that Hawass had confirmed seeing it in its place), a head statue of an Amarna princess, as well as a scarab and several items of his grand father Yuya. The market value of these objects was at least $100 million. . . .

As no artefacts were found with the nine people caught inside the Museum, Osman says that these items were not stolen on the 28th of January, but at some later time. . . . Osman raised the question: have the surveillance recorded the images of those who looted

Tutankhamun's objects, or were they out of work at the time? (For so far these recordings have not been checked by the investigators.) Dr. Zahi Hawass responded to Osman's accusations by saying that: "Osman is an envious man who wants to become a hero while sitting at home in London. How can someone accuse me while I have returned thousands of artefacts to Egypt?"

Hawass, incomprehensibly, insisted to various journalists including the *New York Times,* that all museums in Egypt were safely protected when it was blatantly obvious from eyewitness accounts that *massive looting* was taking place all over Egypt. The more Hawass was pressed to reveal the truth, the more he maintained his position by denying that these eyewitness accounts were true, insisting that he had everything well under control and that looting had been minimal.

For example Mohamed Megahed, an official of the antiquities reported "immense damages to Abusir and Saqqara" where looters had apparently broken into tombs and caused much damage as they took whatever ancient artifacts they could carry. According to Megahed "only the Imhotep Museum [at Saqqara] and adjacent central areas were protected by the military, [but at nearby] Abusir all tombs were opened [by] large gangs digging day and night." Megahed also lamented that "storage facilities in South Saqqara, just south of Cairo have also been looted," although he admitted that he could not assess yet the full extent of the damage and losses.

A police source also reported that looters literally attacked a warehouse with weapons at the Qantara Museum (near Ismailia) that contained three thousand artifacts from the Roman and Byzantine periods (objects that had been mostly found by Israeli soldiers in the Sinai during the 1967 war and had only recently been returned to Egypt). A worker at the warehouse told police that the looters were "searching for gold, but when none was found they continued pillaging the storehouse, smashing items and taking others." Whatever the case, Hawass's obstinate denials of the looting made things far worse than they already were.

When by March 2011 it became obvious that looting had been far more extensive than Hawass was letting out, the Supreme Council of Antiquities (SCA) itself decided to come clean and issued a revised list of objects stolen from the Egyptian Antiquities Museum in Tahrir. Rather than the "very few insignificant" objects previously reported by Hawass, they now admitted that fifty-four important items were stolen, mostly bronze, gold-plated, and limestone statuettes—all worth millions on the black market. The SCA also admitted that the true extent of looting at other sites around Egypt was previously "not accurately reported."

Martin Bailey, an art expert, lamented this pathetic state of affairs in an article in *The Art Newspaper* ("List of looted antiquities finally released," April 2011): "The perfunctory details of the objects and the poor quality images of the missing items suggests that the museum (the world's most important collection of ancient Egyptian artifacts) has poor records and that its contingency planning for an emergency was woefully inadequate." It was clear that the sad state of Egyptian antiquities after the revolution, rather than being reliably reported so that quick action could be taken to recover stolen artifacts, was instead being politicized. While Hawass trumpeted how he had managed to "recover" this or that stolen item, investigation experts in stolen antiquities pointed out that it would have been far more useful for Interpol and other international policing agencies to have been given early and accurate reports and detailed inventories of stolen items from warehouses and museums, so that they could then act quickly to trace them to black markets and illegal dealership networks before such items could be lost in the ciminal underworld. The denials and delays in proper reporting had, sadly, much reduced the chance of finding these artifacts ever again. Egyptologists and archaeologists around the world were exasperated and dismayed.

Realizing that the accusatory finger was now probably being pointed at him, on March 3, an indignant Hawass handed in his "resignation"— now of all times, when he was most needed! In the following statements by Hawass, posted on his blog, he gave a rather garbled explanation for his resignation, and finally admitted (but too late in our opinion) that the looting and damage to antiquites has been extensive!

I am leaving because of a variety of important reasons. The first reason is that . . . in the last 10 days the army has left these posts because it has other tasks to do. The group now in charge of the protection of these sites is the Tourist Police, but there are no Tourist Police to do this either . . . Egyptian criminals, thieves, you know, in every revolution bad people always appear . . . have begun to destroy tombs. They damaged the tomb of Hetep-ka at Saqqara, the tomb of Petah-Shepses at Abu Sir, and the tomb of a person called Em-pi at Giza. They attacked a storage magazine at Saqqara and we do not yet know how many artifacts are missing; they opened two storage magazines at Giza; one tomb dated to the 19th Dynasty, the only one in the Delta in fact, was damaged at Ismaïlia; and a store at El-Qantara East has been broken into and looted for antiquities. People have begun to build houses and to excavate at night, everywhere, putting heritage sites all over the country at risk . . . I cannot stay in Egypt and see antiquities being stolen when I cannot do anything to stop it! This situation is not for me! . . . The second reason is that there are two crooks in the Antiquities Department, who have accused me of stealing antiquities and doing other illegal things all of the time . . . A third person started saying similar things, a university professor who was the Antiquities Director for almost 6 years before me . . . These three people encouraged young Egyptians to protest against me personally, to shout outside my office . . . in response to the horrible rumors that I am stealing antiquities. How could this be?! How could a man who has given his life to protecting and promoting antiquities, be accused later of stealing them? . . . My work is responsible for bringing many tourists to Egypt, which helps our economy. But now I cannot do this! Therefore, I decided to resign . . .

I cannot work during this mess . . . I was writing an article before you came about a situation similar to this that happened 4,000 years ago in Egypt. A nice man, his name was Ipuwer, tells us on a papyrus . . . he describes chaos, how the poor became rich and rich became poor . . . People robbed the pyramids, they robbed everything. That is what is happening now too!

In a volte-face that is very difficult to comprehend, Hawass completely changed his tune: whereas for the two months after the revolution and while he was still in power, he had insisted that the antiquities were safe, now that he had "resigned" he was actually saying the opposite! Also whereas a few months before Hawass had openly supported the despotic president Mubarak, now that the latter was deposed, Hawass presented himself as an ally of the young people of the revolution! But amazing as it may seem, Hawass's bombastic and emotional "resignation" seemed to have touched Prime Minister Essam Sharaf, because on March 30, hardly three weeks later, Sharaf *reinstated* Hawass as minister of state for Antiquities Affairs! Kate Taylor, a columnist at the *New York Times,* reported on this bizarre turn of events.

EGYPTIAN ANTIQUITIES MINISTER RETURNS
LESS THAN A MONTH AFTER QUITTING

Zahi Hawass, who resigned as Egypt's minister of antiquities less than a month ago under criticism for his close ties to former President Hosni Mubarak, was reappointed to the post on Wednesday, Agence France-Presse reported, citing an Egyptian news report; Mr. Hawass, reached by phone, confirmed his reappointment. Mr. Hawass, a powerful figure in the world of Egyptology, was promoted to a cabinet position in the early days of the uprising, and drew the animosity of the revolutionaries by saying at the time that Mr. Mubarak should be allowed to hold power for another six months. He also said that Egypt's museums and archaeological sites were largely secure and that cases of looting were very limited. In the weeks that followed, that turned out not to be the case: several dozen objects were stolen from the Egyptian Museum in Cairo during a break-in on Jan. 28—many have been recovered, though 37 are still missing—and hundreds more were taken from tombs and warehouses elsewhere in Egypt.

After Mr. Mubarak resigned, Mr. Hawass expressed support for the revolutionaries. Criticism of him mounted, however. On March 4, Egypt's ruling military council acceded to the protesters' demands by forcing the resignation of Prime Minister Ahmed Shafiq and replacing him with Essam A. Sharaf. Mr. Hawass, after posting on his blog for the first time a long list of sites that had been looted or damaged, announced that day that he had decided to resign because he could no longer protect Egypt's antiquities. It was Mr. Sharaf who reappointed Mr. Hawass on Wednesday.

Mr. Hawass, who has never been accused of being humble, said on Wednesday that he did not ask to come back, but that there was no one else who could do the job. "I cannot live without antiquities, and antiquities cannot live without me," he said.

The young revolutionaries, however, as well as thousands of poorly paid antiquities workers, were not impressed with Hawass's two-faced performance. Hawass, they felt, was speaking on the rack. They also knew that Hawass was a prominent member of the old regime and a favored crony of the Mubaraks. Furthermore, there were dozens of legal actions lodged against him at the office of the attorney general. How could a man in such a situation be trusted, they argued? They soon started to protest outside his office, calling loudly for his departure as they had done for his mentor Hosni Mubarak.

It was now obvious that Hawass was no longer welcome in post-revolution Egypt. Clearly, the situation was becoming untenable. Yet amazingly, like some blotch that would not wash off, Hawass held on fast to his ministerial post. It began to seem that the "man with the Indiana Jones hat" had nine lives! On July 13, 2011, however, the coup-de-grace finally came in the form of a political thwarter, as reported by Kate Taylor of the *New York Times*.

Until recently Zahi Hawass, Egypt's Antiquities minister, was a global symbol of Egyptian national pride. A famous archaeologist in an Indiana Jones hat, he was virtually unassailable in the old Egypt, protected by his success in boosting tourism, his efforts to reclaim lost artifacts and his closeness to the country's first lady, Suzanne Mubarak. But the revolution changed all that. Now demonstrators in Cairo are calling for his resignation, as the interim government faces disaffected crowds in Tahrir Square. Their primary complaint is his association with the Mubaraks, whom he defended in the early days of the revolution. But the upheaval has also drawn attention to the ways he has increased his profile over the years, often with the help of organizations and companies with which he has done business as a government official. He receives, for example, an honorarium each year of as much as $200,000 from National Geographic to be an explorer-in-residence even as he controls access to the ancient sites it often features in its reports.

He has relationships—albeit ones he says he does not profit from—with two American companies that do business in Egypt. One, Arts and Exhibitions International, secured Mr. Hawass's permission several years ago to take some of the country's most precious treasures, the artifacts of King Tut, on a world tour; its top executives recently started a separate venture to market a Zahi Hawass line of clothing. A second company, Exhibit Merchandising, has been selling replicas of Mr. Hawass's hat for several years. Last year that company was hired to operate a new store in the Egyptian Museum in Cairo. Mr. Hawass says his share of the profits from those products goes directly to Egyptian charities. But the fact that both charities, a children's cancer hospital and a children's museum, were overseen by Ms. Mubarak before the revolution has angered some critics. "We don't know how Egyptians lived all this time under this government or under these people," said Entessar Gharieb, a radio announcer with a degree in archaeology who helped organize a recent protest calling for Mr. Hawass's removal. "Zahi Hawass was one of this system, the system of Hosni Mubarak."

Remarkably, given his Mubarak ties, Mr. Hawass has been able to hold on to his government post through the aftershocks of the revolution, though he resigned briefly in March and was reinstated. He travels a lot, serving as a cultural ambassador, praising the revolution and urging foreigners to visit Egypt. Nonetheless, Mr. Hawass remains dogged at home by unflattering reports in newspapers and on television. The gift shop at the Egyptian Museum had to be closed after a dispute over how the contract was awarded threatened to land him in jail. And critics have gone to Egyptian prosecutors with complaints about Mr. Hawass's relationship with National Geographic and other matters. "I have never done anything at all contrary to Egyptian law," Mr. Hawass said in an e-mail response to questions. "Egyptian law permits government employees to accept honoraria and fees through outside contracts." The accusations against Mr. Hawass are much less serious than those made against other former government officials, but they show how quickly the landscape has tilted. . . .

National Geographic first brought Mr. Hawass on as an explorer-in-residence, one of 16* it has around the world, in 2001 when he was director of the Giza Pyramids. He has appeared in numerous National Geographic films about ancient Egypt, and the organization publishes some of his books and arranges his speaking engagements, for which he asks $15,000. It is not clear how the National

*The National Geographic Explorers-in-Residence are: Robert Ballard, James Cameron, Wade Davies, Jared Diamond, Sylvia Earl, J. Michael Fay, Rereck and Beverley Joubert, Meave and Louise Leakey, Johan Reinhard, Enric Sala, Paul Sereno, Paul Steger (Emeritus), Spencer Wells, Stephen Ambrose (Emeritus), Jane Goodall (Emeritus), Zahi Hawass (Emeritus), Bradford and Barabara Washburn (Honorary). *Data from National Geographic website.*

Geographic payments compare in size to Mr. Hawass's government salary, which he would not disclose. National Geographic says it pays Mr. Hawass to advise it on major discoveries and help shape its policies on antiquities issues. It says it has never received preferential access to archaeological sites or discoveries. . . . But Mr. Hawass also said this week that he has decided to resign temporarily as a National Geographic explorer so that he can focus on protecting antiquities. Mr. Hawass's relationship with Arts and Exhibitions International dates back to 2003, when it approached him about staging a tour of Tutankhamun artifacts. . . . Under the contract with Egypt, the organizers also donated $2 million to what was then known as the Suzanne Mubarak Children's Museum, according to Mr. Norman, the president of Arts and Exhibitions International. Mr. Norman said there is no connection between the Hawass clothing line, which he is producing under a separate venture, Adventure Clothing, and the Tut tour, which was negotiated years earlier. The clothing, he said, is just an effort on Mr. Hawass's part "to leverage his image to benefit Egypt, which to me seems like a good thing." Last year, when Egypt looked to open the new, larger souvenir store at the Egyptian Museum, Mr. Hawass's agency awarded the contract to a state-owned entity that then hired Exhibit Merchandising to run the store. . . . Curt Bechdel, a vice president with Exhibit Merchandising, said that Egyptian officials wanted his company because they were familiar with the Tut exhibit shops and they "wanted a well-run, Western approach to retail.". . . The fact that we sold his hat had nothing to do with it.". . .

On *Bikyamasr,* a popular Internet news site about Egypt, Joseph Mayton reported on February 16, 2011,

Egypt's Zahi Hawass, the man who has become synonymous with Egyptology, known for his cowboy hat wearing, has sparked the ire of Egyptians in recent days, with protests chanting for him to step down from his post atop the country's Supreme Council of Antiquities. Ironically, as reports of stolen artifacts continues to surface since Hosni Mubarak was ousted from power on Friday, Hawass went public during the demonstrations and declared, triumphantly, that nothing has been stolen from the Egyptian Museum in downtown Cairo following the break-in on January 28. "Get out," chanted a crowd of 150 archaeology graduates outside Hawass' office on Monday. The protest was highly personal: demonstrators called Hawass a "showman" who seeks publicity and has little regard for the thousands of archaeology students who are unable to find work in their field. Hawass has been under fire from a number of sides in recent years including from rights groups who accuse the man of dictatorial polices concerning debate and scientific findings. The Arabic Network for Human Rights Information (ANHRI) called out Hawass in 2009 for allegedly pushing aside a researcher for stating views that differed from the SCA Secretary-General's, which led to dozens of investigations. . . . "He has a huge temper," began one archaeologist. "If you don't agree with him, he simply screams at you and threatens to remove your funding."

Other reports show that he takes advantage of those needing internships with the SCA. He takes on American students, promises them adequate salaries, and then refuses to pay, a number of former interns told *Bikya Masr*. "He is paid thousands of dollars for each appearance he makes for the Discovery Channel and every time he writes or appears anywhere. The man makes so much money that it is no wonder he tries to curtail other opinions," an Egyptian researcher told *Bikya Masr*. The researcher, who works for the SCA, says that "everyone in the council knows what goes on, but he is the boss and his rules go, so there is little we can do." It is also well known, archaeologists say, that he takes bribes in order to give permits. "And he is big on cronyism and sexual favors," another American researcher said, adding that "it is well-known in the community that he gives key positions to women for specific reasons."

This has been supported by a number of archaeologists, who added that on trips to New York, "he has often been seen with call girls and escorts." Maybe, as the protests against him say, it is time he goes.

Finally the crunch came on July 17, 2011. Prime Minister Essam Sharaf rather embarrassingly announced that Zahi Hawass was dismissed (again!) from his post as minister of state for Antiquities Affairs. The protesters, however, were not going to let him off the hook that easily. On July 30, as Hawass walked out of the ministry's building for the last time, hundreds of angry protesters mobbed him, shouting "*ya harami, ya harami!*" (thief, thief!). The security police barely managed to get Hawass into a taxi while protesters surrounded the vehicle and cried even louder: "Thief, thief! Get out of the car . . . you thief!" (Youm 7 News).

The taxi driver slowly steered his vehicle past the angry crowd. Happily no one was hurt. A very tense and very shocked Zahi Hawass was driven away to his home . . .

"Celui Qui Convoite Tout Perd Tout. . . ."[*]

---

[*]He who covets everything loses everything . . ." French proverb

Postscripts

"A MESSAGE TO ALL MY FRIENDS"

August 15, 2011: Zahi Hawass puts a message on his blog.

A message to all my friends!
I am sorry that I have not updated my website for the past several weeks.
I have had to spend a great deal of my time dealing with false accusations
that have been made against me. I am now waiting for the Office of the At-
torney General to finish their investigation; after this I will be free to pub-
lish the details of these ridiculous allegations . . . My life as a private per-
son is very different from my life as an antiquities official, and apart from
having to deal with false accusations, I am enjoying my freedom from the
great responsibility I have been carrying for the past nine years . . . I do not
use my private car; I take taxis and walk on the street, enjoying the crowds
of Cairo. Every day I am blessed to see first-hand how so many Egyptians
respect and love me . . . The other day, I sat beside a taxi driver who lives
in Nazlet el-Samman, the village at the foot of the pyramids . . . He also
told me that the Egyptians are proud of me and love me, and that all the
foreigners who ride in his taxi know me, and that this made him happy and
proud. . . . Another time, I was walking on Lebanon Street, waiting to cross.
A car with five young men and women inside stopped and asked if they
could take a picture with me, because I am the "Indiana Jones" of Egypt.
. . . Although I am being attacked regularly in the media, I have decided
not to appear on local television, and not to spend all my time defending

myself. I decided to write this short update simply to tell my friends all over the world that I am fine. . . .

NOVEMBER 2011

November 11, 2011 (11.11.11): The Egyptian authorities decided to close the Great Pyramid and cancel all visits for that day. The official reason given was that the monument required "cleaning inside after the excessive visits during the Muslim Eid." The real reason, however, was that the Internet had been full of rumors that "Jews and Masons" were planning a big gathering at the Giza Pyramids and wanted to "place a Star of David on top of the Great Pyramid." This prompted a large crowd of Islamists who descended to the entrance of the Giza Necropolis and wanted to prevent this alleged ritual by Jews and Masons. So alarmed were the authorities that an international incident might take place, they called in the army as well as the riot police to protect the entrances to the site.

November 28, 2011: The Egyptians went to the polls for the parliamentary elections. There was a massive turnout, as millions cast their votes for the first time ever. The Islamists—mainly the Freedom and Justice Party of the Muslim Brotherhood and the Salafist's Al-Nour (Light) Party—won 70 percent of the seats. The *Al-Ahram Daily* newspaper was to comment

> For most Copts, leftists, and secularists, a projected Islamist-controlled People's Assembly (the lower house of Egypt's Parliament) poses a nightmare wherein parliamentarians would seek to implement an unbearably extreme interpretation of Sharia Law, starkly in opposition to their own beliefs, views, and values. Others fear Islamists would damage the economy, pointing to the likely effect on tourism any imposed dress and ethical code would have . . .

Egypt's future, and consequently the future of the antiquities, hangs precariously in the balance. Time will tell in which direction it will go. A very worrying situation is developing that has sent shock waves across the international community of archaeologists and for all who love and admire ancient Egypt and its legacy.

According to journalist Maggie Michael (Associated Press, December 13, 2011):

> The Salafis of Al-Nour are up front about seeking to impose strict Islamic law in Egypt. The Salafis, who follow the Wahhabi school of thought that predominates in Saudi Arabia, are clear in their opposition to alcohol and skimpy beachwear. And they are still wavering on the issues of unmarried couples sharing hotel rooms and the display of ancient Egyptian statues like fertility gods that they believe clash with conservative Islamic sensibilities. At a Salafi rally in the Mediterranean port city of Alexandria recently, party loyalists covered up mermaid statues on a public fountain with cloth. . . . A leading member of Al-Nour, Tarek Shalaan, stumbled through a recent TV interview when asked about his views on the display of nude pharaonic statues like those depicting fertility gods. "The antiquities that we have will be put under a different light to focus on historical events," he said, without explaining further.

Abd Al-Mun'im Al-Shahhat, a spokesman for the Salafist group Dawa, proudly announced that ancient Egyptian monuments—the pyramids, the Sphinx, temples, and statues—should be covered because, he says, they are "religiously forbidden." Al-Shahhat sees the ancient relics as "pagan idols," which thus must be covered up (or destroyed), such as the pre-Islamic pagan monuments in Makkah. "The pharaonic culture is a rotten culture!" Al-Shahhat said.

MARCH 2012

March 30, 2012: "The Muslim Brotherhood will nominate its number two man Khairat El-Shater to run for the presidency of Egypt, said a leading member of the Islamist group. MB called for a press conference at 8:30 pm to announce the news" (*Al-Ahram,* 31 March, 2012).

March 30, 2012: "The Salafist Nour Party has nominated Hazem Saleh Abu Ismail, a 'hard-liner Islamist, as their presidential candidate. Abu Ismail wants to move toward abolishing Egypt's peace treaty with Israel and cites Iran as a successful model of independence from Washington.' He worries about the mixing of the genders in the workplace and women's work outside the home. And he promises to bring extraordinary prosperity to Egypt, if it turns its back on trade with the West (*New York Times,* 1 April, 2012)."

MAY 2012

May 27, 2012: Mohammad Musri, the "replacement" presidential candidate for the Muslim Brotherhood's Freedom and Justice Party (their first candidate, El Shater, was disqualified), has won the most votes in the first presidential ballot. He was followed closely by Ahmed Shafiq, the last prime minister in the Mubarak government. "For many revolutionaries, the results of the first round of the presidential poll takes them back to square one: having to choose between religious theocracy or a police state," says *Al-Ahram* journalist Dina Ezat. "For many revolutionary forces and some mainstream Egyptians, the rule of either Shafiq or Mursi is a nightmare scenario. The Brotherhood or Mubarak's man . . . it represents, for them, a choice between the return of an oppressive and corrupt police state or moving towards a rigid theocracy" (*Al-Ahram,* 27 May, 2012).

The Paris Obelisk

How and Why Freemasonry Came into Egypt

> *In French Freemasonry the allegorical and metaphorical aspects [of architecture] appear to have been invested with greater significance. . . . Architectural history was equated with the development of society. And architecture was seen as a means of establishing a just and ordered system . . .*
>
> JAMES STEPHEN CURL, *THE ART AND ARCHITECTURE OF FREEMASONRY*

(Appendix 1 has been extracted and adapted from *The Master Game,* by Robert Bauval and Graham Hancock.)

PYRAMIDS AND OBELISKS FOR PARIS

On July 14, 1792, a republican ceremony was held at the Champ de Mars in Paris when a so-called Pyramid of Honor was erected to commemorate those who died during the storming of the Bastille.[1] An etching has survived of another republican ceremony that took place a little over a month later on August 26, 1792, in the gardens of the Tuilleries in front of the Louvre. Again, a pyramid was raised in honor of the martyrs of the revolution. A third pyramid appeared in the Parc Monceau, this one commissioned by Philippe Egalité (then grand master of French Freemasonry) and designed by the architect B. Poyet, next to a pavilion that probably served as a Masonic temple. And there were many other pyramid projects that, though never built, still serve to show the peculiar obsession with the pyramidial form in the decades surrounding the 1789 revolution. There are, for example, the curious projects of the revolutionary architect Claude-Nicolas Ledoux,[2] a Freemason, who the architectural historian James Curl describes as being "involved with Masonic and crypto-Masonic cults." Indeed so involved was he with such interests that when a fellow Freemason from Britain, an architect, attended a Masonic meeting in Ledoux's home in Paris, he was put out by what he felt to be the excessively occult nature of the event. He commented afterward: "It would seem that Ledoux was more involved in the type of heretical Masonry of *Cagliostro*."[3] Many architects have been intrigued by one of Ledoux's most ambitious designs, the so-called Forge a Canon, an iron-smelting plant with massive pyramids and a layout that recalls "various versions of the Temple complex in Jerusalem."[4] Then there are, of course, those most extraordinary pseudo-Egyptian designs by the revolutionary architect Étienne Boullée, the most famous of which was the so-called *Cenotaphe dans le genre Egyptien,* which was a series of gigantic pyramids with their capstones missing— a design very reminiscent of the actual appearance throughout historical times of the Great Pyramid at Giza and of the truncated pyramid seen on the great seal of the United States.[5] James Curl, who is regarded as an expert on Masonic architecture, comments that "in spite of its title *Cenotaphe,* the building was clearly a cemetery or a *center for cults,* to judge from the processions going up and down the gigantic ramps."[6]

IMAGING THE SUPREME BEING

Were Ledoux and Boullée thinking of the Masonic Supreme Being in their designs? Perhaps. But both these men, like many architects of their generation, were much influenced by the famous architect and Freemason Quatremère de Quincy. The latter was known for having presented a prize essay to the Académie des Inscriptions et Belles-Lettres in 1785 on ancient Egyptian architecture and, more specifically, on the pyramids.[7] According to James Curl, "Quincy was not only a Freemason, but was very powerfully influenced by his Masonic convictions."[8]

There is, too, an extraordinary project by Ledoux—Quincy's pupil—which is shown in his book *L'Architecture considérée sous le rapport de l'art, des mœurs et de la legislation,* published in Paris in 1804. There we can see a plan for the theater of the city of Besançon in the form of a gigantic "all-seeing eye," which James Curl describes as "an unquestionably Masonic allusion."[9] The same idea was used by the revolutionary architect Poyet who had designed the Parc Monceau pyramid for Philippe Egalité. Another of Poyet's ambitious plans was for a public hospital in Paris, where a gigantic all-seeing eye can easily be discerned in the general layout.[10]

The eye of vigilance, the all-seeing eye, the eye in the pyramid, and the eye in the triangle were all symbols of the Supreme Being, the Être suprême of Robespierre used in revolutionary propaganda. Thus, for example, we have a poster dating from the revolution, which depicts the hero-philosophers Voltaire and Rousseau pointing to a glowing solar disc within which is the all-seeing eye and a caption that reads: *Être Supreme, Peuple Souverain, Republique Française.*[11] The all-seeing eye is also prominent on a poster of the Fête de la Fédération at the Champ de Mars, dated to 1790, where the rays of the sun shoot down to form a golden pyramid that engulfs two tricolor flags and a red Phrygian cap fixed on a "pole of Liberty."[12]

The association of the all-seeing eye with Voltaire on the first of these posters is particularly interesting. It is a very well-known fact among Freemasons that Voltaire was initiated on April 7, 1778, at the Nine Sisters lodge in Paris by the astronomer Jérôme Lalande and Benjamin Franklin.[13] When Voltaire died a month later, the lodge was converted into a Lodge of Sorrow, a sort of Masonic funerary service, and on November 28, 1778, a service was held there for his departed soul. In line with Masonic tradition, the whole interior of the lodge was draped in black veils. At the far end of the room was a raised stepped pyramid, also draped in black.[14] On the summit of this pyramid was a cenotaph, and at the place where the capstone would normally have been could be seen hovering a glowing triangle with the letter G inscribed in it.

Such a pyramid with the same glowing capstone is, of course, to be seen on the great seal of the United States, the design of which was coordinated by Benjamin Franklin and Thomas Jefferson in 1776.[15] In Masonic symbolism, the eye, representing the Supreme Being, is interchangeable with the letter G, and both symbols stand for God (i.e., the Grand Geometrician or the Grand Architect of the universe"). Professor Michel Vovelle, the French author, also draws attention to a French revolutionary poster where the all-seeing eye is depicted over the breast of the goddess Reason; she holds a victory wreath above a plaque on which appears a small "glowing pyramid with the eye."[16] Indeed, the same glowing triangle with the all-seeing eye found its way to the top of the *Declaration of the Rights of Man and the Citizen* signed in August 1789 at the National Assembly. The text was modeled on essays written by the Marquis de Lafayette and the Abbé Sieyes, two very prominent Scottish Rite Freemasons. Perhaps we ought to recall the telling words of the grand master of the Grand Orient, Paul Gourdot, when he claimed that intellectuals such as Voltaire provided the "spirit of the Revolution" and that the outcome of this—the First Republic—was based on "the Declaration of the Rights of Man *which was formulated in our lodges.*"[17] [author's italics]

NAPOLEON AND THE OBELISK

In a mere two years, Napoleon had risen from being an obscure artillery officer amid the Reign of Terror of 1794, to commander-in-chief of the army by early 1796. A week after his appointment as commander of the French army in Italy, Napoleon had married the exquisitely beautiful Josephine Beauharnais,* widow of the viscount de Beauharnais, a Freemason and nobleman who, like many others of his estate, had ended on the guillotine in 1794. Josephine seems to have been attracted to Freemasonry quite early in her career—perhaps partly because it was considered to be very fashionable among women of the aristocracy and partly because her first husband, the Viscount de Beauharnais, had been a prominent Freemason who came from a family of illustrious Freemasons.[18] Josephine was probably initiated in women's Freemasonry at Strasbourg, while her husband, the viscount, was commander of the Rhine army.[19] Long afterward, their son, Eugene de Beauharnais, who now was about to go to Egypt with Napoleon, would become grand master of the Grand Orient of Italy and also of the Supreme Council of the 33rd Degree of Italy.[20] When she became empress of France in 1804, Josephine was elected as the grand mistress and patroness of women's Freemasonry in Paris.[21] Many ladies close to her also joined the Masonic Sisterhood. Apparently, Josephine's lady of honor, Félicité de Carbonnel de Canisy, was initiated into women's Freemasonry by the wife of the mayor of Strasbourg, Madame Dietrich, and to mark the event, a commemorative medal was struck, showing a golden triangle at the tip of which was placed a star in a crown—almost a premonition of Josephine's future role in France.[22] Josephine's favorite cousin, Emilie de Beauharnais, wife of Antoine Chamans, comte de la Valette, and director general of the Imperial Postal Office, was elected grand mistress of the Adoption lodge Anacreon in Paris.[23]

Being a Freemason initiated in the ancient mysteries, and now with

*Her real name was Marie-Josephe-Rose. She was named "Josephine" by Napoleon after they married in 1796.

all this post-revolution talk of deism, it may be possible that Josephine had begun to take an interest in Islam and may even have privately encouraged Napoleon to bring it into the fold of Western Freemasonry in Europe, for it is well known that her first cousin and closest friend, the beautiful Aimee Dubucq de Rivery, had been kidnapped by Arab pirates and sold to the harem of the sultan of Turkey, Abdul Hamid I, where she soon became his favorite concubine and bore him a son, the Emir Mahmoud. When the old sultan died, Aimee became the mistress of the heir-apparent, the young and glamorous nephew of the sultan, the Emir Selim, over whom Aimee was to wield enormous influence by turning him into a keen Francophile.[24] There thus existed a "dynastic" link between Josephine of France and her cousin the "sultana" of Turkey, a connection that might have brought the Middle East and Islam within Josephine's sphere of attention.* At any rate, whatever was going on secretly in Josephine's and Napoleon's minds, he would one day write to her from Egypt these curious words: "I saw myself founding a new religion, marching into Asia, riding an Elephant, a turban on my head and in my hand a Koran that I would have composed to suit my needs."[25]

Whether or not such words were written in jest, we shall never know.

INSPIRATIONS FOR THE INVASION OF EGYPT

The idea for a French invasion of Egypt was not original to Napoleon. It was the brainchild of Talleyrand, the great French statesman and diplomat. In spite of having reached the position of bishop in the Catholic Church, Talleyrand was a staunch Freemason who, during the early years of the revolution, had been a supporter of the duke of Orléans, who was

---

*The same had happened much later in 1867 when the Empress Eugenie, a great-granddaughter of Josephine, bedazzled the khedive of Egypt in one of the most exquisite and daring flirtations in history that eventually led to the construction of the Suez Canal by her cousin, the engineer Ferdinand de Lesseps.

grand master of French Freemasonry. Talleyrand had been a member of the prestigious lodge Les Philaletes in Paris and of the lodge Les Amis Reunis (to which Marat, Sieyes, and Condorcet also belonged).[26] Les Philaletes in Paris had been much involved with Cagliostro's Egyptian Rite back in 1784 to 1785, where it was said that many of their members joined his lodge in Paris. The Freemason Henry Evans explains:

> The controversy between Cagliostro and the Lodge of Philalethes (or Lovers of Truth) is Masonic history. On February 15, 1785, the members of the Philalethes, with Savalette de Langes at their head, met in Paris to discuss questions of importance regarding Freemasonry, such as its origin, essential nature, relations with the occult sciences, etc., . . . among them being French and Austrian princes, councillors, financiers, barons, ambassadors, officers of the army, doctors, farmers, a general, and last but not least two professors of magic. M. de Langes was a royal banker, who had been prominent in the old Illuminati. A summons had been sent to Cagliostro to attend the convention, and he had assured the messenger that he would take part in its deliberations. But he changed his mind and demanded that the Philalethes adopt the constitutions of the Egyptian Rite, burn their archives, and be initiated into the Mother Lodge at Lyons ["Triumphant Wisdom"], intimating that they were not in possession of the true Masonry.

Could any of this Masonic "Egyptian" hype have influenced Talleyrand in any way when he later began to push the idea of an Egyptian expedition to Napoleon Bonaparte? It seems quite plausible.

A few centuries before the French Revolution, in 1672, the famous mathematician and philosopher, Gottfried Leibniz, presented Louis XIV with a secret plan for a full-scale invasion of Egypt.[27] Louis XIV was then at war with Holland and ultimately turned down the plan—

the real object of which may have been to divert his attention from European conquests by getting him to focus instead on a "universal mission" to unite East and West in the style of Alexander the Great. Scholars suspect Leibniz to have been a member of the "invisible" Brotherhood of the Rosicrucians.[28] It is also known that he was for a long while in contact with the Jesuit and Hermetic-Kabbalist, Athanasius Kircher, with whom he shared an interest in Egyptian hieroglyphs and obelisks.[29] Kircher appears to have influenced Leibniz in his mathematical and philosophical researches and especially in his studies of ancient languages, which in due course would become a personal obsession.[30] The idea of an invasion of Egypt still did not go away. Other similar plans were later proposed by Étienne François, the duke of Choiseul, minister of Foreign Affairs under Louis XV.[31] François was among the very first of the high aristocrats of France to become a Freemason.[32] He was also a bitter enemy of the Jesuits, whom he eventually managed to have banned from France in 1764. His wife, the duchess of Choiseul, was a regular participant in La Loge Isis, which Cagliostro had opened in Paris in 1785, and had even been nominated as the lodge's grand mistress at one stage.[33] Being the man responsible for the modernization of the French fleet, François was the authority on any naval invasion France cared to consider. But his project, too, was eventually shelved.

On March 5, 1798, amid eloquent orations evoking France's "universal mission" and the alleged need to thwart British trade with India, the directory voted in favor of a military expedition to Egypt to be headed by Napoleon. The vote was kept secret until the fleet actually set sail from Toulon on May 19, 1798.[34] Apparently, a rather odd exchange of words took place between Napoleon and Josephine as he prepared to board the flagship, *l'Orient,* bound for Egypt:

"When will you return?" She murmured.

"Six months, six years, perhaps never." Bonaparte replied indifferently.

As the boat pushed off from the quay, Josephine stepped forward with one last message: "Good bye, Good bye! If you go to Thebes [Luxor], do send me a little obelisk . . ."[35]

When the French fleet reached Alexandria on July 1, 1798, an excited Napoleon issued a rather curious proclamation to the Egyptian people, who were under the supposedly oppressive rule of the Mamluks.*

> People of Egypt! You will be told that I come to destroy your religion. Do not believe it. Reply that I come to restore your rights and punish the usurpers, and that I venerate more than the Mamluks, Allah, his Prophet and the Koran. . . . There formerly existed in Egypt great cities, great canals, great commerce; by what means have they all been destroyed if not by the avarice, the injustice, and the tyranny of the Mameluks? . . . Sheikhs! Imams! Go tell the people that we are the friends of true Muslims.† Is it not we who have destroyed the Pope who preached that war must be made on Muslims? Is it not we who have destroyed the Knights of Malta because these madmen believed that God willed them to make war on Muslims? Is it not we who have been long friends with the Sultan and the enemies of his *enemies?* . . .[36]

There is a very revealing color etching by the Parisian printer Basset dating from that time, which shows what Napoleon might have had in mind.[37] In the top register, Napoleon is seen in the center of the scene standing next to the pyramids of Giza and receiving the key of Egypt from two Arabs kneeling at his feet. Above Napoleon are two angels

---

*A military-political class made up of the descendents of freed slaves.
†Napoleon also told the Imams of Egypt, "In the name of Allah . . . tell your people that the French are also Muslims . . . they have [occupied Rome and] ruined the Papal See, which was always urging the Christians to attack Islam."

holding a wreath-crown; one angel represents Glory and the other Renown. In the lower register, Napoleon is shown pointing to a large glowing triangle (the Supreme Being) hovering next to him and seems to be inviting representatives of all the known religions to venerate the universal God symbolized by the glowing triangle.

After Napoleon's capture of Cairo in late July 1798, the Arabs played along with his offer of a covenant between the new French republic and Islam, all the while secretly hating him and his troops as much as they had hated the Crusaders of bygone days. But it was a case of bargaining now with the devil until a way could be found to throw him out. The *folie egyptienne,* as historians would later call Napoleon's Egyptian campaign, was to cost France dearly: the complete destruction of the French invasion fleet at Abukir by the British under Horatio Nelson and the loss of nearly 40 percent of the expeditionary army, which, at the outset, had totaled

Figure A.1. Napoleon introducing the Masonic "Supreme Being" (the glowing pyramid) to the Muslims, Christians, and Jews of Egypt in 1798

some 54,000 men. Worse still was the humiliating surrender of the survivors to the British forces under Sir Ralph Abercrombie at Alexandria.

Napoleon himself returned to France long before the surrender and somehow managed to survive this military and political disaster. Soon enough an effective propaganda campaign began to convert the reality of the defeat into the perception of a cultural victory.

We recall how Napoleon had taken along to Egypt 167 savants—scholars and the erudite from many different disciplines all hand-picked from the Institut National de France. It was the mathematician Gaspard Monge who had personally recruited them. Monge was one of Napoleon's closest friends and advisers and considered the young general his "adopted son."[38] Monge was a prominent Freemason from the famous Nine Sisters Lodge in Paris (claiming illustrious members such as Voltaire and Benjamin Franklin) and was responsible, along with Charles-Gilbert Romme, for introducing the so-called republican calendar modeled on the ancient Egyptian calendar. It was also Monge who founded the Institut d'Egypt in Cairo and acted as president (with Napoleon acting as his vice president).[39] Many of the other savants and officers who accompanied Napoleon to Egypt were also Freemasons, notably his right-hand man, General Jean-Baptiste Kléber.[40]

There are no primary source documents that prove Napoleon was a Freemason. There has, however, been much learned speculation by Masonic scholars arguing vehemently that he *was* an initiated Mason.[41] Indeed, many continental Freemasons in the nineteenth century certainly acted as though Napoleon was a member of the brotherhood. There were dozens of Masonic lodges in Europe that bore his name, such as the Saint Napoleon lodge in Paris, the Napoleomagne lodge in Toulouse, the Napoleone lodge in Florence, La Constellation Napoleon in Naples, the Etoile Napoleon in Madrid, and so on—with other lodges also choosing names that evoked Napoleon's military, social, and cultural achievements.[42] It is well known that Napoleon's entourage was filled with prominent Freemasons such as Talleyrand, Monge, Kléber, Massena, and others, and that most members of Napoleon's family were

Freemasons, including his own father, Charles Bonaparte; his brothers Jérôme, Louis, and Joseph; his wife, Josephine; and his brother-in-law, Joachim Murat.[43] Historian and Masonic author François Collaveri asserts with confidence that ". . . the initiation of Napoleon is not a legend; he was initiated into Freemasonry probably in Egypt as is expressly claimed by the Grand Orient of France."[44]

Other authorities go so far as to argue that Napoleon, as well as his General, Jean-Baptiste Kléber, underwent their Egyptian Masonic initiation inside the Great Pyramid of Giza at the hands of a Coptic sage.[45]

Kléber, who took control of the French occupation of Egypt after Napoleon's departure, was a prominent Freemason. According to historian Paul Naudon, Kléber founded Egypt's first modern Masonic lodge, which he predictably named La Loge Isis.[46] Just before he died on St. Helena, Napoleon was asked why he had invaded Egypt. He calmly replied: "I came to draw attention and bring back the interest of Europe to the center of the ancient world."[47] Or was it the other way around: to bring Freemasonry back in direct contact with its original source? We can but wonder.

Alexandre Lenoir was a staunch Freemason and once the superintendent of the king's buildings before the 1789 revolution. Lenoir was a keen adept of the Masonic Scottish Rites,[48] an "initiate of the cult of Isis,"[49] and also the publisher of *La Nouvelle Explication des Hieroglyphes* in 1808. When Champollion began his own work on the Egyptian hieroglyphs, he had condescendingly called Lenoir *un oison* (a little goose) and stated that he only respected the older man because he was "in the good books" of the empress Josephine.[50] In 1814, Lenoir had published a book entitled *La franc-maçonnerie rendue à sa véritable origine* (Freemasonry brought back to its true origins), in which he linked the origins of the brotherhood to the cult of Isis, which may explain why Lenoir, as Champollion himself had dryly noted, was highly regarded by Josephine.

During the Napoleonic era, there had existed in Italy a curious Masonic society called the Société Secrète Egyptienne. It is thought that one of the founders of this society was Mathieu de Lesseps, father of the famous engineer, Ferdinand de Lesseps, who built the Suez Canal in Egypt.[51] In 1818, the Austrian police raided a Masonic lodge in Venice and among the confiscated documents was one revealing the existence of this secret society, which, oddly enough, had as one of its members no less a figure than Egypt's first modern ruler, Muhammad Ali.[52] Mathieu de Lesseps was a staunch Bonapartist and also a keen adept of the Egyptian rites of Freemasonry.[53] He was a very close friend of the khedive and from 1803 to 1806 had been France's commercial attaché in Egypt, after which he had served as French consul in the city of Livorna.[54]

In 1828, a few years after Napoleon's death, the restored King Charles X offered to sponsor Champollion to undertake a feasibility study for bringing an obelisk from Egypt to Paris, which had been donated to France by Muhammad Ali.[55] In July of that year, Champollion headed a small team of scientists and artists, including the French archaeologist Charles Lenormant and the architect Antoine Bibent, and set sail from the port of Toulon toward Egypt. They reached Alexandria on August 18, 1828, where Champollion was received by the French consul, Bernardino Drovetti, and a friendship quickly developed between the two. Since 1818, Drovetti had been the grand copte of the Egyptian Masonic lodges in Alexandria.[56] And like Mathieu de Lesseps before him, Drovetti had become a close friend of Muhammad Ali. During his eighteen-month visit to Egypt, Champollion managed to get an agreement from Muhammad Ali to take to France one of the two obelisks that stood outside the temple of Luxor. The khedive would have been quite happy to let Champollion take both obelisks, but it seemed that one was all that the French could cope with, for the job of bringing the ancient monolith to France proved to be no easy task (it weighed an estimated 230 metric tons and was twenty-three meters tall).[57]

It took from April to July of 1831 for the French engineer Jean Baptiste Apollinaire Lebas to get the purpose-built ship, the *Luxor,* to transport the obelisk from the city of Luxor in Upper Egypt to the French port of Toulon. Two further months followed while the obelisk was dragged the few hundred meters to the shore of the Nile and finally hoisted onboard the *Luxor.* Lebas had to wait till July of the next year for the inundation of the Nile in order to be able to sail downstream to Alexandria. After a delay of three months at Alexandria, the *Luxor* finally crossed the Mediterranean and arrived at the French port of Toulon on May 11, 1833. From there, it was brought by river to Paris, where it waited at the docks for three more years. It was the so-called citizen-king Louis Philippe I who decided that the obelisk should be raised in the center of the Place de la Concorde.[58] On October 25, 1836, a crowd of 200,000 people gathered at the Place de la Concorde to witness the event. Lebas personally supervised the difficult lifting operations, which, to everybody's admiration and delight, went without a hitch. Amid cheers of jubilation and joy, Paris at long last had its very own solar talisman from ancient Egypt adorning its skyline. The beautiful obelisk standing in the Place de la Concorde was and still is, by virtue of its great antiquity, the oldest monument in Paris. It witnessed the story of Egypt from about 1500 BCE, and now in Paris, it was to see the passing of the French monarchy and the creation of the Second Republic in 1848; the rise of the Second Empire under Napoleon III, the grandson of Napoleon Bonaparte and its fall in 1871; the formation of the Third Republic* under the "Masonic" government of Leon Gambetta;[59] the First World War; the Second World War; and finally, in 1958, the present Fifth Republic founded by General Charles de Gaulle.

---

*Five of the founders of the Third Republic were Freemasons, including their leader Leon Gambetta.

In 1981 François Mitterrand, then president of France, launched the so-called Grands Travaux, the Great Works, which involved the construction of a series of impressive architectural projects to the glory and culture of France. Mitterrand planned huge celebrations for the bicentennial of the French Revolution in 1989. The two monuments that Mitterrand took great personal interest, a glass pyramid at the Louvre and the Grande Arche at La Defense, evoked ancient Egypt as well as the Masonic Supreme Being or "Great Architect of the universe." Although Mitterrand was not a registered Freemason,[60] he was none-theless extremely sympathetic to the lodges—so much so that many in France remain convinced to this day that he was a clandestine Mason.

Much has been made in recent years of the fact that Guy Penne, one of Mitterrand's closest political advisers, was a member of the council of the Grand Orient of France.[61] There is also the scandal involving Mitterrand's son, Jean-Christophe, who, in 1982, joined the office of Guy Penne and in 1986 took over Penne's job. Jean-Christophe was recently exposed by the French press for his embroilment in the so-called Falcone Affair, involving shady arms deals in West Africa, which also implicated some senior African politicians who were members of Masonic lodges.[62]

The full dramatic effect of the ensemble of these Masonic and Egyptian monuments in Paris was revealed when the French composer Jean Michel Jarre performed a special concert at the foot of the Grande Arche at La Defense on July 14, 1990. It was an amazing extravaganza of sound, light, and fireworks, the likes of which Paris had never seen before. During the concert, all the relevant monuments on the histori-cal axis—the Grande Arche, the Arc de Triomphe, the Luxor obelisk, and, of course, the Louvre glass pyramid—were lit up as if to reveal a magical Masonic landscape for Paris. The orchestra of Jarre was positioned at the foot of the Grande Arche inside a huge, makeshift, metal-framed pyramid that was lit up with laser lights. The lasers also projected images onto the facades of adjacent skyscrapers—with many of these images evoking odd Hermetic-Masonic symbolism, especially a set of large eyes projected on the sides of the pyramid.

Eight years later, in May 1998, Jarre would be commissioned to perform a similar show in Egypt involving the Great Pyramid of Giza. This was announced during a state visit to Paris by President Hosni Mubarak of Egypt and other officials of his government. The Egyptians had come to witness a special ceremony at the Place de la Concorde, during which a golden capstone was placed on top of the Luxor obelisk.[63] It was there and then that Egypt's minister of culture, Farouk Hosni, announced that a golden capstone would also be placed on top of the Great Pyramid of Giza at midnight on December 31, 1999, as a symbol for the new millennium. Later in October 1998, Farouk Hosni announced to the Egyptian press that French composer Jean Michel Jarre had been commissioned to organize this event at Giza. What the Egyptian authorities omitted to say—or perhaps were unaware of—was that Jarre intended to project images on the pyramid, which included a giant eye.

There are several curious connections to the ceremony that took place at the Place de la Concorde on May 14, 1998. But first let us note that Charles X, who commissioned the Luxor obelisk in 1828, was a staunch Freemason, and it may well have been the lodges that were really behind the bringing of the obelisk to France. This is a likely supposition, for it is well known that other obelisks also taken out of Egypt a few decades later were clearly masterminded by British and American Freemasons, namely the two famous Cleopatra's Needles, which had stood at the Eastern Harbor of Alexandria and which today stand at the Victoria Embankment in London and in New York's Central Park near the Metropolitan Museum of Fine Arts. The London obelisk was commissioned and paid for by a prominent Freemason, Sir Erasmus Wilson, and the raising ceremony was attend by hundreds of Freemasons in

September 1878 under the auspices of the Prince of Wales, the grand master of United Grand Lodge. That same year former U.S. President Ulysses S. Grant* and General William T. Sherman† saw the remaining obelisk at Alexandria during a tour of Egypt and suggested that America should also have an ancient Egyptian obelisk of its own.[64] Henry W. Gorringe,[65] a prominent American Freemason,‡ was selected for the task of bringing the obelisk to New York. The obelisk was raised in October 1880 outside the newly built Metropolitan Museum, with nearly ten thousand Freemasons attending the ceremony in full Masonic regalia.§

On May 14, 1998, when the golden capstone on the Paris obelisk was being unveiled in Paris, huge celebrations were also taking place in Tel Aviv for the fiftieth-year jubilee of the declaration of the State of Israel. At first glance, this choice of date for the ceremony at the Place de la Concorde may seem just a coincidence. But on closer examination, coincidence should, in our opinion, be ruled out.

---

*His full name was Hiram Ulysses Grant—but always called Ulysses, his middle name by his friends. Hiram was, and still is, a popular Masonic name (from Hiram Abiff, the legendary "architect" of Solomon's Temple in Masonic rituals). This choice of name was clearly intended as a Masonic label, since Ulysses's father, Jesse Grant, had been Master Mason of a prominent lodge in Ohio.

†Although there is controversy whether General William T. Sherman was a Freemason, his own father, Charles Robert Sherman, certainly was a senior Freemason, as confirmed by his Masonic apron located by the Lancaster, Ohio, Historical Society. Sherman is credited for being the first to suggest to Khedive Ismail that the obelisk should be donated to the United States. He got the financial backing from a prominent Freemason, William H. Vanderbilt, who in turn got the political support from of Gen. Henry G. Stebbins, New York's Commissioner of Public Parks. It was Stebbins who petitioned the U.S. Secretary of State, William M. Evarts, to personally write to Elbert Farman, the American consul-general in Egypt, to persuade the khedive of Egypt to donate the obelisk to the United States.

‡On their way to the Mediterranean during a two-year survey with the *Gettysburg*, a tired old paddlewheel ship, Gorringe and a fellow Freemason, Lieutenant Seaton Schoeder, used equipment to measure depth and "snagged the top of a submerged mountain in the Atlantic Ocean which they claimed was the 'Lost Atlantis,' and received a congratulatory telegram from President Grant for this 'discovery.'"

§The important symbolic aspect of an obelisk is not its tall stem but its top, which is shaped like a small pyramid.

The metal plaque that was fixed at the foot of the Paris obelisk contains the following text (translated from the French).

This obelisk, offered by Egypt to France in 1830, to serve eternally as a bond between the two countries, has been dressed by its pyramidion of origin on 14th May 1998, under the presidency of Jacques Chirac in the presence of Catherine Trautmann, Minister of Culture and Communication, and Dr. Maher El Sayed, Ambassador of Egypt for the occasion of the Year France-Egypt "Shared Horizons" and the visit of the president of the restored Arab Republic of Egypt, Hosni Mubarak. The monument thus restored is dedicated to Jean-François Champollion, founder of Egyptology, who chose it from the temple of Luxor. This pyramidion is realized thanks to the support of Yves Saint Laurent, Pierre Bergé and the House of Yves Saint Laurent.

The name of the famous fashion designer Yves Saint Laurent and his ex-lover Pierre Bergé pricked our curiosity. We discovered that there was much controversy on the Internet surrounding *La Vilaine Lulu* (Nasty Lulu), a comic book that Yves Saint Laurent wrote and illustrated, which was published in 1967. It has been described as a sort of satanic-cum-Masonic manual by advocates of conspiracy theories and the so-called illuminati. The book concerns a young girl called Lulu who, among other warped actions, goes around decapitating, hanging, and burning people. What we found out about Pierre Bergé was even more intriguing. There was without a doubt a connection with Bergé and Zionism that, to say the least, makes his name on the ancient Egyptian obelisk's plaque somewhat disturbing.

Bergé is a notorious French billionaire and philanthropist, who was a keen and active supporter of François Mitterrand during the latter's presidential campaigns. Cofounder of the Yves Saint Laurent empire and one-time director of the Paris Opera, Bergé is a well-known patron of the arts and, partly because of his Jewish faith, a staunch crusader against anti-Semitism. Bergé is the founder of the Musée Dreyfus at the

Figure A.2. The plaque at the Luxor Obelisk in Paris, placed on May 14, 1998

Figure A.3. The Luxor Obelisk at the Place de la Concorde in Paris, with golden capstone (photo courtesy of Kandis Twa)

Maison Zola, to be opened in 2012. The Musée Dreyfus, as the name implies, is dedicated to Alfred Dreyfus, a French artillery officer of Alsatian Jewish origins who, in 1894, was condemned to life imprisonment by a military court for allegedly spying for Germany. This famous Dreyfus affair exposed the rampant anti-Semitism in France and created a huge controversy when the famous writer Emile Zola published an open letter in the French newspaper *L'Aurore* in January 1898, in which he exposed the anti-Semitism of the French army and government.

It is also well known that the Dreyfus affair was the catalyst that gave birth to modern Zionism. This happened when Theodore Herzl, the Paris correspondent for the German newspaper *Neue Freie Presse,* was so incensed by the anti-Semitism that surrounded the Dreyfus Affair and by the crowds chanting "death to the Jews" that he was prompted to organize the First Zionist Congress in Basel, Switzerland, in 1897. Thus, the deep connection of Pierre Bergé with the Dreyfus Affair coupled with his involvement with the ceremony of the golden capstone on the Paris obelisk makes the choice date of May 14, 1998 (the fifty-year jubilee of the State of Israel) an odd "coincidence," to say the least.[66]*

The bridge that Farouk Hosni created between the 1998 ceremony in Paris at the obelisk and the 2000 millennium ceremony in Egypt at the Great Pyramid, both of which involved capping these two ancient monuments with golden capstones, reached its climax when the Egyptian press that opposed the Mubarak government got hold of the story in early June 1999; that is, a few months before the planned millennium ceremony at Giza. At first, three million people were scheduled to attend the millennium ceremony at Giza, but the Egyptian authorities put a limit of 250,000 for security reasons. A massive worldwide promotional campaign was organized in cities such as New York, Los Angeles, Sydney, and various capital cities in Europe. Preparations then

---

*Curiously, a relative of Emile Zola, a certain Salvatore Zola, was a prominent Freemason in Egypt in the 1800s and, of all things, was assigned by Khedive Muhammad Ali to help the Americans move an obelisk from Alexandria to New York's Central Park.

began for a huge stage to be erected in the desert south of the Great Pyramid, with a seating capacity for VIPs. All was apparently going as planned until senior members of the Egyptian parliament began to complain of the costs involved and also that the millennium celebrations coincided that year with the holy month of Ramadan, when devout Muslims fast from dawn to dusk. To counteract such criticism, culture minister Farouk Hosni stated that a ban would be placed on alcohol during the celebrations and that no music would be played until after the official end of the fast was announced. To add fuel to the growing controversy, the radical Egyptian press, notably the newspaper *Sawt Al Shaab* (Voice of the People), reported that Jean Michel Jarre was Jewish* and that he intended to project an eye, among many other images, on the Great Pyramid using laser beams. *Sawt Al Shaab* accused the organizers of staging a Masonic event in collusion with the Jews. The newspaper claimed that the eye in the pyramid planned for this ceremony was intended to evoke the well-known Masonic symbol of the eye in the triangle and, more specifically, the eye in the pyramid seen on the U.S. one dollar bill (and also the great seal of the United States), also suspected to be of Masonic significance. More such accusations of Masonic-Zionist infiltration ensued in the Arab press; all hotly denied, however, by culture minister Farouk Hosni as "groundless," and by Hawass, who meekly stated that "the celebration has nothing to do with Masonic beliefs. The design on the U.S. dollar is a faulty imitation of the pyramids of the Middle Kingdom."

It came as no surprise, therefore, that with these allegations and rumors of Masonic-Zionist plots flying about, in early December 1999, under heavy pressure from the Egyptian press and also from members of parliament, the Egyptian authorities cancelled the decision to place a golden capstone on the Great Pyramid, admitting that this was because of public outrage over the Masonic and Zionist implications of the ceremony.

---

*Jean Michel Jarre has Russian origins, but we could not confirm if he is Jewish.

Although the alleged Zionist-Masonic conspiracy is generally seen as a secular evil, the Freemasons are often associated with the mysterious and satanic figure of a supernatural entity akin to a false prophet or a false messenger, who, in Muslim lore, is supposed to appear before Yom el Kiyama on the day of judgment. In the Koran, the Dajjal has a single eye, which is inevitably associated with the single eye in the pyramid on the U.S. one dollar note and, of course, the eye in the triangle in Freemasonry and also Judaic symbolism. It was thus no surprise that a few days before the planned millennium celebrations at the Giza Pyramids, the Egyptian newspaper *Sawt Al Shaab* accused minister of culture Farouk Hosni of allowing the "Jew" Jean Michel Jarre to present a Masonic-Zionist event on the soil of Egypt, to be seen live on television on a global scale by billions of viewers. The newspaper printed a large composite image showing a Freemason with a huge eye (clearly representing the Dajjal) on whose chest was pinned the Star of David and the Masonic triangle.

In early November 2011, after the January 25 revolution and weeks before the parliamentary election (when Islamists were vying for a majority seats), accusations and rumors of a Jewish-Masonic plot involving the Giza Pyramids again was rife, this time on the Internet rumor mill. An alleged huge gathering of Jews and Masons was supposed to take place near and inside the Great Pyramid, when a Star of David symbol was allegedly going to be placed on the top of the Great Pyramid. The Islamists were outraged and apparently marched in protest to the gates of the Giza Necropolis and threatened to take over the site. The army and riot police had to be called in, and the decision to close all the pyramids to visitors and groups that had obtained permits for private sessions inside the Great Pyramids. According to Middle East correspondent Adrian Blomfield of *The Telegraph* ("Pyramids closed by 11.11.11 threat," November 11, 2011):

Egypt's Supreme Council of Antiquities succumbed to pressure after protest groups behind the revolution that overthrew Hosni Mubarak in February demanded that the Pyramids be sealed off for the whole of "Magic Friday." It was claimed that 1,200 Jews were planning to attend the ceremony with the intention of erecting a Star of David above the Great Pyramid to assert their claim that it was built by ancient Israelites rather than ancient Egyptians. There were also allegations that Masons, who are sometimes associated with Satanism by people in the Arab world, were also planning to attend. A tour agency with some Jewish links is involved in the ceremony, but has insisted that had no plans to erect any symbol above the sarcophagus of King Khufu, who is buried in the Great Pyramid. Seeking to avoid further controversy, the Supreme Council of Antiquities said the closure was for "maintenance" reasons.

APPENDIX 2

Discoveries and Achievements— or Personal Agenda?

TOMBS OF THE PYRAMID BUILDERS

Becoming a great discoverer is, understandably, the dream of every archaeologist. For Zahi Hawass, however, it became an obsession. He somehow had to come up with major discoveries, come what may—even if such discoveries had to be staged or usurped.

Discovering the tombs of the pyramid builders, for example, was the reverie of many Egyptologists who had worked at Giza, and for Hawass this became a fixation when in 1982, then a young chief inspector, he attended a lecture by Dr. Gamal Mokhtar (then director general of the Supreme Council of Antiquities [SCA]) at the Metropolitan Museum in New York. Mokhtar's poignant words must have resonated deeply in Hawass's mind: "We are still awaiting the discovery of the pyramid builders. If it happens, the discovery will be more important than the finding of the tomb of the golden Pharaoh Tutankhamun." In April 1990, a lucky twist of fate obliged in favor of Hawass.

The story goes that a guard rushed into Hawass's office at Giza to inform him that an American tourist was thrown off her horse when the animal stumbled over an ancient mud-brick wall south of the so-called Wall of the Crow (located a few hundred meters south of the Sphinx). The hooves of the horse had exposed the roof of an ancient structure. Hawass immediately rushed to examine the place and, without even a basic preliminary scientific examination of the ruins, decided there and then what it was: "As soon as I saw the place, I knew that we had found the tombs [of the pyramid builders], just as I had predicted." Hawass then began to turn his "discovery" into a political victory by telling ordinary Egyptians: "Many people have claimed the pyramids were built by slaves, or even aliens. . . . With the discovery of the Cemetery of the Pyramid Builders, however, I was finally able to reveal the truth to people around the world!"

The truth is that from an archaeological and scientific viewpoint, in spite of Hawass's bombastic claims, there was no convincing evidence found at the site to prove that the tombs he had discovered belonged to the actual workers who built the pyramids. Indeed, and for this very reason, the SCA not only abstained from endorsing Hawass's conclusion, but Ali Hassan, director general of the SCA at the time, admitted to us that these tombs belonged not to the workers but to people responsible for *guarding and serving* the Giza Plateau, which is a very different thing altogether. When Mokhtar asked Hawass to produce evidence to back his claims, no evidence from him was forthcoming.

The reality is that the building of the Giza Pyramids, which took place in the Fourth Dynasty, circa 2500 BCE, would have required far more workers than the meager six hundred skeletons that Hawass uncovered at his alleged tombs of the pyramid builders. The Great Pyramid alone contained some 2.5 million blocks averaging two tons each. Herodotus, who visited Egypt in the fifth century BCE, quoted Egyptian priests claiming that one hundred thousand men worked for twenty years to build the pyramid. But it's easy to build the Great Pyramid on paper! So Hawass simply reduced the number of workers to match his discovery. In an *Al-Ahram Daily* article dated September 9, 2000, he is quoted as saying:

It is likely that according to our search in the area that those who worked in the Giza burial ground and the building of the pyramid did not exceed 20 thousand in Khufu's time . . . the new discoveries indicate that the hieroglyphic writings which we call graffiti left by the workers in red ink over the stones of the pyramids and tombs . . . were the remains of scripts left by the builders of the pyramid . . . They had names like "friends of Kufu" . . . "Overseer of the Burial Ground of the Pyramid," "Head of the Artists," "Overseer of Building Work," "Head of Workers," "Supervisor of Professional Labour" . . . "Head of the King's Works," "Head of the Pyramid Side" . . . we found that it [sic] indicate the existence of a dwelling location . . . and [we found] pottery that goes back to the fourth and fifth dynasties . . .

However, Hawass conveniently omitted saying that the pyramid area also included a burial ground for the nobles and high officials, as well as temples, storehouses, and many other auxiliary buildings. It is to be expected, therefore, to find the remains of other workers, such as guards, officials, priests, artists, and other professionals who administered, maintained, and supervised the region and the pyramids themselves. At any rate, what indicated that the owners of these tombs *were not the workers who built the pyramids* is that many of the skeletons belonged to women and children—individuals hardly capable of moving multiton blocks!

THE SMILING SPHINX

On May 15, 1998, Hawass celebrated the completion of a ten-year program to restore the Great Sphinx. In *Al-Ahram Daily* (November 27, 2010 "Secrets of Egypt"), he is quoted saying:

I went to see the Sphinx one day and saw that it was smiling again. It was happy that we had saved it, this great statue that has kept all of Egypt's secrets for thousands of years. I will never forget the moment in 1998 when President Hosni Mubarak came to celebrate our successful restoration work. We arranged a great event in front of the Sphinx, within its sanctuary with an orchestral symphony, and the President honored us all with medals.

However, a few years later, it became clear that the "smile" of the Sphinx was hiding much agony and suffering. Rather than dealing with the real problem facing the Sphinx, Hawass was able to hide, whether inadvertently or not, the Sphinx's real problems (it was flaking profusely!) by placing a facade of more than 120,000 new stones to hide the deteriorated areas from view.

The Great Sphinx is generally believed to represent King Khafre (Chephren), the fourth ruler of the Fourth Dynasty, circa 2500 BCE. Although the Sphinx is more than 4,500 years old, it has only shown rapid deterioration since the 1960s. After the Giza Necropolis was abandoned at the end of the Old Kingdom around 2181 BCE, the Sphinx became buried up to its shoulders in sand. About eight centuries later, Tuthmose IV was the first to clear the sand off the Sphinx, and he erected his Dream Stela between its paws around 1400 BCE. However, the sand later covered the body of the Sphinx again. For more than two thousand years, the Sphinx was buried up to its neck in sand, which protected it from the elements. In 1817, Captain Caviglia supervised the first excavation, uncovering the statue's chest completely. Then in 1926, the French Egyptologist Émile Baraize dug the Sphinx out in its entirety.

Since it was uncovered by Baraize, the Sphinx has suffered from modern pollution and rising subsoil water. As the Sphinx was carved directly from the living limestone bedrock right on the edge of the Giza Plateau, it is affected by the level of groundwater. It became clear to experts trying to restore the Sphinx that much of the damage was caused by water coming from nearby drainage systems. Underground water had been rising inside the rock of the Giza Plateau, causing salt to form inside the Sphinx's body. There are two reasons for this: the building of the High Dam by the late president Nasser and the emergence of a new village lying at the foot of the Sphinx, Nazlet El Simman. Until 1960, this area was sparsely inhabited; now, Nazlet El Simman, with more than a quarter of a million inhabitants, extends between the ancient canal and the Giza Plateau, coming as close as a few meters to the Sphinx. The village causes serious environmental damage with its overflowing sewers and air pollution. The dozens of tourist coaches and buses in the massive parking lot of the Sound and Light Show constantly run their engines, filling the air with diesel fumes, which also causes significant air pollution. Climatic factors such as acid rain and unusual fluctuations in humidity and temperature, the pollution from industrial factories in the area, and vibrations from aircraft and vehicular traffic in the immediate vicinity have all contributed to the problem. The Sphinx has further suffered from vandalism over the years. In medieval times, a Muslim fanatic hacked off the nose; also missing is the ceremonial beard, which a British explorer removed in 1836 and which is now displayed in the British Museum in London.

In their attempt to save the ailing Sphinx, the Egyptian Antiquities Organization (EAO; later the SCA) carried out a restoration program between 1982 and 1987. However, they ill-advisedly applied a large amount of cement and gypsum mortar directly to the rock from which the Sphinx is made. As a result, the rock of the Sphinx could not breathe; thus the humidity trapped inside began to wither and flake the rock from the inside, and more deterioration and salt appeared on the newly repaired parts outside. In an online article titled "History of the Conservation of the Sphinx," Hawass criticized these early restoration attempts.

> In my opinion most of the conservation campaigns in the past were conceived as stop-gap solutions, with no long-term strategy in mind for protecting the Sphinx. Some of these temporary measures even damaged the Sphinx more than benefited it.

While the Sphinx continued to deteriorate, repeated efforts by experts from around the world have all failed, prompting suggestions for drastic remedies. When in February 1988, a chunk of limestone on the southern shoulder of the Sphinx fell off (which led to the dismissal of Kadri from his job as a director general of the EAO; see chapter 1), an Italian Egyptologist, Joseph Fanfoni, suggested that the base of the Sphinx should be sawn off and that glass chips should be inserted underneath the grand statue to protect it against subterranean leakage and water. According to Fanfoni: "This method has been used in the Samaakhana in Islamic Cairo and it should prove effective in protecting the Sphinx" (see Egypt State Information Service, www.sis.gov.rg/En/Pub/Spring1998).

However, such very drastic measures were, understandably, rejected by the EAO. In January 1989, the EAO decided to launch its own Sphinx Restoration Project and appointed Hawass as the director of the project. As the Sphinx was part of UNESCO's human heritage, they agreed to pay the $3 million restoration bill. The first stage of restoration consisted of carrying out scientific studies as well as doing restoration work in select areas at the southern paw, the southern flank of the body, and the tail of the Sphinx. The repair blocks and mortar previously used were removed and the natural (mother) rock was treated with special sealants. New repair blocks were quarried at Helwan, after analysis confirmed these were consistent with the natural limestone that formed the Sphinx, and were placed against the mother rock in overlapping courses. The chest of the Sphinx was given a protective course of limestone matching the original ancient repair methods. Then in May 1990, the Getty Conservation Institute of the United States installed a solar-powered monitoring station on the back of the Sphinx, designed to measure potentially destructive environmental factors, such as wind, precipitation, relative humidity, and condensation. During the next stage of the project, which started in September 1992, the chest, the northern, middle, and lower parts of the Sphinx and the neck were treated. The final phase of restoration work on the Sphinx came to an end on December 25, 1998. Hawass, who was responsible for the restoration project, proudly commented on his achievement, in an article in the *Giza Journal* (July 11, 1991): "I believe that the Sphinx project is the only restoration project that has been done scientifically in 50 years. . . . The Sphinx is now back to its youth for the first time."

What Hawass didn't mention—or didn't realize—was that the cosmetic treatment of the Sphinx avoided dealing with the real cause of the problems (the rising water) and only concealed the damage, by covering the deteriorated areas with new stones brought from the quarries. Professional restorers were not involved in the Sphinx project, neither Egyptians nor foreigners; instead the responsibility was given to architects under the supervision of the artist Adam Hinain. Furthermore, Ali Hassan, director general of the EAO during the early stages of the project, had actually complained that Hawass did not consult him at any stage of the restoration project. Hassan had openly expressed his worries and fears about Hawass's methods because the restoration work did not deal with the source of the problem but was merely superficial. This view was also shared by Ali El-Kholi (who became the director general of the EAO in May 1999, at the end of the restoration project). He pointed out that, unfortunately, what could now be seen after Hawass completed the project was not the original Sphinx body but the new stone covering it. Furthermore, as reported in the Cairo weekly *Akhbar al-Adab,* Mohamed Abdel Hadi, dean of the Luxor College for Restoration, accused the restorers of using the chemical substance Nemex in the restoration of the Sphinx's neck and chest, which, he claimed, produced salts on the surface of the stone and would lead to the formation of a solid layer that could eventually fall off.

THE TOMB OF OSIRIS

In the summer of 1999, Hawass excavated a water-filled shaft inside a small tunnel that runs north–south under the causeway of King Khafre at Giza and which was believed by many New Age enthusiasts to lead to the Great Pyramid. After pumping out the water, Hawass found the first segment of a shaft, almost 10 meters deep, leading to an empty chamber. Through the northern part of this chamber, a second vertical shaft was found leading down for another 13.25 meters and ending in a second small chamber surrounded by six smaller side chambers and a recess from which yet another shaft descended. Three of the side chambers contained sarcophagi belonging to the Twenty-sixth Dynasty (about 650 BCE). In addition to the side chambers, Hawass found a recess in the southeastern corner of the main chamber from which yet a third vertical shaft descended, ending in a chamber of about 9 square meters.

Here, Hawass found what he regarded to be the most interesting discovery: in the center of this chamber was a rectangular platform carved from the living rock on which was placed a sarcophagus, containing the remains of a skeleton as well as amulets dating from the Late Period (747–332 BCE). For some strange reason based not on archaeological or textual evidence but on pure speculation, Hawass announced that this chamber represented a "symbolic tomb for Osiris," the legendary Egyptian god of the underworld. The rectangular shape of the central elevated platform (which was connected at one side with the entrance of the chamber that had the same elevated level) was taken by Hawass to represent the hieroglyphic sign *pr* meaning a "house." And even though neither the name of Osiris nor his image was found in this chamber, Hawass insisted that the shape of the central platform represents the word for house, and so it must mean, according to him, the "house of Osiris"! By using his position of authority, the announcement that the tomb of the legendary lord of the dead, Osiris, had been found sent ripples of excitement in the various occult and New Age communities around the world, and the inevitable plethora of articles, interviews, documentaries, and lectures ensued—all potential sources of fees and funding.

THE TOOTH OF HATSHEPSUT

In 2006, Hawass looked for a new "discovery." Having exhausted the mysteries of the Giza Plateau, the possible "secret chambers" under the

Sphinx and inside the Great Pyramid and the "unopened tombs" of the golden mummies, he now set his sights on the alleged mummy of the legendary and celebrated Queen Hatshepsut. The archaeological "discoveries" exploited by the big international channels with the exclusive participation of Zahi Hawass was paying off: millions of U.S. dollars and huge international publicity were being generated, along with the acquisition of scan and DNA equipments for the SCA, the awarding to Hawass of medals, academic honors, and prizes, and even private audiences with royalty and heads of state. In fact Egypt's Indiana Jones had reached world celebrity status, surpassing Spielberg's fictional Indiana Jones. With such huge notoriety, as well as the cronyism he shared with the Mubaraks and Farouk Hosni (the minister of culture) and his position appointment in 2002 as director general of the SCA, Hawass felt invincible. No one in Egypt would dare to oppose him. And so it was announced on his website (http://guardians.net/hawass/Press%20Releases/identifying_hatshepsut.htm) that

[u]pon the approval of the Minister of Culture, Farouk Hosni, an Egyptian archaeological mission led by Dr. Zahi Hawass, Secretary General of the Supreme Council of Antiquities (SCA), found Hatshepsut's mummy inside tomb KV 60 in the Valley of the Kings on Luxor's west bank.

The unidentified mummy—which Hawass now claimed was Hatshepsut—had in fact been discovered in 1903 in the Valley of the Kings. It was Howard Carter (the discoverer of Tutankhamun's tomb) who had found it along with another mummy, in an obscure and undecorated tomb (labeled KV60), one of which was inside a coffin inscribed for a royal nurse, the other, the mummy of woman, was on the floor. However, nothing much was done about this find, and the mummies were just left in place. In 2006, Hawass began his investigation at KV60 and examined the mummy on the floor. He noticed that the left arm was bent at the elbow with the hand over the chest, while the right arm lay against the mummy's side. Although Kathryn A. Bard of Boston University pointed out that royal mummies were usually laid out with both hands crossed at the chest (the *New York Times*, June 27, 2007), Hawass was convinced that the mummy belonged to a royal person, a king or queen. Hawass began to see Hatshepsut in this pathetically dilapidated and unnamed mummy—and set about to prove it.

Although a woman, Hatshepsut was crowned as pharaoh in the Eighteenth Dynasty. She ruled over Egypt for about fifteen years (1473–1458 BCE) and was one of only two women known to have assumed the throne of Egypt (the other being the celebrated Cleopatra VII). She was the daughter of Thutmose I, third king of the Eighteenth Dynasty, and was married to her half brother, Thutmose II. When the latter died, she ruled as regent with her stepson Thutmose III, but effectively took over the throne. During her rule, Hatshepsut apparently dressed like a man and wore a false beard. After her death, her name was obliterated from the records in what is believed to have been her stepson Thutmose III's revenge. Hatshepsut's funerary temple at Deir el-Bahari was built against the side of a mountain to the east of the Valley of the Kings on the west bank at Luxor. It consists of three colonnaded balconies, and its holy of holies was built on the same axis as that of the queen's burial chamber inside a tomb labeled KV20.

When Howard Carter also discovered KV20 in 1902, the queen's mummy was missing. When he returned to the tomb in 1920, Carter found two sarcophagi, one for Hatshepsut and the second for her father Thutmose I, but both were empty. Canopic jars and *ushabti,* or funerary, figurines of Hatshepsut were also found along with stone pots bearing the names of Ahmose Nefertari, the queen's great-grandmother, wife of Ahmose I, who established the Eighteenth Dynasty, and of Hatshepsut herself.

Now the mummy that Hawass identified as Hatshepsut was found not in KV20, as would be expected, but in the uninscribed and unassuming tomb KV60. So how did Hawass prove that the unidentified mummy on the floor of KV20 was, in fact, that of Queen Hatshepsut?

Hawass made a deal with the U.S.-based International TV company, Discovery Channel, to donate $5 million to establish his own DNA laboratory in the Egyptian Museum. Apparently the laboratory was principally set up for the making of an exclusive TV documentary on Queen Hatshepsut, but Hawass announced to the world press that he also planned to test the DNA of all the royal mummies in the Cairo Museum. Oddly, Hawass had always objected to the using DNA tests on Egyptian mummies. Indeed, only two years earlier, Hawass had used another method, a CT scan, on Tutankhamun's mummy, but when some Egyptian scientists contested the validity of this method, Hawass had stated in the *Al-Ahram Weekly* (March 2–9, 2005) that

[f]our Egyptian individuals objected to the recent examination of King Tut. Their objection was not based on scientific evidence. Rather, one of the objectors wanted his name in the media. . . . The second was upset because in the past he had wanted to do DNA testing on the mummy but the minister of culture, Farouk Hosni, refused his request because DNA testing had not been found to be accurate when dealing with mummies.

In the same vein, the highly respected London *Sunday Times Magazine* ("King Tut Tut Tut," May 22, 2005) reiterated Hawass's obstinate and seemingly unchangeable objection to DNA testing on royal mummies: "Finally we come to the question of DNA. Hawass is quite clear about this. He rejects DNA testing, and forbids it . . . he will not permit 'invasive' techniques that damage the mummies . . ."

Yet, here was Hawass DNA testing not only his alleged Hatshepsut mummy but also proposing to DNA test all other royal mummies in the Cairo museum! So what brought about this amazing volte-face? Could it be that now that Hawass had his very own DNA laboratory at the Cairo Museum, bought with Discovery Channel money, so any DNA tests—and results—would be under his complete control? Making sure that those working in the laboratory were under his authority, Hawass refused access to foreign DNA experts. In an Associated Press report (December 23, 2007), he stated "it's time Egyptian scientists took charge. . . . Egyptology, for the last 200 years, it has been led by foreigners."

Hawass appointed Dr. Yehya Zakariya Gad, a professor of molecular genetics from Egypt's National Research Center, to be in charge of the laboratory. DNA samples from the alleged "Hatshepsut," her great grandmother Ahmose Nefertari, her father Thutmose I, and the wet nurse Sitre-In were taken by entering the same puncture hole from a number of different angles with a bone marrow biopsy needle, which is a less invasive technique than ones that had been used by previous researchers.

But as everyone knows, DNA tests can take a lot of time to be correctly completed (and properly double-checked). So here was the snag: When Discovery Channel financed the DNA laboratory for the Cairo Museum, it had already allocated a slot for its documentary on Hawass's findings (just as Fox TV had so successfully done back in 1998, 1999, and 2002 with other live programs involving Hawass). When Hawass made his announcement on June 27, 2007, the Discovery Channel allocated July 15 for airing its exclusive documentary *Secrets of the Lost Queen of Egypt*. But as the broadcasting date approached, it was clear that the Egyptian scientists at the Cairo Museum DNA laboratory would not be finished with the testing. Gad and his Egyptian team were following correct procedures by comparing DNA bone samples taken from the mummy's pelvic bone and femur with those of the mummy of Amos Nefreteri (Hatshepsut's grandmother), which is a very time-consuming activity, especially for a new laboratory and with local scientists who had little experience with such tests on mummies.

As it became apparent that the results of the DNA tests would not be available, Hawass dropped the DNA testing of the mummy and decided instead to use CT scans to meet the Discovery Channel's deadline. Correspondent John Noble Wilford in a *New York Times* article ("Tooth May Have Solved Mummy Mystery," June 27, 2007) reported a confused statement by Hawass.

> Dr. Hawass said the DNA research into the possible Hatshepsut mummy was continuing, and he was vague about when the results would be reported. But early tests of mitochondrial DNA, he said, showed a relationship between the mummy and the matriarch Ahmose Nefertari.

So although the evidence—at least most of it—that had led Hawass to declare that the KV60 mummy was Hatshepsut came from CT scans, the scientists in the Discovery Channel documentary were shown extracting DNA from the mummies of KV60, and it was clearly stated that the DNA results proved that the mummy under investigation belonged to Hatshepsut. On the other hand, Hawass said that the identification of the mummy was made a few weeks earlier, when a CT scan of a sealed wooden box that bore the name of the queen revealed a broken tooth. The broken tooth, Hawass claimed, "fits exactly" into the jaw socket and broken root of the mummy of an obese woman originally found in Tomb KV60. Hawass also had radiologists make CT scans of a wooden box bearing the name Hatshepsut (which had been recovered from yet another tomb). In the same *New York Times* article, Wilford reported the following observations and conclusions.

> The container held some of the viscera removed from the body during embalming. . . . Late one night recently, the box was subjected to the CT scan. . . .
>
> The images revealed a well-preserved liver and a tooth. A dentist, Galal El-Beheri of Cairo University, was called in. He studied the images of the mummy collection, and the tooth seemed to belong to the obese mummy.
>
> Further CT scans led physicians to conclude that the woman was

about 50 when she died. She was overweight and had bad teeth. She probably had diabetes and died of bone cancer, which had spread through her body.

Much of Hawass's evidence for the identification of Hatshepsut rests on a broken tooth inside a sealed box. Furthermore, the box in question was not even found in the queen's tomb, and no independent confirmation based on forensic dentistry was produced. Far from looking for more scientific evidence to confirm or negate his conclusions, Hawass told the Associated Press that "[we] are 100 percent certain" that the mummy belongs to Hatshepsut (Associated Press June 28, 2007), and Peter Lovering, Discovery Channel's senior programming executive, also told the Associated Press (December 23, 2007) that

> [t]he reason why we went with such a strong claim was because the CT scan was conclusive and the fact that the missing tooth provided the missing clue. . . . I don't think that the DNA testing will indicate otherwise.

The notion that a queen's tooth would be sealed inside a box or canopic jar seemed strange to some Egyptologists, as in no other case did ancient embalmers place teeth in boxes or jar–only internal organs. Many scientists, therefore, protested that Hawass had rushed his conclusions. Understandably, these scientists said they would reserve judgment until they had themselves studied the results of the DNA analysis and when the tooth evidence could also be confirmed by other independent researchers. "You have to be so careful in reaching conclusions from such data," said Bard, an Egyptologist at Boston University (*New York Times*, June 27, 2007). Molecular biologist Scott Woodward, director of the Sorenson Molecular Genealogy Foundation in Salt Lake City (and very experienced in DNA testing on mummies), also expressed cautions to the Associated Press (June 28, 2007): "It's a very difficult process to obtain DNA from a mummy.

To make a claim as to a relationship, you need other individuals from which you have obtained DNA, to make a comparison between the DNA sequences." Such DNA material would typically come from parents or grandparents. With female mummies, the most common type of DNA to look for is the mitochondrial DNA, which reveals maternal lineage. Said Woodward: "What possible other mummies are out there, they would have to be related to Hatshepsut. . . . It's a difficult process but the recovery of DNA from 18th Dynasty mummies is certainly possible."

But not everyone was convinced. According to Salima Ikram, a professor of Egyptology at the American University in Cairo, a mummy's age, the mummification process, and the condition in which it was stored all contribute to a high degree of contamination and results that are not foolproof. In an Associated Press article (December 23, 3007), Ikram made these cautious observations:

> It is exciting and it can be useful. But please, use it with a little bit of caution. . . . Months after Egypt boldly announced that archaeologists had identified a mummy as the most powerful queen of her time; scientists in a museum basement are still analyzing DNA from the bald, 3,500-year-old corpse to try to back up the claim aired on TV. Progress is slow. So far, results indicate the linen-wrapped mummy is most likely, but not conclusively, the female pharaoh Queen Hatshepsut. . . . Running its own ancient-DNA lab is a major step forward for Egypt, which for decades has seen foreigners take most of the credit for major discoveries here.

It must be emphasized that even if the DNA laboratory in Cairo Museum would publish results confirming that this mummy belongs to Hatshepsut (which they so far have not), this will not be the final evidence by any means, because before any DNA results can be published in a scientific journal, the Egyptian Museum laboratory must duplicate its initial findings—which have not yet been completed—and then the samples must be sent to an independent lab to be replicated. As Ikram noted to the Associated Press:

> The ancient-DNA world goes by a very stringent set of criteria. . . . One of the biggest is replication by an independent lab. . . . If you don't do it, particularly with something as famous as this mummy, no peer review journal will publish it. . . . And if you don't get it published in a peer review journal, as a scientist, you haven't done anything.

However, in order to avoid his results having to be scrutinized by an independent lab, Hawass cunningly started looking for a *second DNA laboratory* to be established in Egypt. In the same article (December 23, 2007), the Associated Press reported Hawass's plan to acquire another lab.

> The Discovery Channel paid for the current lab in exchange for exclusive rights to film the search for the Hatshepsut mummy. Hawass said he's offering other companies a similar deal, namely the rights to film a highly coveted expedition—possibly the search for King Tut's family—in exchange for a second lab.

The matter remains controversial and unresolved.

APPENDIX 3

"LIVE" Egyptology

Whatever is said about the Secretary-General of the Supreme Council of Antiquities (SCA)—and a great deal is—one thing is certain, he is never going to be accused of being a wallflower. Since being appointed to the post . . . Zahi Hawass has courted the media spotlight with a fervour few would have imagined in the rarefied world of archaeology. Strolling across our television screens in his trademark Indiana Jones hat, he has no doubt about his own abilities. "I'm damn good," he says at one point in our interview. And later: "I am already famous and powerful . . ."

NEVINE EL-AREF, "ZAHI HAWASS: A HAT IS A HAT,"
AL-AHRAM WEEKLY

A FOX IN THE SCENE

Starting sometime in 1998, Hawass developed a close relationship with Fox TV, owned by News Corporation, the giant media conglomerate created by the Australian-American business mogul Rupert Murdoch. Whatever the deal, if any, that was struck between Fox TV and Hawass, what is certain is that it brought about two things: several big budget "live" television shows that were extremely profitable to the channel, and also the opportunity to turn Hawass into a superstar of archaeology or, more aptly, a real-life Indiana Jones.

It would very much appear that Hawass's longtime dream of becoming famous led him into the exciting and glamorous (but dangerous and fickle) world of big media and big budget television—the kind of media that can make or break presidents and turn men and women into superstars overnight, and destroy them just as quickly. News Corporation (which is presently under FBI investigation following, inter alia, a massive scandal in the United Kingdom involving one of its newspapers, *The News of the World*) set its eyes in the mid-1990s on Egyptian archaeology. Fox TV, one of its major subsidiaries, became particularly interested by the discovery of an alleged door inside the Great Pyramid in March 1993 (see below), followed by a prime-time BBC *Everyman Special* in February 1994. The BBC, however, did not manage to get exclusivity for the "live" *opening* of the door in the Great Pyramid, leaving this incredibly lucrative television deal open for grabs. This golden opportunity for a mega live documentary was tossed about for several years, partly because of the politics involved and the conflict of interests that arose among the parties involved and partly—perhaps even mostly—because Hawass was not (yet) in full control of the Supreme Council of Antiquities (SCA), but only director of the Giza Pyramids. Eventually another company of News Corporation, National Geographic Channel, would land this highly coveted show, but not until 2002, when Zahi Hawass would finally become the head of the SCA. Meanwhile, Fox TV sniffed around for other "discoveries" that they could exploit with Hawass.

Around mid-November 1998, Fox TV acquired from the SCA the exclusive rights for a two-hour live special: *Opening the Lost Tombs: Live from Egypt*. A crew led by Fox TV's producer Nancy Stern arrived in Cairo on November 12 to start filming. To assist Hawass in the show were Fox's celebrity presenters Maury Povich and Suzy Kolber. The allegedly lost tombs awaiting to be opened "live" were the small pyramid of Queen Khamerernebty II, which lies south of the Third Pyramid at Giza (Menkaure's), and also a tomb of an unknown person. In addition, the mummy of a nobleman from the Old Kingdom called Nefer at Saqqara was to be examined in front of Fox's cameras "live." This, apparently, was the first time that ancient Egyptian tombs were to be excavated "live" on television, and naturally Fox TV made hay with massive publicity and hype around this event. No expenses seemed to have been spared. According to Mahmoud Kassem of the *Cairo Times* (June 1–7, 2000):

> [F]or over a month a legion of American television producers, aided and abetted by Video Cairo and Israeli freelance cameramen, have bewildered residents of the town of Bawiti with their Indiana Jones costumes, convoy of busses and vast satellites.

Fox TV then launched a huge promotional campaign worthy of the best and purest Hollywood schmaltz, with clips of old mummy movies (Boris Karloff) and speculation running wild as to what would be found. Richard C. Carrier, an American archaeologist who was among the dumbstruck academics who saw the trailers and also the live show on Fox TV in March 1999, was to write:

> I couldn't believe my eyes . . . the graphic behind the announcer, on a backdrop of the Gizeh pyramids, asks the question: "Alien Architects?" The announcer plugs the upcoming Fox television network special "Opening the Lost Tombs: Live from Egypt," then segues into the story with the campy introduction, "There are many mysteries in Egypt, like the pyramids. Who built them and how did they do it?" With that she introduces Fox News correspondent David Garcia, who begins his voice-over to video of the pyramids: "The ancient future, a civilization of contradiction . . . Still, modern-day scholars debate not only what they are, but why they are—who, or what, built them . . ."

Then we see a man identified onscreen as Fadel Gad, Egyptologist: "Were the Egyptians thinking of UFOs at that time? Yes! A very sophisticated, highly intelligent species that had intercepted this planet Earth and had caused the evolution and the exploration of the human consciousness." . . . Fadel Gad just happens to be a co-executive producer of "Opening the Lost Tombs.". . . Why hype what could have been a beneficial and educational examination of an ancient tomb with such foolishness? The answer is clear: Lies sell better than truth . . .

Mara Greengrass, an archaeologist, also wrote a scathing review in CSICOP online and concluded by saying that "[o]pening the Lost Tombs was an embarrassment to archaeology, to Egyptology, and to television . . ."

Another archaeologist, Chris Andersen, also commented to Fox TV that

I was unsure what the point of this show was supposed to be but as a professional archaeologist I was progressively embarrassed, dismayed, disgusted, annoyed, angered, and appalled by this program on all levels. . . . This show proved to be an embarrassment both to Hawass and the Supreme Council of Antiquities, to Egypt, and to archaeology as a whole. By taking advantage of every opportunity the show provided in order to trot out every hare-brained bit of pseudo-scientific claptrap to come down the pike from Edgar Cayce and Atlantis to the "face" on Mars, the Fox Network and Mr. Povich effectively dishonored the ancient Egyptians who created these magnificent monuments and served only to add fuel to the fire of all the "New Agers" and other irrational cranks, crackpots, and "conspiracy theorists" who would rather believe in "X Files" than the often awe-inspiring accomplishments of our own ancestors. What's more, the manner in which the tombs were entered and "investigated" was clearly very thoroughly stage-managed, and very poorly even at that.

Even my 10- and 13-year-old sons could immediately tell that the mummy found in the wooden sarcophagus had been very recently placed there. . . . And with all due respect to Dr. Hawass, no archaeologist worthy of the title would have torn apart a newly-discovered sarcophagus with his bare hands just to see what was inside!

This sorry performance was followed soon after by the appalling scene of your female reporter [Suzy Kolber] stomping around a stone sarcophagus in the Queen's tomb, all the while audibly crunching what turned out to be human bones beneath her feet—a fact which was confirmed for all the world to see by Dr. Hawass a bare few moments later. This broadcast performed a real disservice to the causes of archaeological exploration, cultural heritage preservation, and public education. And all for the sake of television ratings!

FOX TV 2000: *OPENING THE TOMBS OF THE GOLDEN MUMMIES: LIVE!*

Seemingly unaffected or undiscouraged by the harsh criticism coming from his peers (and much of the public) over the sensationalism and unprofessionalism he displayed with the Fox TV show, Hawass again happily participated with Fox TV on yet another live extravaganza titled "Opening the Tombs of the Golden Mummies: Live!," this time with Hollywood superstar Bill Pullman and TV presenter Lisa Guerrero. And again, not surprisingly, this show proved to be a great embarrassment to the Egyptians and the scholarly community. The most damning scene was when Hawass and Pullman used their heavy desert boots to kick open a sarcophagus during the live broadcast. The *Al-Ahram Weekly* (23–31 May 2000, "Mummy's the Word," by Tarek Atia, issue 483), a popular English language newspaper in Egypt usually supportive of Zahi Hawass, this time could not restrain its disgust and summed up the public outrage.

A lot of people might consider the events that culminated in Baharija Oasis early Wednesday morning as a farce . . . "Opening the Tombs of the Golden Mummies Live!" was "the second time in recent years that FOX has mined ancient Egyptian history for compelling subject matter . . ." says the [FOX TV] web-site. Mined it for money is more like it. . . .

In the pre-press for the show, co-producer Leslie Greif said, "I can only tell you that the man inside the mummy [which will be opened up live for the cameras] is dead." Then he added wistfully: "Just think of the ratings we would get if he were alive."

Actor Bill Pullman of *Independence Day* fame would be "discovering" the mummy with Zahi Hawass, Director-General of Giza Plateau. Veteran announcer Hugh Downs and Fox Sports reporter Lisa Guerrero were the co-hosts.

Fox had everything covered. There was a separate team standing right outside the "location" filming live promos to Fox affiliates across the U.S.—doing the all-important lead-up to the show, pumping the audience's expectations. . . . We're only hearing the announcer's side of the conversation as he speaks with the 5 and 6 o'clock news anchors in Cleveland, Ohio, Miami, Florida, and so on.

"I understand they found something very, very special," he's saying, a big grin on his face, "just earlier today, that will be opened tonight, someone who was a ruler in the area, so it's going to be special today." David Moss does this over and over again. Live with another affiliate, Moss is almost bursting with this false excitement. "You know when you are a little kid who is reading a book about mummies and you think the mummy is going to get up and come alive . . . well tonight, it's going to happen for real, live!" . . .

Another surreal moment: Lisa Guerrero describes the wine-making region of ancient Bahariya as the "Napa Valley" of Egypt, falling into the trap of comparing Ancient Egypt with modern America. . . .

The show makes it all look so simple, with archaeologists and movie stars discovering the tombs of mummies, to the delight of couch potatoes across the world.

Zahi Hawass, referred to as the "animated" Hawass on the website, is indeed the star here, while everyone else is an extra.

Hawass says Fox likes him because he can provide an American-style commentary on history. "No other Egyptian archaeologist can give them that. . . . This needs action, and easy to digest information." At one point on the show he claims that "this is the most interesting moment in the history of archaeology."

At another point, Pullman asks Hawass how much these mummies are worth, and Hawass says, "It's priceless. This is history. We learn from history, we never sell it."

That said, the Supreme Council for Antiquities got $100,000 from Fox for the right to film, an increase on the $65,000 paid for the previous special at the Pyramids.

Surely the alleged $100,000 given by Fox TV to the Egyptian authorities was a pittance compared to the millions of dollars such a big budget television extravaganza would normally generate? We do not have Fox TV's accounts for this project, of course, so it is not possible for us to know.

Earlier when Hawass, on March 2, 1996, announced that he discovered what he called the Valley of the Golden Mummies, he had claimed that he, with his Egyptian team, found about 250 mummies going back to the time when Egypt was part of the Roman Empire. On his website, Hawass gave details of the discovery: "When people ask me which of my discoveries has meant the most to me personally, I often think first of the Valley of the Golden Mummies at Bahariya Oasis."

However, Nasri Eskander, the director of research and restoration in the Department of Egyptian Antiquities, also announced that the mummies found in Bahariya Oasis were not discovered by Hawass in 1996, as the latter had claimed, but were found five years earlier in 1991 to 1992. Moreover, Eskander denied that these were golden mummies, as he pointed out in an article in the *Al-Wafd* newspaper (April 20, 2001).

> The mummies discovered recently in the Baharia Oasis are not golden mummies. The small burial amulets found with these mummies are not made of gold, although it is used to decide the date of the tombs. The discovered bodies have masks that point to the Roman period.

When Hawass announced the discovery of the golden mummies in 1996, it was declared to be the most important find since Howard Carter's discovery of Tutankhamun's tomb in 1922.

Eskander told us that he personally took part in the work at the Bahariya tombs when it was accidentally discovered in 1991 when a guard riding his donkey on the way to work fell into a hole in the ground, revealing ancient ruins. The guard reported this to El-Ashri Shaker, the local director of antiquities, who quickly realized that there were tombs under the roadside. Shaker excavated the area and found forty bodies. According to Eskander, these were badly preserved bodies wrapped in linen shrouds, instead of the usual bandages used for proper mummification. And except for a few thin gold plates, no other gold was discovered in these tombs—only simple amulets of semiprecious stones. Also no copy of the traditional Book of the Dead or hieroglyphs were found in these tombs, and most of the so-called mummies were nameless. In other words, the discovery had very little historical or scientific value (indeed, these type of Late Period mummies had been previously unearthed by the thousands in the nineteenth and early twentieth century and sold to credulous foreigners who believed them to have medicinal properties). It was because of these reasons that the antiquity authorities, at the time of the original discovery decided neither to carry on clearing the tombs nor to announce the discovery to the press. Nonetheless, as we have seen, Fox TV and Hawass turned the "discovery" into a huge publicized and hyped television production. As Hollywood was getting ready to release its new production *The Mummy* in 1999, the mas-

sive Fox media machine set about turning the Baharia "golden mummies" into the most important discovery of the century, with Hawass
as the hero-cum-real Indiana Jones. Hawass, who was director of
the Giza Pyramid and Baharīya antiquities, enthusiastically joined the
media hype in selling the "Valley of the Golden Mummies" as a new
and dramatic discovery. The Fox TV documentary was earmarked to
be a two-hour big budget production to be shown "live" on May 24,
2000, featuring actors/presenters Hugh Downs and Bill Pullman and,
of course, Zahi Hawass wearing the now-famous Indiana Jones–style
Stetson hat. As Fox TV news reported:

> For the first time, the secrets of ancient Egypt yielded themselves
> to television cameras early Wednesday as Fox TV broadcast the live
> opening of several mummies' tombs on its two-hour special, "Opening
> the Tombs of the Golden Mummies: Live!"

Hawass went as far as welcoming Fox's blockbuster *The Mummy*
as a great event that helps to "educate people about Egyptian history." (Following the box-office success of this movie, Fox released
Return of the Mummy to coincide with Hawass's announcement of
more golden mummies he discovered at Baharīya.)

Except for the body of the Twenty-Sixth Dynasty governor of
the oasis, the other corpses at Baharīya, estimated by Hawass to
number ten thousand, have no or little historical importance. These
were ordinary people who left no record. Indeed, this was the view
of Ahmed Fakhri, the great Egyptian archaeologist, half a century ago.
Fakhri had excavated at Baharīya in 1947 and discovered a temple
dedicated to Alexander the Great—only one kilometer from the
so-called golden mummies' tombs. And although Fakhri reported
the location of these tombs, neither he nor indeed his successors
deemed it worthy to waste valuable funds to dig out these bodies of
no historical value.

Egyptian mummies represent the age-old belief in resurrection and
eternal life. No self-respecting country would allow the desecration

of their dead for television entertainment as has been the case in Egypt. It was for this very reason that in 1980 President Anwar El Sadat ordered the hall of the royal mummies in Cairo Museum to be closed (it was reopened in 1993). Yet while the financial benefit of showing the royal mummies to visitors is perhaps justified, this is surely not the case in exposing ten thousand decayed and unnamed corpses. Egypt has a huge archaeological wealth of ancient pyramids, temples, artifacts, and wonderful sights, which are more than plentiful for attracting tourists. At any rate, Hawass published the inevitable glossy coffee-table book on the "Golden Mummies"; and tourism in Bahariya returned to normal once it was realized that only a few late period mummies were worthy of display, and that in any case many such similar mummies could be seen in the various museums of the world. As for the "Bahareya Golden Mummies," these ended up in a small museum at the Bahareya Oasis where very few tourists bother to visit.

NATIONAL GEOGRAPHIC CHANNEL: SECRET CHAMBERS REVEALED—LIVE!

It has long been known that narrow shafts emanating from the King's and Queen's Chamber in the Great Pyramid had stellar alignments and were directed to important stars associated to the rebirth rituals of the pharaohs.

On August 5, National Geographic announced to the world that they were about to commence a daring exploration inside the southern shaft of the Queen's Chamber and attempt to see what was behind a small trapdoor discovered in 1993 by Rudolf Gantenbrink, a German robotics engineer.

Secret Chambers Revealed was aired "Live" by National Geographic to many TV networks around the world on September 17, 2002 (September 16 in the United States). Wearing a red shirt down to his thighs and an Indiana Jones–style hat, Hawass was hailed by presenter Laura Greene as the "most famous archaeologist in Egypt." Hawass beamed and told Greene: "Welcome to my beautiful country, Egypt." Throughout the show, Hawass sweated profusely and often looked nonplussed in the live scenes. "I have been waiting all my life for this moment!" he told Laura Greene, ". . . to reveal the secret of the Pyramids . . ." When asked to explain the task of the robot, he looked at Greene and said: "As you can see, the shaft is very small, so we will have to use the robot and not you, Laura!" Later, when Greene reminded Hawass that he was awaited by Jay Schadler elsewhere to attend to the opening of the sarcophagus, he exclaimed: "I know your heart will be broken to see me go, but I will be back soon!"

The opening of the overseer's sarcophagus turned out to be a big flop, as "live" discoveries go. No golden mummy, not even a simple wrapped mummy, just a pile of old bones. True, they were 4,500 years old, but not very exciting for viewers who waited all night for the big moment. Hawass was undeterred. He lovingly brushed the dust off the skull, which he called a "beautiful face" and declared to the world that this proved that the Egyptians had built the pyramids and not slaves and that all the "idiots who spoke of lost civilizations and such nonsense" must now shut their mouths. All this, mind you, "live" around the world. He then appeared to talk on behalf of the 4,500-year-old dead man, saying that he was happy that he could tell the world for him that the Egyptians were a great people. Asked by the presenter, Jay Schadler, to give his expert comments on the disappointing skeleton, Hawass said: "He is looking at the rising sun. But the most important thing I want you to learn from this is that these are the fingerprints of the workmen, the Egyptians, who built the pyramid! This can shut the mouths of all these idiots who talk about lost civilizations and all this kind of nonsense. This man is existing, he's a skull, at the time of Dynasty 4 when mummification was very rare . . . Give me this brush. . . . I can clean this beautiful face and let this man tell the world that the Egyptians were the builders of the pyramid . . . this is really a message from this Sut Weser [the name of the alleged overseer], and I'm glad that this man saved his body . . ."

Then Schadler attempted to help Hawass with the point he clearly wanted to make. "This is one of those principal points that you want to make, isn't it, Zahi? That the Egyptians were not the slave culture . . ." Schadler said. Hawass beamed: "Exactly! . . . Pyramids had to be built by love. . . . This is exactly what I expected . . . and when I look at his face [the skeleton], I can really see him alive in front of me and telling the world about the Egyptians, they were like us . . ." Trying to look serious and excited at the same time, Schadler cut him short by saying: "So now begins the hard archaeology in some ways. But one incredible discovery for tonight! I can't quite believe that we've had this one . . . more perhaps ahead over at the Queen's Chamber . . ."

The next day, Sandra Laville of the *Daily Telegraph,* who had watched the whole painful experience, gave this account of what followed.

After 4,500 years and centuries of speculation the answer to one of the riddles of the Great Pyramid of Giza was about to be answered. In front of a live television audience . . . there were gasps from those watching the flickering pictures transmitted via a tiny probe. "We can see . . ." said Dr. Zahi Hawass, the commentator broadcasting to millions of viewers, "we can see . . . another sealed door . . ." A collective breath was exhaled as Dr. Hawass struggled to recover from what appeared to be the greatest of anticlimaxes. "What we have seen tonight is totally unique within the world of Egyptology," he said, with utter conviction. "The presence of a second door only deepens the intrigue." But for many who watched the ambitiously entitled "Pyramids Live: Secret Chambers Revealed" broadcast by Fox TV on the National Geographic channel, no amount of spin could transform a rather boring limestone slab into the gold and treasure some had predicted would be discovered.

Zahi Hawass, it seemed, had taken Egyptology on yet another embarrassing live romp around Egypt's antiquities. Many felt that he could have, for instance, stayed calm and given his professional view on the finding of the "second door," but instead it went this way:

Greene: This is really the moment of truth that we've all been waiting for, isn't it Zahi? The camera is now lined up . . . we are going to follow its progress through the hole to find out if and what is behind that stone door. . . . Let's see what's happening. OK, the lights are on, you can see the camera making a steady progress across the hole now. Now Zahi, talk us through what's happening . . . !

Hawass: "Just the camera getting into the hole now, but I can't see anything . . ."

Greene: "Okay . . . now, oh my God, look at that! There's shrieks inside here, I gotta tell you, this team of archaeologists have been waiting for this moment for months and months. . . . This is incredibly exciting! What are we seeing, Zahi . . . ?'"

Hawass: "We can see . . . another . . . sealed door . . . another . . . another sealed door . . . but it looks to me we have a discovery . . . But it looks like it's really something, we are here in front of a discovery, and I'm really happy we did this, we found another sealed chamber . . . Laura, this is very important, this is something I am very proud that finally we revealed the first mystery of the Great Pyramid of Khufu . . . We will study this, we will find out how we can reveal more secrets of the Pyramid, but this is very important that what we are showing now . . . it shows the amazing [skills] of those people, the great Egyptians . . ."

It was clear that Hawass was extra keen to remind the world that it was the "great Egyptians" who built the pyramids and not slaves. But how could the finding of the second door and an ancient skeleton prove this? And even if they were slaves, surely they were also Egyptians? So what was the problem? Did Hawass have something else in mind that prompted such declarations? Hawass was known in Egypt for often declaring to the press that he was at war with all those who attacked Egyptians by falsely claiming that it was the biblical "Jews in Captivity" who had built the pyramids. For example, not long ago, in an Arabic language publication, Hawass accused Jews of "stealing the pyramids" by claiming to have built them. "The Jews are thieves of history and civilization," he is quoted by Egyptian reporter Mushira Moussa:

> The discovery of the tombs of the workmen who built the pyramids was tremendously important to Egyptians because it proved that the greatness of Egypt was a project of both Egyptian genius as well as Egyptian labor. It is especially important vis-à-vis Israeli claims that it was their Jewish slave ancestors who built the pyramids, but also vis-à-vis theorists who would have that the pyramids were built by Atlanteans or aliens.

We can detect in the above statement certain key words like *the greatness of Egypt, Egyptian genius, Jewish slave ancestors,* which are reminiscent to what Hawass also said to National Geographic presenter Jay Schadler and Laura Greene and later to the press. This question thus begs the asking: Had Hawass been making the same point, that is, that it was not Jewish slaves who built the pyramids, on the National Geographic show?

At the press conference at the luxurious Mena House Oberoi hotel after the show (and where I, Robert Bauval, was also present), Hawass was visibly agitated. No sooner had he started talking than he told the press that "bad people" had booked to stay overnight at the hotel just to sabotage the event (later it was reported by the *Asharq Al-awsat* newspaper that he had been more specific and said that one of these bad persons was a "Jew"). Hawass exclaimed,

I feel that the opening of the sarcophagus and that skeleton that we found shows the importance of the discovery and this completely discards the theory about the pyramid built by slaves, because slavery cannot build something genius like the pyramid, and I will tell the public that everyone who tries to talk against the Egyptians should shut their mouths!

Later the next day Hawass told *Al Gomhoreya* newspaper: "The results of the robot's exploration . . . refutes the allegations reiterated by Jews and some Western countries that the Jews built the pyramids."

Notwithstanding the polemics and rhetoric that followed the airing of *Secret Chambers Revealed,* it was noted that when the show was aired live on the large TV screen at the Mena House Oberoi hotel banquet room, there were long gaps of total darkness and silence, indicating places in the show where advertisements were being shown in the United States and other countries. A total of 30 minutes, fragmented into 4 to 5 minutes intervals, was devoted to such advertisements. Considering the extremely high profile of this extravaganza TV show, the huge promotional campaign that had been done before its airing, and the estimated six hundred million viewers worldwide glued to their TV set waiting for the secret chambers to be revealed in the Great Pyramid, the revenue of advertising space alone would have run in over a million dollars. Again, we have not seen the accounts for this project, and cannot therefore know how much was generated.

By 2010, and largely thanks to the very effective and very aggressive U.S. media machine, Zahi Hawass had been properly imaged and packaged as the real Indiana Jones who single-handedly makes stunning archaeological discoveries in Egypt to thrill and delight adoring television audiences around the world. Hawass became a regular feature on U.S. television, giving interviews, talking on chat shows, and appearing on just about every program that had to do with ancient Egypt. A household name to many, Hawass became the cultural voice of Egypt, and was heard more loudly and more often than Hosni Mubarak or any other minister in the Egyptian cabinet. But like all who have been lured into the limelight of the world stage by a media who loves to create heroic or notorious images, the person involved is compelled to feed, promote, and push this image to higher and higher levels, which, inevitably, leads to a downfall or, in some cases, total self-destruction.

Hawass, as the world now was accustomed to see him, was portrayed as a passionate man, oozing with enthusiasm and filled with bravado, loving his work and unabashedly confessing his love of archaeology and ancient Egypt, and ready to fight, to use his own rhetoric, "anyone who attacks Egypt and Egyptians." But then, in 2010, eager to show himself as he really was to the world, Hawass made the near-fatal mistake of agreeing to be the star of a reality show proposed by the History Channel: a ten-part series titled *Chasing Mummies*. It would be a huge hit for the TV channel—and a total disaster for Hawass, for instead of his media-image of the passionate, enthusiastic, adventurous, dashing, friendly, flirtatious, and lovable archaeologist, he came across instead as a megalomaniac, a bully, rude, abusive, and a rather violent person. In the show he is seen running around with a bunch of adoring students, busting open tombs, rescuing damsels in distress, telling subordinates off, screaming at cameramen and producers, and even fighting off a deadly royal cobra. The highlight was a student actress called Zoe, who Hawass was trying to make into a "real" archaeologist—which amounted to bullying, cajoling, ignoring, and flattering Zoe (with a tête-à-tête dinner with Egyptian one-time heartthrob actor Omar Sharif) and finally seeing the poor girl humiliating herself to a world audience by peeing on camera inside the Great Pyramid!

The trailer for "Chasing Mummies" announced that

[t]he Greatest ruins in the world belong to one man. One hundred thousand years of history are his. Follow this legendary archaeolo-

gist and unearth a history the world has never seen before: "Chasing Mummies" premiers Wednesday, July 14, on history made every day!

[Hawass then says]: "Can YOU dig it?"

The reviews were scathing. The History Channel message board was swamped with e-mails expressing disgust, shock, and anger at this parody of archaeology, and many demanded that the show be taken off the air. Neil Genzlingler of the *New York Times* in "The Pharaoh of Egyptian Antiquities" (July 13, 2010) wrote:

Zahi Hawass, secretary general of the Supreme Council of Antiquities in Egypt, seems to get his name in the papers and his face on television every time anyone sticks a shovel in the ground there.

The resulting fame—the man has become ubiquitous on history-heavy American cable channels—has apparently given Dr. Hawass, like many celebrities before him, the mistaken impression that any sort of personal behavior will be embraced by his adoring public, because he sure is obnoxious on "Chasing Mummies," an annoying new show that begins Wednesday night on History.

Dr. Hawass has allowed a History crew to tag along as he does what he does, but, at least from the evidence of the premiere, this does not result in many revelations about the science of archaeology. It results instead in a fair amount of footage of Dr. Hawass verbally abusing those around him: the film crew, college-age interns who have come to worship at his feet, and so on. Any infraction or no infraction at all, seems sufficient to warrant one of Dr. Hawass's tirades.

The show is also intent on forcing drama into the proceedings in a way that seems artificial. In the opening installment, an intern and a cameraman become stuck in a pyramid tunnel, but the bit feels about as genuine as one of those fake injuries we kept seeing in the World Cup.

Sure, some Egyptology occasionally creeps into this irksome spectacle. In the opening episode Dr. Hawass finds a never-before-breached sarcophagus, a rare thing these days, and when it is opened, he imparts interesting tidbits about why this mummy is not in very good shape. But this scene doesn't last as long as you want it to; gotta go look for someone else to dress down.

There are two possibilities here. One is that the program is accurately capturing Dr. Hawass's personality. The other is that, as on many reality shows, the people in this one are putting on personas that they think will make good television, and Dr. Hawass, having studied his Simon Cowell and Donald Trump, has concluded that American audiences want to see underlings browbeaten. But there's a big difference between enjoying Mr. Cowell's antics in the artificial construct of "American Idol" and seeing the same thing out in the real world, where college kids are just trying to learn, and film crews are just trying to film.

Whichever explanation is correct, one hopes that this show will, like some of those ancient pharaohs, die young, or that Dr. Hawass will unearth some ancient Egyptian chill pills and swallow a generous helping.

The Death
of Tutankhamun
The Cover-up

This is a personal account of Ahmed Osman's controversial battle with
Zahi Hawass, which began in 1992 regarding the circumstances surround-
ing the death of the pharaoh Tutankhamun.

Since the discovery of his tomb in 1922, a great mystery has surrounded the premature death of Tutankhamun. The boy king was only
ten when he ascended the throne of Egypt around 1361 BCE and died
mysteriously nine years later. So far, all medical examinations of his
mummy have confirmed that he suffered from no physical disease. In
1992, while studying the various works regarding this king, I came to
the conclusion that Tutankhamun had met a violent death by hanging, as his head and neck were found separated from the rest of the
body. Looking for a possible assassin, I surmised that the young king
was killed by Pa-Nehesy, the high priest of his father, the "heretical"
king Akhenaten. At the time, Zahi Hawass rejected outright my conclusion, insisting that the young king died of natural causes. Yet seven
years later, American Egyptologist Bob Brier, in his book *The Murder of
Tutankhamun,* agreed with me that the king had been killed (according

to Brier by a blow on the back of his head)—practically now forcing Hawass to accept this conclusion. Later, when R. G. Harrison, late professor of anatomy at Liverpool University, suggested in a BBC interview that Tutankhamun was killed by a blow on the back of his head, nearly all other Egyptologists seemed to agree with this view.

Allow me, therefore, to review here the genesis of this fascinating story . . .

It may be an understatement to say that when Howard Carter discovered the tomb of Tutankhamun in 1922, it reignited interest in the history of ancient Egypt as intensely as the "Egyptomania" that had swept across Europe after Napoleon's 1799 expedition in Egypt (see chapter 3). Until 1922, almost nothing had been known about this mysterious pharaoh of the Eighteenth Dynasty, and indeed little was revealed even after the tomb was found. The general belief was that the role of the boy king in Egyptian history had been of little significance. Thomas Holving, a former head of the Metropolitan Museum in New York, drives this point:

> Tutankhamun is one of the most famous and at the same time least known rulers of the ancient world, or to use Carter's words, "We might say with truth that the one outstanding feature of his life was that he died and was buried."

Yet despite—or perhaps because of—the mystery surrounding Tutankhamun, hordes of people have queued for hours to catch a glimpse of his breath-taking golden treasures and iconic tomb. The tomb's riches, over five thousand artifacts (many gold plated) to accompany the pharaoh on his journey into the afterlife, has fired the imagination of millions all over the world. So how do we explain this fascination with King Tut? Is it because his is the only pharaoh's tomb to have been found perfectly intact? Or is it the hauntingly beautiful gold mask that overlaid his face? Or, as it was in my case, the mystery of his early death?

The first X-ray examination of Tutankhamun's mummy ever to be carried out was in 1968 by R. G. Harrison and A. B. Abdallah, professors of Anatomy at the universities of Liverpool and Cairo respectively. Although they failed to find any evidence of disease being the cause of the king's death, it was nonetheless clear from the state of his remains that Tutankhamun's mummy had suffered extensive damage, which, one supposes, could have been inflicted either in ancient times or following the discovery of his tomb. Still, the report these scientists drew up would not be out of place in a modern legal thriller.

> When the bandages around the remains were removed, it was immediately obvious that the mummy was not in one piece. The head and neck were separated from the rest of the body, and the limbs had been detached from the torso . . . Further investigation showed that the limbs, as well as being detached from the body, were broken in many places. The right arm had been broken at the elbow, the upper arm being separated from the forearm and hand . . . The left arm was broken at the elbow and, in addition, at the wrist . . . The left leg was broken at the knee. The right leg was intact . . . The heads of the right humerus [upper arm bone] and both femora [thigh bones] had been broken off the rest of the bone . . . The head and neck had been distracted from the torso at the joint between the seventh cervical and first thoracic vertebrae . . ."

Young Tut had come on the throne during a very troubled and confusing period in Egyptian history. His father, Akhenaten, who had ruled for seventeen years, had abolished the old Egyptian gods in favor of a single deity, Aten, whom he had forced upon his people (and thus becoming, according to most historians, the first monotheist). When Amenhotep III, Akhenaten's father (and coregent), had died, the new king closed all the ancient gods' temples, confiscated their lands, dispersed their priests, and gave orders that the names of all deities be expunged from monuments and inscriptions throughout the land. He also began the construction of a new capital, Akhetaten (Horizon of Aten), at the site known today as Tell el-Amarna. In the brand-new temple complexes Aten was worshipped in the open sunlight (rather than in dark temple enclosures as had been the previous custom). Akhenaten had imposed his religious reformation ruthlessly, using the army to destroy the powerful old priesthood and to force his new monotheistic religion on his people. However, the army, whose commanding general was Horemheb, shared the same religious beliefs as the rest of the people and could not go on suppressing these beliefs in favor of the new monotheistic religion of the king. There are indications that General Horemheb led the first military coup in history to depose Akhenaten in favor of his young son, who was then still called Tut-ankh-Aten.

For the first four years of his reign, Tut-ankh-Aten continued to live at Tell el-Amarna, leaving in place his father's religious revolution. In year four of his reign, upon reaching the age of fifteen, the young king introduced his dramatic religious counter reform. He started by inviting the deposed priests of Amun to accompany him in a surprise visit to the temple of Karnak (which his father, Akhenaten, had closed and ransacked). Noting the sorry state of the temple, he ordered this and all other old temples reopened and their properties returned. He also restored the priesthood, changed his own name to Tut-ankh-Amun (and also that of his wife's to Ankhsenpa-Amun). The young king, clearly very wise (or very well advised), realized that his people could not grasp the abstract idea of a singular god who neither manifested himself in a visible form nor favored one nation against the other (although Tutankhamun seemed to have still regarded Aten as the one and only universal and invisible god—as attested by Aten's name found on the back of his throne—the young king nonetheless understood that the people needed some visual "angelic mediators" of the Aten to communicate with). Having thus launched his religious counter reform, Tutankhamun left Tell el-Amarna for Memphis, and three years later, he was dead.

As I previously pointed out, the very fact that Tut's skull was found separated from his body strongly suggests that he could have been killed by hanging or a massive blow on the head. Who, then, might have been responsible? By allowing the old deities to be worshipped again as well as changing his royal name from "the living image of Aten" to "the living image of Amun," Tut not only blatantly betrayed his father's (Akhenaten's) priesthood who had adopted Aten as their sole god, but also he was almost certainly regarded by the Aten followers as an apostate. It was for these very reasons that, in 1992, I suggested that it was Pa-Nehesy, Akhenaten's high priest, who had been responsible for the killing of Tutankhamun.

Eight years later, my hope of examining more evidence regarding Tut's death was raised, for in November 2000, the Egyptian authorities announced that they had given official permission to scientific experts from Japan's Waseda University to use DNA tests on two royal mummies, that of king Tutankhamun and his supposed grandfather Amenhotep III, in order to confirm Tut's royal ancestry. In addition to funding this project, the Waseda University was donating a specialized laboratory to the Supreme Council of Antiquities (SCA) to conduct the DNA tests. A joint team from Waseda University and from Cairo's Ein Shams University were given permission to carry out the test under the supervision of Gaballah Ali Gaballah, then head of the SCA. In early December 2000, the team, headed by Gaballah, traveled to Luxor in Upper Egypt to take samples from Tutankhamun's mummy (which was still inside the tomb in the Valley of the Kings). The joint Egyptian-Japanese team was to open the coffin and take samples of hair, bone, and intestines from Tut's mummified body. These samples would then be returned to Cairo, about six weeks later, and analyzed at the new high-tech laboratory financed by Japan (in order to compare it with Amenhotep

III, presumed grandfather of King Tut). It was hoped that the tests would resolve his paternity despite the previous poor record of DNA testing in earlier archaeological studies. However, while the Japanese mission was at Luxor with Gaballah, there came orders from Cairo to halt the operation. According to Sabri Abdel-Aziz, the SCA's chief archaeologist in southern Egypt, the Japanese experts assigned to this project did not have security clearance. Why this was so, however, Abdel-Aziz did not say. A short while later, the Egyptian authorities announced that the permit issued to the Japanese-Egyptian team was withdrawn on the grounds that it represented a "threat to the National Security!" But it soon became known that it was Zahi Hawass who had been behind this last-minute decision to cancel the DNA tests on Tutankhamun's mummy. Here's what happened behind the scenes: because the SCA had officially agreed to the DNA testing by the Japanese-Egyptian team under Gaballah, Hawass could not himself stop the operation simply on archaeological grounds, so he convinced his crony friend Farouk Hosni, the minister of culture, that these tests could be used to revise Egyptian history. The Associated Press (December 13, 2000) quoted Hawass saying to the Arab newspaper *Akhbar El Yom* that he has "refused in the past to allow foreign teams to carry out such [DNA] tests on the bones of the pyramids builders, because there are some people who try to tamper with Egyptian history."

DNA, deoxyribonucleic acid, is a nucleic acid that contains the genetic instructions used in the development and functioning of all known living organisms. As it contains the instructions needed to construct other components of cells, such as proteins and RNA molecules, DNA is often compared to a set of blueprints. The DNA segments that carry this genetic information are called genes. With the advances in science technology, DNA testing can now help Egyptologists in their quest to construct the definitive chronology of

Egyptian kings. The process involves taking minute amounts of tissue samples from a donor, which can be broken down into their constituent parts, allowing the identification of individuals, by comparison to other known samples.

It is clear that Hawass, who was then the director of the Giza Plateau, opposed DNA testing on mummies because, he claimed, it might open the door to a range of false theories. Commenting on the cancellation of Tut's DNA tests, Mark Rose wrote in the American magazine *Archaeology* (March/April 2002 issue):

> Just before an Egyptian-Japanese team took tissue samples from Tutankhamun's mummy last spring, the Egyptian government abruptly halted the work for what it said were national security reasons. Press reports, however, pointed to concern that some people might misinterpret the results to further claims that Akhenaten was the biblical Moses. This far-fetched link . . . has been made in *Moses: Pharaoh of Egypt,* authored by Egyptian-born amateur historian Ahmed Osman . . .

Although Hawass on the face of it seemed to have changed his mind on DNA testing and even accepted Brier's account of the king's death, it is very likely that he never really believed it. When Hawass was appointed secretary general of the SCA in 2002, he used his high authority to prove that Tut was not killed, as Brier and I had claimed, but rather that he died of illness. Deep in his mind, Hawass rejected the idea that Tutankhamun was killed probably because he wanted to project an ideal picture of pharaonic Egypt, which did not include acts of murder, treachery, or deception. The other reason—and probably the main reason (knowing him)—was the nagging fact that it was not he who first came up with this idea.

At any rate, in a concerted and final attempt to unlock the

mystery of the king's death, a team of researchers under the orders of Hawass removed Tutankhamun's mummy from its tomb in the Valley of the Kings one evening in January 2005 and laid bare his bones for a CT scan inside a van standing nearby. The team of radiologists, pathologists, and anatomists worked under the supervision of Madiha Khattab, dean of medicine at Cairo University. Under rare cloudy skies on the west bank of the Nile at Luxor in Upper Egypt, the quasi-covert removal of the wooden box that holds Tut's mummy from underneath the stone sarcophagus in his tomb began. The blackened mummy was left in its box when it was placed inside the scan machine, in the specially equipped van parked near the tomb. The machine, brought from Germany, was donated by Siemens, while the American National Geographic Channel was there to directly transmit the operation live on air.

Hawass, who was personally supervising the operation, told reporters that King Tut's remains were inserted inside the machine for a fifteen-minute CT scan, which captured more than 1,700 three-dimensional images of his bodily remains in order to provide a detailed view of the bones that make up his mummy. Amazingly, Hawass spoke of Tutankhamun as residing at Luxor (ancient Thebes) at the time of his death when it is well known that Tut's residence was at Memphis and—even more amazing—before knowing the outcome of the tests, Hawass confidently said that the result would only confirm his own views in the matter. Some two months later, on March 8, 2005, Hawass released his verdict: *"We don't know how the king died, but we are now sure that it was not murder."*

The CT scan confirmed the 1968 X-rays, which had revealed two bone fragments inside the king's skull and a broken section at the base of the skull, but these fragments were dismissed by Hawass's team as having been done *after* Tut's death, probably by Howard Carter. These bone fragments could not possibly have been from an injury *before* death, as they would have become stuck in the embalming material; the scientific team therefore believed that these were broken during the embalming process or, perhaps, by Howard Carter's team in the 1920s. Moreover, the CT scans revealed a picture of a well-nourished nineteen-year-old pharaoh in good health. According to the reports: *"Judging from his bones, the king was generally in good health. . . . There are no signs of malnutrition or infectious disease during childhood . . ."* But if Tutankhamun was indeed in good health and was not murdered, how then did he die at such a young age? According to Hawass, *"Maybe he died on his own . . . the case is closed!"*

And here we have it: rather than identifying the real cause of Tut's death, the CT scan confirmed Hawass's pet theory that Tutankhamun was *not killed* but died of natural causes. It is no wonder, therefore, that many scholars refused to accept the results of the CT scan made by Hawass.

Hawass, however, was unrepentant and relentless: he decided to arrange a more spectacular show in front of the TV cameras to show that Tutankhamun was not killed. If the CT scan hadn't worked to close the case, then why not use DNA testing this time?

Because his earlier conclusions about Hatshepsut's mummy had been deemed inconclusive when he did not allow a second laboratory to verify the results, this time Hawass, in an effort to neutralize this argument, asked the Discovery Channel to provide him with yet another DNA laboratory so that this second laboratory could confirm the results of his first laboratory. Once the second laboratory was set up, Hawass immediately started his DNA tests on the mummy of Tutankhamun, as well as ten other mummies that he thought were related to the young king. The primary analysis was carried out in the new DNA laboratory (funded by the Discovery Channel) at the Egyptian Museum, while the second laboratory (also funded by the Discovery Channel) was set up at the Faculty of Medicine at Cairo University. The tests were carried out by an all-Egyptian team recruited by Hawass himself.

Some DNA experts, however, such as Eske Willerslev, director of the

Center of GeoGenetics in Copenhagen, openly objected to the method of DNA analysis used by Hawass and his team. Rather than extracting and sequencing DNA, the team used a technique called genetic fingerprinting, which involves measuring the size of the DNA products that have been amplified by polymerase chain reaction. This method, say critics, is rarely used in ancient DNA studies because it is especially difficult to rule out contamination. And on a much-handled mummy such as Tutankhamun's, contamination could be rife. Indeed, in the TV documentary, Hawass is seen several times examining the mummy without the obligatory protective clothing or even sterilized gloves.

In any case, on February 17, 2010, Hawass finally announced the results of the DNA tests on the mummies of Tutankhamun and his ten relatives. This time, however, Hawass made sure to give three different causes for Tut's death. Having confirmed his old view that the young king was not killed, he then declared in an article he wrote for *National Geographic* ("King Tut's Family Secrets," August 2010) another reason for Tutankhamun's death, which has nothing to do with the DNA tests.

> The study showed that Tutankhamun died . . . soon after he suffered a fracture of his left leg.
>
>   . . . Ashraf Selim and his colleagues discovered something previously unnoticed in the CT images of the mummy: Tutankhamun's left foot was clubbed, one toe was missing a bone, and the bones in part of the foot were destroyed by necrosis . . . Both the clubbed foot and the bone disease would have impeded his ability to walk. Scholars had already noted that 130 partial or whole walking sticks had been found in Tutankhamun's tomb, some of which show clear signs of use. Some have argued that such staffs were common symbols of power and that the damage to Tutankhamun's foot may have occurred during the mummification process . . . of all the pharaohs, only Tutankhamun is shown seated while performing activities such as shooting an arrow from a bow or using a

throw stick. This was not a king who held a staff just as a symbol of power. This was a young man who needed a cane to walk.

But here Hawass was deliberately misleading: Ashraf Selim was not an active member of the DNA team and none of the fifteen samples taken from Tut's mummy during DNA testing indicated a missing bone. (Selim was, however, one of the CT-scan team members in 2005.) It also was not true to say that Tutankhamun was always shown seated; many statues show him standing with his arms crossed at his chest, and there is the famous statue of Tutankhamun the Harpooner standing in a boat of papyrus and holding a rope in his left hand. According to Hawass, in the same *National Geographic* article:

> Tutankhamun's bone disease . . . on its own would not have been fatal. To look further into possible causes of his death, we tested his mummy for genetic traces of various infectious diseases. . . . Based on the presence of DNA from several strains of a parasite called *Plasmodium falciparum,* it was evident that Tutankhamun was infected with malaria. . . .

After the CT scan of Tut's mummy in 2005, Hawass had declared that there were no signs of infectious disease, and now, six years later, he contradicted his own conclusion by stating that Tut had been infected with malaria. At any rate, malaria (which was also found in three other mummies examined) could not be proved to be the cause of the king's death. Hawass notes in his *National Geographic* article that "malaria was probably common in the region at the time, and Tutankhamun may have acquired partial immunity to the disease."

So far the evidence of the DNA tests has not provided conclusive results to explain Tutankhamun's death, but this did not prevent Hawass from stating, in the same article, that

[i]n my view, however, Tutankhamun's health was compromised from the moment he was conceived. His mother and father were full brother and sister [like the majority of Egyptian pharaohs]. Pharaonic Egypt was not the only society in history to institutionalize royal incest, which can have political advantages. . . . But there can be a dangerous consequence. Married siblings are more likely to pass on twin copies of harmful genes, leaving their children vulnerable to a variety of genetic defects. Tutankhamun's malformed foot may have been one such flaw. We suspect he also had a partially cleft palate, another congenital defect. Perhaps he struggled against others until a severe bout of malaria or a leg broken in an accident added one strain too many to a body that could no longer carry the load.

Notwithstanding the scientific jargon, Hawass's strategy was clear: he was using his position of authority and credibility as head of the SCA and the heavy support of National Geographic media to convince the public that Tutankhamun was *not killed* but died from a mixture of natural causes.

Let us note that the results of the DNA tests of 2009 were only partially published in February 2010 (while the Y-DNA results were filed away). Using this partially available DNA information (which was revealed by Hawass on the Discovery Channel) scientists at a Zurich-based DNA genealogy center reconstructed the DNA profile of Tutankhamun, Akhenaten (his supposed father), and Amenhotep III (his supposed grandfather). The results were as shocking as they were controversial: contrary to what was expected, these results showed that Tut, his father, and his grandfather belonged to a Western European rather than an Egyptian ethnic group with a genetic code known as haplogroup R1b1a2—which is found in less than 1 percent of modern-day Egyptians but in 50 percent of Western Europeans. Apparently, before migrating into Europe, this racial group originated in the vast area surrounding the Black Sea in

Asia (Reuters, August, 2, 2011). That area east of the Black Sea was the original home of Ashkenazi Jews before they spread over Russia, Germany, and Eastern Europe. *Did Tut have Jewish ancestral origins?* This conclusion, however, is contradicted by much artistic representation of the Egyptian Pharaohs of the Eighteenth Dynasty, as well as by anthological evidence. Be that as it may, there is a bizarre political twist to this "Tutankhamun ethnic origin" controversy, which was recently brought into the investigation by none other than the Director of Egypt's archaeological sites, Nour Abdel Samad. Samad accused Hawass and the former first lady Suzanne Mubarak of receiving millions of dollars to doctor the results of the DNA on certain royal mummies. In the same vein, Abdel Samad also revealed that the medical doctor in charge of the study of the royal mummies at Kasr el Aini Hospital resigned his position when he discovered the plot (Egyptian Al-Wafd TV, February 17, 2011). These hard-to-believe accusations by Abdel Samad are currently being investigated by Egypt's attorney general.

Meanwhile, contrary to Hawass's claim that the case of Tutankhamun's cause of death was closed, I believe it has now become more open than before. For although the result of the CT scan suggests that the young king did not die from a blow on the back of the head, it does not remove the possibility that Tutankhamun was killed in a different way. When I investigated this issue back in 1992, I offered that Tut had died from hanging and not by a blow on the back of the head. The "blow in the head" theory was not from me but from Bob Brier. Both conclusions, however, were inspired by the fact that Tut's head had been found severed from his body. Hawass took it for granted, however, that Tut's head was separated from the body either during the mummification process or much later in modern times when Howard Carter removed the (world-famous) golden mask from the mummy. Because of this, Hawass did not consider the separation of the head in his CT-scan research.

Going back now to 1968, X-rays were made of Tutankhamun's

skull by a team from the University of Liverpool under the supervision of R. G. Harrison—and a TV documentary of the conditions under which the X-rays were made, as well as Harrison's conclusions, were aired on the BBC in 1969. Harrison pointed out that the X-rays suggested that a piece of bone was fused with the overlying skull, and this, according to him, was consistent with a depressed fracture that had healed. This, therefore, meant that Tutankhamun could have died from a brain hemorrhage caused by a blow to his skull from a blunt instrument. But much later, and according to R. C. Connolly, a member of Harrison's team, Harrison had regretted making that conclusion on the BBC program (see box).

The Skull and Cervical Spine Radiographs of Tutankhamun: A Critical Appraisal. Richard S. Boyer, Ernst A. Rodin, Todd C. Grey, and R. C. Connolly in *American Journal of Neuroradiology* (2003 24: 1142–47)

(ABSTRACT)

BACKGROUND AND PURPOSE: Tutankhamun, the last pharaoh of the XVIIIth dynasty, died unexpectedly at approximately age 18 years. A cause of death has never been established, but theories that the young king was murdered by a blow to the head have been proposed based on skull radiographs obtained by a team from the University of Liverpool in 1968. We recently had the opportunity to evaluate the skull and cervical spine radiographs of Tutankhamun. The purpose of this study was to report our critical appraisal of the radiographs of Tutankhamun regarding the findings alleged to indicate traumatic death.

METHODS: Copies of lateral, anteroposterior, and submental vertex skull radiographs of Tutankhamun were reviewed with special attention to the claims of a depressed skull fracture, intracranial bone fragments, and calcified membrane of a posterior fossa sub-dural hematoma. A phantom skull was radiographed to reproduce the appearance of the floor of the posterior fossa in the lateral projection.

RESULTS: The skull radiographs of Tutankhamun show only postmor-tem artifacts that are explainable by an understanding of the methods of mummy preservation used at the time of his death. Some findings also relate to trauma inflicted by an autopsy performed in 1925. The alleged calcified membrane of a posterior fossa subdural hematoma is easily reproduced with a skull phantom.

CONCLUSION: Our critical review of the skull and cervical spine radiographs of Tutankhamun does not support proposed theories of a traumatic or homicidal death.

It is generally agreed that Tutankhamun, the last pharaoh of the XVIIIth dynasty, died unexpectedly at approximately the age of eigh-teen years. The cause of his death has never been conclusively estab-lished. It has been alleged that a blow to the head murdered the young pharaoh. Skull radiographs obtained in 1968 by a team from the University of Liverpool headed by Professor R. G. Harrison have been used as supportive evidence of this allegation. A video documen-tary of the conditions under which the radiographs were obtained and Harrison's conclusions about the radiographic findings were shown on British television in 1969. The radiographs were never published in the medical literature, but an article by Harrison "Post Mortem on Two Pharaohs: Was Tutankhamun's Skull Fractured?"—was published in the December 1971 issue of *Buried History.* Harrison stated, "While examining X-ray pictures of Tutankhamun's skull, I discovered a small piece of bone in the left side of the skull cavity. This could be part of the ethmoid bone, which had become dislodged from the top of the nose when an instrument was passed up the nose into the cranial cavity during the embalming process. On the other hand, the X-rays also suggest that this piece of bone is fused with the overlying skull and this could be consistent with a depressed fracture, which had healed. This could mean that Tutankhamun died from a brain hemorrhage caused by a blow to his skull from a blunt instrument."

This evidence, taken together with the knowledge that the pharaoh was only 18 years old when he died, and considered against the troubled times during which he lived, poses an intriguing question. Was Tutankhamun murdered?

A second article by Harrison (and coauthor Abdalla), "The Remains of Tutankhamun" was published in *Antiquity*. In that publication, Harrison's team reported that Tutankhamun's body had been dismembered during the first autopsy, which was had been performed by Carter and Derry in 1925. This process was necessary because the mummy was glued to the innermost coffin by an excessive use of unguents and had to be literally chiseled out to unwrap the body and retrieve the artifacts, which are now in the possession of several museums and have been displayed around the world. In the process, the head and cervical spine were severed from the remainder of the spinal column below the seventh cervical vertebra. Harrison described the radiographic findings as follows: "The most prominent feature, however, is the presence of two attenuated shadows, the first along the vertex of the skull, and the second occupying the back (posterior) region of the skull. Each of these shadows possesses a fluid level, suggesting that radio-paque [*sic*] fluid was introduced into the cranial cavity with the skull lying vertex downwards, and then with the body lying horizontally, so that the posterior region of the skull was most dependent. In addition a small fragment of bone is seen in both lateral and frontal views of the skull, lying in the posterior aspect of the left parietal region of the skull. This, at first sight, looked like a piece of bone from the thin bony roof of the nasal cavity (the cribriform plate of the ethmoid bone), and perusal of the frontal X-ray of the skull confirms that this bone has disappeared from both sides of the floor of the skull.

This would be very understandable, and could fit in well with known theories of the practice of mummification. It is a generally accepted view that an instrument is passed through the nostril, up into the nasal cavity to perforate or remove this bone, allowing extraction of the brain, and the introduction of any preservation fluid into the cranial cavity. On closer analysis, however, after further X-rays were developed and became available for study, several main objections to this theory were apparent and an alternative explanation suggested itself. This additional analysis will be discussed in a future publication."

No further publication was produced. However, on the previously mentioned BBC videotape in which the events surrounding the second autopsy as performed by Harrison's team are shown, the radiographic findings are explained by Harrison. As recorded on this tape, he regarded the bone splinter as a postmortem artifact. However, in the same video documentary, Harrison raised a question about the appearance of the posterior fossa of Tutankhamun on the lateral radiograph. Pointing to the floor of the posterior fossa, which he called "eggshell thinning" of the occipital bone, he said: "This is within normal limits. But in fact, it could have been caused by a hemorrhage under the membranes overlying the brain in this region, and this could have been caused by a blow to the back of the head, and this in turn could have been responsible for death."

These sentences have since been taken to indicate that the pharaoh had, in fact, been murdered. However, we propose that all findings alleged to indicate a traumatic death are explainable by an understanding of normal anatomy and the process of Egyptian mummification in practice at the time of Tutankhamun's death. Some artifacts are also due to an entry into the cranial vault at the time of the autopsy performed by Carter and Derry in 1925. For full article see www.ajnr.org/content/24/6/1142.full

At any rate, it was on this conclusion that much later in 1998 Bob Brier developed his theory that Tutankhamun was killed by a blow on the back of the head.

To clear this historical conundrum, and following Hawass's CT scan, I decided to pay a visit to R. C. Connolly in Liverpool, who was still working at the Department of Human Anatomy and Cell Biology at the University of Liverpool. It was a very cold day that Monday of December 17, 2007, when I met Connolly at the Department of Anatomy in the Sherrington Building on Ashton Street in Liverpool. In contrast to the weather, I was warmly welcomed by Connolly. I immediately went to the point: Was Tutankhamun killed? Connolly replied with a flat no. He was very familiar with all the points of the argument. Even *before* the latest CT scan was conducted he had already concluded that the broken bone at the back of the king's skull could not have been the cause of his death. Relying on Harrison's X-rays (which he used to explain his conclusion), it was clear to Connolly that the bone in question had not broken *before* Tut's death. It was, in fact, the tilted position of the skull when radiographed that had created a dark area at the back of the skull giving the wrong impression of a brain hemorrhage. He also did not agree that the broken bone of the knee could have caused Tut's death, as it probably took place in modern times, as a result of Howard Carter's examination of the mummy in 1925. According to Connolly, Tutankhamun's mummification did not follow the usual method of embalming because his brain was not removed through the nose as was usually the case and the embalmers placed resin inside the skull. He also saw evidence of bones on the mummy's chest deliberately broken by the embalmers. According to Connolly, the reason for this unusual behavior could be the fact that the inside organs were deteriorating as the result of a long time having passed between the time of death and the time of embalming. This is why the brain became soft and could not be removed in the usual way by an opening in the nose. The foul smell caused by not removing the brain in the normal manner was probably the reason why resin was poured inside the skull. Also the embalmers needed to remove the heart quickly before it deteriorated further, and this is probably why he had to cut open the chest bones. All this to Connolly fortified his view that a long time must have elapsed between the king's death and his mummification. This, albeit not proven, nonetheless supports my argument that Tut was killed away from his residence, and that a week or more must have passed before his body could reach the royal embalmers in Thebes. I informed Connolly that my argument of the killing of Tutankhamun was not based on broken bones; I believed that the king had been tortured and then hanged, which resulted in breaking his neck and separating the head from the body. Fortuitously, it turned out that Connolly had in fact carried out special research on how people died by hanging. He could confirm, therefore, that Tut's head and neck were distracted from the torso at the joint between the seventh cervical and first thoracic vertebrae. But to my dismay, Connolly told me that this did not prove that Tutankhamun was hanged, for if he had been dropped with a rope around his neck, his skull would have been severed from the base of the neck, which, quite clearly, was not the case. Feeling somewhat dejected by what Connolly was telling me, I made my way back to London (where I live). While on my journey back home, I was struck by a thought: What if Tutankhamun was not hanged by the same method used today, which is by being dropped with a rope around the neck, thus causing the skull to break at the base? What if, instead, as I originally suggested, the king had been held by a group of people who placed a rope around his neck, then dragged him to the nearest tree, and hauled him above ground, where he slowly suffocated to death? I decided to phone Connolly to ask his opinion on what would have happened to the king's head and neck. Connolly replied, "In this case you have a point. If Tut was hanged by a group of ordinary people who wanted him to suffer as much as possible by not dropping him [but rather by letting him dangle till he died], his skull and neck would not break. He would die of suffocation. The evidence of X-ray and CT scan cannot *disprove* that."

The jury is still out. But I remain convinced that Tutankhamun was indeed murdered, or to be more precise, he was brutally executed by slow suffocation through hanging for political reasons—almost certainly by the orders of the high priest of Aten, who, in my opinion, had the strongest motive for this regicide. I also remain convinced that Hawass's theory was not based on unbiased scientific evidence but rather on a personal agenda that had to do with his own inflated ego and his xenophobia on the ethnic origins of the pharaoh. Hawass was trying to fit the evidence to an already formulated conclusion. And rather than let the evidence speak for itself, he added his own personal spin to it. We may well wonder why.

At any rate, only further unbiased and fully independent scientific investigations will hopefully resolve this intriguing historical mystery.

ADDENDUM

As well as his desire to prove his own theory that Tutankhamun was not killed, Hawass's DNA tests also aimed at establishing Tut's family relatives, especially his supposed father Akhenaten. But as the latter's remains had not been found, Hawass decided to identify a mummy in tomb KV55 as belonging to Tut's father. In his article for the August 2010 *National Geographic,* he gives his interpretation of the evidence.

Once the mummies' DNA was isolated, it was a fairly simple matter to compare the Y chromosomes of Amenhotep III (father of both Akhenaten and Smenkhkare) in KV55, and Tutankhamun and see that they were indeed related. . . . our team was able to establish with a probability of better than 99.99% that Amenhotep III was the father of the individual in KV55, who was in turn the father of Tutankhamun. . . . But not all the evidence pointed to Akhenaten. Most forensic analyses had concluded that the body inside was that of a man no older than 25—too young to be Akhenaten, who seems to have sired two daughters before beginning his 17-year reign. Most scholars thus suspected the mummy was instead the shadowy pharaoh Smenkhkare. New CT scans (not DNA) of the KV55 mummy also revealed an age-related degeneration in the spine and osteoarthritis in the knees and legs. It appeared that he had died closer to the age of 40 than 25, as originally thought. With the age discrepancy thus resolved, we could conclude that the KV55 mummy, the son of Amenhotep III and Tiye and the father of Tutankhamun, is almost certainly Akhenaten (Since we know so little about Smenkhkare, he cannot be completely ruled out.) . . . what about better than 99.99 percent.

Typically, Hawass contradicted himself by saying, on the one hand, that his team was able to establish with a probability of "better than 99.99 percent" that the remains in tomb KV55 belonged to Akhenaten, but then, on the other hand, saying that "not all the evidence pointed to Akhenaten" and, then again, saying that "Smenkhkare . . . cannot be completely ruled out." Furthermore, and as at least four medical examinations by prominent international medical experts showed, the mummy in question had a wisdom tooth that was just breaking in, thus strongly indicating a young individual; so how could Hawass's team conclude that the mummy in tomb KV55 belonged to a man of forty! Let us retrace the full genesis of this strange story.

On January 1907, a small tomb—known as tomb KV55—was found in the Valley of the Kings. The excavation was sponsored by Theodore M. Davis, a rich retired American lawyer and amateur archaeologist, who employed the British archaeologist Edward R. Ayrton to conduct the digs. The tomb is one of only three discovered closed with both mummy and funerary equipment inside, the others being that of Yuya and his wife Tuya and of Tutankhamun. Tomb KV55, which was used during the reign of Tutankhamun, is located near the entry of the inner valley, close to the site where the tomb of Tutankhamun was subsequently found. It consists of a small, rock-cut chamber approached by a sloping passage and does not seem to have been intended originally for a royal burial. The burial appears to have been carried out in haste, with a minimum of equipment. The tomb's deteriorated condition, resulting from a great deal of rainwater dripping into it through a fissure in the rock, made it difficult to establish ownership of the tomb. Inside the tomb, the remains of a large wooden gilded shrine were found, with inscriptions indicating that it was dedicated by Akhenaten to the burial of his mother, Queen Tiye. A coffin was found in another part of the chamber, with inscriptions that included the titles and cartouches of Akhenaten; nearby, there were four canopic jars. Four magic bricks to protect the deceased in the underworld were also found in situ, inscribed with the name of Akhenaten. The coffin was originally made for a woman, but adapted for a male burial by the addition of a beard and the alteration of the inscriptions. The face on the coffin had been broken off, and the royal names on it, which would have perhaps identified its occupant, had been removed. The coffin had originally lain upon a bier, but when the wood had eventually rotted away because of the damp, it collapsed, and the mummy partly projected from under the lid. The flesh of the mummy had consequently also rotted away leaving the skeleton as the only bodily remains. When the mummy was first discovered, Davis thought it was of Queen Tiye, the mother of king Akhenaten. But later Davis was disappointed when the remains were examined by Grafton Elliot Smith, professor of Anatomy in Cairo Medical School, who concluded that the skeleton was that of a man. However, the debate about the identity of the owner of the skeletal mummy in tomb KV55 has continued up to the present time: Is it Akhenaten or his brother/son-in-law Smenkhkare?

Akhenaten is the most mysterious and most interesting of all ancient Egyptian pharaohs. His religious revolution introduced the first monotheistic form of worship in history, and his artistic innovations produced new romantic and realistic schools of art. The son of Amenhotep III and Queen Tiye, he married his half-sister Nefertiti to gain the right to the throne when his father had made him his coregent. Soon after, Akhenaten abandoned the worship of Egyptian traditional gods in favor of a single god, Aten, and removed himself and his court to Akhetaten, the Horizon of Aten (modern Tell e-Amarna), a city he built midway between Egypt's two traditional capitals of Memphis and Thebes. Akhenaten's new beliefs and artistic ideas, however, were not popular with his people. I believe that he was forced to abdicate the throne in favor of his son Tutankhamun by a military coup, and following the end of his rule, his name was removed from all official documents in Egypt. What actually happened to Akhenaten after this is not known, nor is known his place of burial.

The debate about the ownership of tomb KV55 has rumbled on for a whole century and is still going on till now. It was Cyril Aldred, the Scottish Egyptologist, who insisted that the skeletal remains of tomb KV55 belonged to Akhenaten. Aldred came to this conclusion because he believed that Akhenaten had peculiar physical characteristics as a result of suffering from a disorder known as Frohlich's syndrome, which slows down physical development. He relied on an apparently nude statue of Akhenaten at Karnak—one of four colossi—which showed the king seemingly deformed and without genitalia. At the end of the day, this proved to be something of a storm in teacup, however, when it was demonstrated eventually that the seemingly nude colossus at Karnak was actually an unfinished statue awaiting the kilt that was seen on the other adjacent three colossi.

The age of skeletal remains in tomb KV55 was the key to the mystery. Before Hawass appeared on the scene, almost all examinations of the skeleton showed that it belonged to a young man in his early twenties. Indeed, Grafton Eliot Smith, who first examined the mummy, concluded that the remains belonged to a man of about twenty-five. Another examination was carried out by D. E. Derry, professor of anatomy in the faculty of medicine at Cairo University. Derry, whose examination included restoring the skull, reported that the conformation of the skull does not support Aldred's conclusion that the person to whom it belonged suffered from hydrocephalus, instead it was a type known to anthropologists as platycephalic, in which the skull is flattened from above downward and correspondingly widened—the reverse of the shape produced by hydrocephalus. Derry further concluded that the remains were those of a man no more than twenty-four years of age. Derry also noticed a similarity between the skull in tomb KV55 and that of Tutankhamun. A third examination in 1963 under the supervision of R. G. Harrison (the late Derby professor of anatomy at the University of Liverpool) confirmed that the skeleton belonged to a man about five feet seven inches tall whose death occurred in his twenties. Harrison also confirmed Derry's view of the similarity in facial appearance with Tutankhamun and concluded that he found no evidence of abnormality.

> There is no evidence of hydrocephalus in the skull of these remains
> . . . The presence of a pituitary tumour may also be excluded . . .
> The bodily physique and proportions are within normal limits and
> unlike those which occur in established endocrinopathies.

A fourth examination of tomb KV55's skeletal remains was conducted in 2002 by Joyce M. Filer, British Museum Egyptologist and anthropologist. According to the report, which was published by the American journal *Archaeology* in March 2002, Filer's conclusion was categorical and clear.

> The human remains from Tomb 55, as presented to me, are those
> of a young man who had no apparent abnormalities and who was
> no older than his early twenties at death and probably a few years
> younger. If those wanting to identify the remains with Akhenaten
> demand an age at death of more than mid-twenties, then this is not
> the man for them.

Hawass's attempt to use DNA tests and CT scans to conclude that the skeletal remains in tomb KV55 belonged to Akhenaten rather than Smenkhkare is a premeditated action—almost certainly because for the thirty years before all these tests were made on the mummy, Hawass's mentor and superior (and a staunch Mubarak crony) Farouk Hosni, the minister of culture, *had already long made up his mind that it was Akhenaten.*

Let us also note that since the discovery of tomb KV55, its contents have been exhibited in the Cairo Museum under the name of Smenkhkare. In 1931, the golden base of the sarcophagus, which had collapsed due to the dampness, disappeared from the museum! Fifty years later, in 1980, Dietrich Wildung, director of the Egyptian Museum in Munich, discovered the disappeared base of the sarcophagus—apparently left in the Munich museum by its owner, a Swiss antique collector who casually had brought it in for restoration. The deteriorated base had some golden sheets with hieroglyphic inscriptions as well as some colored semiprecious stones attached to wood, which had much deteriorated. The Munich museum spent more than 200,000 marks in restoration, and therefore was not in favor of returning the base of the sarcophagus to Egypt. However, when the prime minster of Bavaria visited Cairo on May 3, 2001, he agreed to return it to its home country.

On January 27, 2002, after seventy-one years of being lost, Egypt received the base of the sarcophagus. But here is another mystery: when the base disappeared from the Cairo Museum, it was labeled under the name of Smenkhkare, but the minister of culture Farouk Hosni surprised everyone by announcing the return of *Akhenaten's* sarcophagus! Hosni did explain his reason for changing the label on the coffin's occupant from Smenkhkare to Akhenaten. Not surprisingly, Ali Radwan, professor of Egyptology at Cairo University, rejected outright Hosni's identification as being "not correct."

In finality, let us be clear on this issue: Akhenaten, who is known to have ruled for at least seventeen years, had been first married on coming to the throne or shortly before, with his first daughter, Merytaten, being born either late in his first year or during his second year of reign. Consequently, Egyptologists believed that he must have been about thirty-three at the end of his rule. It seems that the Mubarak old boys' school of cronies, to which Hawass and

Hosni belonged, were for some reason bent to support the shaky theory that Akhenaten had suffered from some physical disorder, which decelerated his growth and thus made him look younger than his true age.

Fitting a camel through the eye of a needle comes to mind here.

APPENDIX 5

Egypt, My Native Country

OUT OF EGYPT

By Ahmed Osman

In 1947, when the United Nations announced the partition of Palestine into an Arab state and a Jewish state, the Muslim Brotherhood began calling for volunteers to go and fight the Jews in Palestine to prevent the establishment of a State of Israel. I was told that if I joined the fight against the Jews I could expect one of two results: either I would be victorious and help defeat the enemies of God, or I would die a martyr and go straight to paradise. To me, this sounded like the best deal I could possibly get, a free ticket to heaven. However, when I went to the volunteers' camp to join, I was refused because of my age. I was only thirteen at the time.

By the early 1960s, my views had completely changed. The continuous conflict between Egypt and Israel compelled me to understand the ancient roots of our unexplained enmity. After all, the Israelites came to Egypt as a tribe and left, in their exodus, as a nation; Joseph the Patriarch lived and died in Egypt; Moses the law giver was brought up in the pharaoh's royal house; and the Torah was revealed on the top of Mount Sinai—which is in Egypt. Because of this historical confusion, I decided to leave Cairo and go to London, where I joined the Egypt Exploration Society and enrolled in a three-year evening course on the history of Egypt, followed by another three-year study of hieroglyphics.

I also studied some Hebrew, which, after all, is a Semitic language, same as Arabic. It took me more than twenty-five years of research at the British Library to make my first breakthrough. In 1987, I wrote a book titled *Stranger in the Valley of the Kings,* in which I argued that Joseph (of the coat of many colors) was probably the same person as Yuya, an important Eighteenth Dynasty courtier whose mummy was displayed in the Cairo Museum, and who had been minister to the pharaoh Amenhotep III. Yuya eventually had become Pharaoh Akhenaten's grandfather (his daughter, Queen Tiye, was Akhenaten's mother).

It was now the right time for me to go back to Egypt, equipped with my new and full understanding of the relation between ancient Egypt and the tribe of Israel. Back in Egypt, however, instead of being welcomed and given the opportunity to present my conclusions with Egyptian intellectuals, I was attacked by the press—especially by members of the Egyptian Antiquities Organization (EAO). They considered that my identification of an Egyptian mummy to an Israelite character was a national crime! Zahi Hawass, who was still working on his Ph.D. in the United States, dismissed my research as part of a "Zionist plot" to steal the identities of Egyptian pharaohs and bestow them on Hebrew characters. So incensed was Hawass that he sent a letter to refute my argument, which was published in the Egyptian weekly *Akhbar el Yom.* Also on March 23, 1984, writing in *The University Museum* (the newspaper of the University of Pennsylvania), Hawass addressed the journalist who had interviewed me in *Akhbar el Yom:*

My dear brother Mr. Mohammad,
I followed the two subjects published by Akhbar el Yom *about Yuya's mummy, and its connection with Our Master Joseph, peace be upon him. I found it was my duty to explain some points in this matter, as I have found that, after the publication of the two subjects, some points have still to be clarified to the reader especially that this subject was transmitted by the news agencies in the American press, and was published more than once. I have been faced with many questions on this subject during my lectures here in America, where*

everyone asked me: Have they found the mummy of Our Master Joseph?

Yesterday a newspaper in Philadelphia published an interview with me, where I gave my personal archaeological view in the matter: "If we look at the view that was published by Brother Ahmed Osman, we will find that it is a view that can be added to many views which . . . got great media uproar especially as it is related to the prophets who visited Egypt in different parts of the ancient history of Egypt. I found that most of these views do not rely on texts or scientific suppositions, established on confirmed evidence for which reason it goes away from the truth and so creates scientific confusion which does not come to an end without Egyptologists refuting it."

If we return to the research of Mr. Ahmed Osman, and before I explain the position of the archaeology, I would like to remind him of the Noble Qur'an. The Noble Qur'an mentioned that Our Master Joseph, peace be upon him, was connected to Egypt's Aziz (Potiphar) and his wife. However, when the noble verse mentioned Moses, peace be upon him, it referred to his connection with Pharaoh and not the Aziz.

By applying this to archaeology, we will find that with the beginning of the First Dynasty around 3200 BC until the Seventeenth Dynasty, the word Pharaoh was not mentioned at all. This title (Pharaoh) was only found with the kings from the Eighteenth Dynasty. . . . Now, we have what the Noble Qur'an has mentioned and what is known for us from Antiquity of texts suggesting in a definite proof, that Joseph, peace be on him, came to Egypt during a time when the title Pharaoh did not exist, before the Eighteenth Dynasty which could be during the Hyksos period. Thus relating Yuya's mummy to our Master Joseph could not be possible, (because of) the much archaeological evidence as well as the Noble Qur'an.

There was no "archaeological evidence," of course, in Hawass's letter. Not only was he apparently ignorant of the story of Joseph in the Bible, which mentions Pharaoh, he also misunderstood the story in the Qur'an by mistaking Al-Aziz (Potifar), who bought Joseph in Egypt, to be the ruling king!

It was then in the mid-1960s that I decided to stay in London where I would carry on with my research without fear of political backlashes or censorship. I have now been living in London for over forty-five years.

I have two homes: England, my adoptive country, and Egypt, my native country. Having one foot in the West and the other in the East, so to speak, coupled with my decades of researching biblical and Egyptian histories, gives me the right intellectual mix, I think, to seek the truths in biblical as well as ancient Egyptian historical mysteries and anomalies.

My feud with Hawass thus started in the 1980s and has been going on until this day. When I met Robert Bauval in 1998, I realized that I was not the only "windmill" in Hawass's Don Quixotian portfolio of enemies. Bauval had also known and endured Hawass's sharp tongue and criticism and was also on the hit list.

LOSING ALEXANDRIA
By Robert Bauval

I have recently learned that my family was in Egypt in 1785, thirteen years before the Napoleonic invasion (1798). My great-great-grandparents (Joseph Siouffi and Therese Tutungi) were born in Cairo in 1785–1786. My grandmother Caroline (Siouffi) Bauval was born in Alexandria in 1876. My father, Gaston Bauval, was born in Alexandria in 1905. I was born in Alexandria in 1948.

I was, and still am, one of the so-called *khawagas* of Egypt. Khawagas are non-Egyptians born in Egypt. In my case, my Egyptian connection goes back more than three generations, not counting myself. My paternal grandfather came to Egypt from Belgium in 1894 to work on the Ramleh tramway lines that were being installed in Alexandria. His name was Charles Bauval, and he was a welder who, like many from his native village near Charleroi, had been apprenticed in canal-barge building. He married Caroline Siouffi, a Frenchwoman born in Alexandria with ancestral origins going back to the Napoleonic invasion of Egypt in 1789. Their only child, Gaston, my father, was born in Alexandria. He became a half orphan at the age of five when Charles died in 1910. To sustain a living, Caroline worked as a seamstress in khawaga households, which took her and Gaston to Kom Ombo, where there was a small Belgian community managing the paper mills near the ancient Temple of Sobek. They eventually resettled in Alexandria, where my father found a job as a draftsman with the French Lebon company, which maintained the city's gas and electricity. In 1939, he married Yvonne Gatt, my mother, who was ten years his junior. Yvonne was born in a khawaga family of Maltese origins. Her father, Robert Gatt, was a well-to-do stockbroker in the cotton trade and also owned a small bottling factory in Ras el Soda outside Alexandria. In the 1920s, Robert had built a large three-story villa at Buckley, then a very lush district of Alexandria. It became the family home until 1984, when it was sold to an Egyptian company (which partially turned it into a storehouse for car tires). It is where I was born with my twin sister, Therese, in 1948—four years before the toppling of King Farouk by the Free Officers (see chapter 5) in the military coup/revolution of 1952.

I grew up in Buckley, a leafy suburb of Alexadria, where I spent much of my time playing on the golden sands at Stanley Bay, a very fashionable beach favored by the large khawaga communities—predominantly of Italian, Maltese, and Greek origins. My childhood was a happy one in this cosmopolitan society, which existed then in this ancient city. Khawagas and Egyptians lived peacefully side by side, and I was weaned in this multilingual, multiracial, and multifaith society not as a European or an Arab but as an Alexandrian. To outsiders, I would introduce myself in French (my home language): *"Je suis Alexandrin."* In Arabic, I was *"ana Eskandarani"*—an Alexandrian. Although my parents, and thus myself, had retained our Belgian citizenship, I always saw myself as an Alexandrian. I was first sent to Catholic schools—Notre Dame de Sion and Sacred Heart in Rushdy—and eventually was enrolled in 1955 at the secular British Boys' School in Chatby.

A year later everything suddenly changed with the Suez War of 1956. The anger aroused in Egyptians by the "tripartite enemy" (Britain, France, and Israel) was directed against the khawagas. Our property, down to the house, furniture, and my father's car, was "sequestrated" by Nasser's military government. My father lost his

Figure A.5. Ex-British Boys' School in Alexandria, 1962–1963.
Robert Bauval is in the third row, third from right.

thirty-year-old job, and I was taken out of school. A mini exodus took place, with hundreds of khawaga families being "expulsed" out of Egypt. Thanks to my father's connections, however, we managed to remain in Egypt. Happy days were no more, not just for my family and me, but for all in Egypt. Gamal Abdel Nasser's nationalization and sequestration programs and his abortive attempts to introduce socialism and industrialization led to economic collapse, corruption, and cultural chaos. By 1967, the situation became intolerable, especially for the remaining khawagas in Egypt. My father had died the previous year. He had been out of work for many years, and the meager reserve of money we had was now nearly depleted. In late May that year, it became obvious that Egypt was on a collision course with Israel and its allies. Nasser's rhetoric became more and more aggressive by the day, and war now seemed inevitable and imminent. My older brother, Jean-Paul, had left Egypt a few years before and had settled in Geneva, Switzerland. The decision was made that my mother, my sister, and I would leave Egypt. I was nineteen at the time. I recall my last day in my home country, running with my old Jawa motorbike from house to house, saying good-bye to friends and places I loved. I recall the strange feeling of loss when we sailed away on the Italian liner *Esperia,* while watching for hours as the Alexandria coastline slowly faded until it finally disappeared below the horizon. I remember, most of all, the confusion that filled my heart and mind, not understanding why it was that I was obliged to leave my homeland and the friends I loved. I resented being made to feel like a foreigner in my own country, different and despised because of my European origins and appearance. The term khawaga began to take on a completely new and negative meaning for me. I suddenly realized a weird truth that would affect me the rest of my life: I would be seen as a foreigner not only in my homeland Egypt but also anywhere else I would be.

I went first to Geneva, where I spent my first three months. Then I was sent to England, where I entered as a boarder at the Franciscan

College in the small market town of Buckingham, in Buckinghamshire. Two years later, armed with the minimum entrance requirement for higher education, I enrolled in a higher diploma course at the University of the Southbank in East London. Three years later, armed with a diploma in building construction and now married (to my first wife, Linda Bauer), I looked for a job overseas. I desperately wanted to find a job in Egypt, but things had deteriorated so much under the corrupt Nasserite military government that it was useless to even try. I took my first overseas contract in Muscat, in the Sultanate of Oman. There, to my surprise and delight, I discovered the simple Arab world, the Arabia Felix of old. It was like taking a time machine and traveling back to the caliphate era! I loved Oman: its exotic, gentle people, its rugged coastline and beaches, its wild deserts and mountains, and the peaceful and congenial atmosphere that reigned everywhere. Time seemed to have stood still here, devoid of all the turmoil, rat race, and bewildering complexity of Western living. Life was simple here, and it was then that it struck me how much I had missed Arabia and, most of all, how truly non-European I was! I was, for all intents and purposes, an Arab in Western clothing.

My overseas working romp kept me in Oman until 1977, then several years spent in Iran, Sudan, French West Africa, and Saudi Arabia. In 1985, I took my now little family of four (my second wife, Michele, and our two children, Candice, then five, and Jonathan, then one) to Spain, where my brother Jean-Paul now lived with his own family, and then immigrated to Australia to join my mother and sister who had moved there in the early 1970s. Like many khawagas who had lost Alexandria and Egypt, I was hoping for a new life in a new country and a new continent. Australia was kind to us and would have indeed served our need to settle, but destiny had other plans for me.

It was while in Australia that I made the radical decision to change my career from construction engineering to trying my hand at being a writer. It was there, from 1988 to 1989, that I wrote my first book, *The Orion Mystery*. Frustrated that I could not find a publisher, I became aware that if I was going to succeed in this fickle and very competitive world of publishing, I would have to be in a major center such as New York or London. So again, I unrooted my family; we sold our home in Sydney and moved to England. We resettled in Buckinghamshire, in the small and dainty village of Beaconsfield. While putting the last touches on my manuscript and beginning the long and trying search for a publisher, I studied for a post-graduate degree in marketing, just in case my writing career did not materialize. While still looking for a publisher, I set up a small one-man consultancy operation at our home and took up research assignments in France, Pakistan, and India.

Finally, in early 1993, I found a publisher for my book. It took a year to rewrite it (for popular readership), and it eventually was published by William Heinemann in February 1994—and to my delight (and surprise!) the book quickly became an international bestseller (now in more than twenty-five languages). It was during that time that I became entangled in the affairs of the Egyptian Antiquities, partly because Zahi Hawass saw himself as critic and opponent to my work (and person!), and also because I had become deeply and inextricably involved in the stunning discovery made by Rudolf Gantenbrink of a door in one of the so-called air shafts of the Great Pyramid (see chapters 5 and 6). From that day on, Hawass and I became rivals over the mystery of the Giza Pyramids. Infuriated that my work was featured on a major BBC documentary, which I also copresented with Emma Freud and my coauthor Adrian Gilbert, he openly attacked me in the media, calling me—among other things—a Zionist, an amateur, and uneducated.

From then on, Hawass started a feud and a media campaign against me that lasted for many years. He can still be heard throwing abusive and derisory remarks on the many television documentaries in which he has appeared in the last seventeen years and which are repeated like some neverending mantra.

And Now . . .

Zahi Hawass was fired from his post in July 2011. My eighth book on Egypt is *Breaking the Mirror of Heaven*.

As for Alexandria itself, the city has much changed since my days there. There was a ray of hope for the revival of its cosmopolitan culture in the 1990s when the Bibliotheca Alexandrina was founded; but this hope was quickly muffled by the rising Islamism in Alexandria. It is now, ironically, the main stronghold of the so-called Salafists (Followers of the Ancestors), an ultra-radical and conservative Islamic faction that has won 30 percent of the Parliamentary seat in this year's election and whose Presidential Candidate, Abu Ismail, is gaining popularity by the day.

Tout passe, tout lasse, tout casse . . .

A Last-Minute Update

On the front page of the Egyptian newspaper *Al-Ahram* of April 12, 2012, ex-Minister of Antiquities, Zahi Hawass, and ex-Minister of Culture, Farouk Hosni, made a most bizarre attack on our book *Breaking the Mirror of Heaven*. Bizarre because the book was not yet published in April 2012 and, furthermore, even more bizarre, because the attack was a sort of anti-Semitic tirade of the worst kind packed with blatant misinformation. The title of this article was "Farouk and Hawass: American book attributes Egyptian Civilization to the Jews." The article also claimed that Robert Bauval's parents were "Belgian Jews from Alexandria."

Notwithstanding the fact that this book definitely does not attribute Egyptian civilization to the Jews, it is also a fact that Robert Bauval's parents were Christian Catholics. His father, Gaston Bauval, was baptized in Alexandria in 1905 at the Church of St. Catherine; and his mother, Yvonne Gatt, was baptized in Alexandria in 1915 at the same church. They are both buried in the Latin Christian Cemetery in Chatby, Alexandria.

Notes

CHAPTER 1. THE MAKING OF EGYPT'S INDIANA JONES

1. Smith and Cayce, *About My Father's Business,* 249–50.
2. Ibid.
3. Bauval, *Secret Chamber,* xviii.
4. *Al-Ahram Weekly,* November 27, 2008.
5. *Al Wafd,* August 5, 1993.
6. Phone conversation with Bakr on March 17, 1995.

CHAPTER 2. OUT OF DARKNESS

1. *Akhbar el Yom,* January 8, 1994.
2. *Egyptian Gazette,* May 16, 1997.
3. *Al-Ahram Weekly,* January 16, 2001.
4. For a detailed overview of this bizarre phenomenon, see Wynn's article, "Shape Shifting Lizard People, Israelite Slaves, and Other Theories of Pyramid Building: Notes on Labor, Nationalism, and Archaeology in Egypt," 272–95.
5. Miller, *Freemasonry in the Mind of the Islamist.*
6. Benjamin and Simon, *The Age of Sacred Terror.*
7. 2008 Update: Saudi Arabia's *Curriculum of Intolerance,* published by the Center for Religious Freedom of the Hudson Institute with the Institute for Gulf Affairs; www.hudson.org/files/publications/saudi_textbooks_final.pdf.
8. Interview with *Rose al-Yusef,* "Israel Is Robbing the Pyramids as It Robbed Palestine," May 5, 1997.

9. Ibid.

10. Memri TV: Arabic Video, English transcript, Broadcast February 11, 2009, see: www.memritv.org/clip/en/2049.htm.

11. "Egyptair," *Horus Magazine,* Summer 1999.

12. *Al Shaab,* December 10, 1999; December 18, 1999; January 4, 1999. Not unexpectedly, Farouk Hosni had this newspaper closed a few months later.

13. See *The Sunday Times,* December 5, 1999, 22.

14. Fagan, *The Rape of the Nile,* 6, 10.

15. Asclepius III, *Hermetica.*

16. The texts of the *Corpus,* which are believed to be of ancient Egyptian origin [*The Egyptian Hermes,* Garth Fowden, Cambridge: Cambridge University Press, 1986; and R. Jasnow and Karl-Th. Zausich, "A Book of Thoth," paper given at the seventh International Congress of Egyptologists Cambridge, September 3–9, 1995], were likely redacted between the first and the third centuries CE. Sir William Flinders Petrie believes that some texts in the Hermetic corpus date back to the sixth century BCE. [*Historical References in the Hermetic writings, Translations of the Third International Congress of Religions,* Oxford I, 1908, 196–225; and *Personal Religion in Egypt before Christianity,* New York: Harpers, 1909, 85-91]. Parts of the *Hermetica* were also found among the Nag Hammadi Coptic texts, discovered in Upper Egypt in 1945, one of which was not previously known. This Coptic treatise, called *The Ogdoadand the Ennead,* contains a very lively description of a hermetic initiation into hidden knowledge.

17. Bruno, *Dialoghi italiani.*

18. White, *Isaac Newton: The Last Sorcerer.*

19. Yates, *Giordano Bruno and the Hermetic Tradition.*

20. Fagan, *The Rape of the Nile,* 15.

21. Bauval, *Secret Chamber,* 177.

CHAPTER 3. THE PASHA

1. Bauval, *Secret Chamber,* chapter 7.

2. Strathern, *Napoleon in Egypt,* 424.

3. "Nevine el Aref, 'The Rose of the Nile,'" in *Al-Ahram Weekly,* November 24–30, 2005.

4. Fagan, *The Rape of the Nile.*

5. Bauval and Brophy, *Black Genesis,* appendix 3.

6. Rodenbeck, *Cairo: The City Victorious,* 39–43.

7. Ibid.

8. Ibid.

9. Sinoué, *Le Dernier Pharaon.*

10. Fagan, *The Rape of the Nile,* 252.

11. Sinoué, *Le Dernier Pharaon*, 233.

12. Ibid., 234.

13. Ibid.

14. Ibid., 253.

15. Ibid., 234.

16. Ibid., 239.

17. Ibid.

18. Ibid.

19. Ibid., 238.

20. Ibid., 459.

21. Bauval and Hancock, *The Master Game,* 498–503.

22. Morrow, "The Shoes of Imelda Marcos."

CHAPTER 4. SAVING ANCIENT EGYPT

1. Fagan, *Rape of the Nile,* 282.

2. Starbo, *Geographica,* vol. 17, sect. 32, 89.

3. Malek, "Who Was the First to Identify the Saqqara Serapeum?" 65–72.

4. Fagan, *Rape of the Nile,* 267.

5. *Al-Ahram Weekly,* August 26–September, 2004, no. 705.

6. Ibid.

7. Ibid.

8. Ibid.

9. Ibid.

CHAPTER 5. THE END OF AN ERA

1. Rodenbeck, *Cairo: The City Victorious,* 210.

2. Eames, *The Nile,* 139.

3. Sadat, the Internal Ministry radio show, July 23, 1952.

4. Khan, *The Long Struggle,* 58.

5. Rodenbeck, *Cairo: The City Victorious,* 218.

CHAPTER 6. SECRET CHAMBERS

1. Bauval, *Secret Chamber,* chapter 9.

2. Ibid.

3. Ibid.

4. Ibid.

5. Ibid.

6. Lehner in private correspondence with the authors, October 15, 1955.

7. *ARCE Newsletter,* 132, 1985, p. 44.

8. Bauval, *Secret Chamber,* chapter 9.

9. Ibid., chapters 9, 10.

10. Ibid.

11. Boris Said interview by Kenneth and Dee Burke, "Secret Tunnels in Egypt," *Leading Edge Newspaper,* January/February 1998 issue. See also Bauval, *Secret Chamber,* chapter 10.

12. Bauval, *Secret Chamber,* chapter 11.

13. *Daily Mail,* September 14, 2002.

14. Ibid.

15. Zahi Hawass website: www.drhawass.com/blog/dr-hawass-named-vice-minister-culture -egypt.

CHAPTER 7. REVOLUTION!

1. BBC 1, *The Andrew Marr Show,* February 6, 2011.

APPENDIX 1. THE PARIS OBELISK

1. Kerisel, *La Pyramide a Travers les Ages,* 158.

2. Fagiolo, *Architettura e Massoneria,* 44.

3. Curl, *The Art and Architecture of Freemasonry,* 118.

4. Ibid.

5. Kerisel, *La Pyramide a Travers les Ages,* 161.

6. Curl, *The Art and Architecture of Freemasonry,* 129.

7. Ibid., 129. For a detailed review on the pyramid design and the French Revolution, see Mouilleseaux, *Les Pyramides ephemeres de la Revolution Francaise*, Revue FMR 21, vol. 6, August 1989.

8. Ibid., 129.

9. Ibid. 117.

10. Fagiolo, *Architettura et Massoneria*, 53.

11. Legaret and Courtines, *Paris Story*, 83, plate 3.

12. Ibid., plate 6.

13. Ovason, *The Secret Zodiacs of Washington DC*, 116.

14. Curl, *The Art and Architecture of Freemasonry*, 132–33.

15. Fagan, *The Rape of the Nile*, 252.

16. *Vovelle, la Revolutopn contre L'Eglise*, frontispiece.

17. Faucher, *Les Francs-Maçon et le Pouvoir*, 34.

18. Hivert-Messeca, *Comment la Franc-Maçonnerie vint aux Femmes*, 159.

19. Ibid., 160.

20. Ibid., 159.

21. Naudon, *Histoire Générale de la Franc-Maçonerie*, 172.

22. Collaveri, *Napoléon: Enpereur Franc-Maçon*, 26–27.

23. Ibid., 168.

24. See Mostyn, *Egypt's Belle Epoque*, 17.

25. Ibid., 17.

26. Faucher, *Les Francs-Maçon et le Pouvoir*, 9, 32–33.

27. Iversen, *The Myth of Ancient Egypt and Its Hierogyphs in European Tradition*, 125.

28. Yates, *The Rosicrucian Enlightenment*, 154.

29. Iversen, *The Myth of Ancient Egypt and Its Hierogyphs in European Tradition*, 100.

30. Lacouture, *Champollion: Une Vie de Lumieres*, 382.

31. Ibid., 34.

32. Faucher, *Les Francs-Maçon et le Pouvoir*, 18.

33. Chevallier, *Histoire de la Maçonnerie*, vol. 1, 261.

34. Lacouture, *Champollion: Une Vie de Lumieres*, 35.

35. Aubrey Noakes, *Cleopatra's Needle*, 1.

36. Moorehead, *The Blue Nile*, 65.

37. Foreman and Phillips, and *Napoleon's Lost Fleet*, 69.

38. Ibid., 49.

39. Moorehead, *The Blue Nile,* 124.

40. Naudon, *Histoire Générale de la Franc-Maçonerie,* 224.

41. Collaveri, *La Francs Maçonnerie des Bonaparte;* also see Galtier, *Maçonnerie Egyptienne, rose-croix et neo-chevalierie,* 139; see also Naudon, *Histoire Générale de la Franc-Maçonerie,* 97.

42. Collaveri, *La Francs Maçonnerie des Bonapartes,* annex iv.

43. Ibid., 67.

44. Ibid., 68.

45. *The Kneph,* vol. 3, no. 6, June 1883, 45; see Galtier, *Maçonnerie Egyptienne, rose-croix et neo-chevalierie,* 139–40.

46. Naudon, *Histoire Générale de la Franc-Maçonerie,* 124.

47. Lacouture, *Champollion: une vie de lumieres,* 38; see also Lacouture, *Memorial de Sainte-Helene,* coll. "l'Integrale" chap. 1, 67.

48. Galtier, *Maçonnerie Egyptienne, rose-croix et neo-chevalierie,* 40.

49. Lacouture, *Champollion: une vie de lumieres,* 33.

50. Ibid., 190.

51. Galtier, *Maçonnerie Egyptienne, rose-croix et neo-chevalierie,* 150–51.

52. Ibid.

53. Ibid.

54. Ibid.

55. Lacouture, *Champollion: une vie de lumieres,* 727.

56. Galtier, *Maçonnerie Egyptienne, rose-croix et neo-chevalierie,* 151.

57. Lacouture, *Champollion: une vie de lumieres,* 731.

58. Ibid., 742.

59. Faucher, *Les Francs-Maçon et le Pouvoir,* 9, 85.

60. Ibid., 8; Francois Mitterrand is often confused with Jacques Mitterrand who was a Grand Master of Grand Orient of France in the 1960s (see ibid., 169–70).

61. Ibid., 275.

62. BBC News, Africa, December 22, 2000, 16:01 GMT.

63. Bauval, *Secret Chamber,* prologue and epilogue.

64. See Kiesel's article in the September 1983 issue of *The Masonic Philalesist;* also J. E. Bebrens's article in October 1983 issue of *Knight Templar Magazine.*

65. D'alton, *The New York Obelisk,* 10.

66. See Hancock and Bauval, *Talisman,* 446.

Bibliography

Aref, Nevin el. "A Man with a Mission." *Al-Ahram Weekly,* August 26–September 1, 2004.

———. "Long Road to UNESCO." *Al-Ahram Weekly,* November 27–December 3, 2008.

———. "Zahi Hawass: A Man with a Hat." *Al-Ahram Weekly,* August 25–31, 2005.

Bauval, Robert. *Secret Chamber.* New York: Arrow Books, 2000.

Bauval, Robert, and Thomas Brophy. *Black Genesis.* Rochester, Vt.: Bear and Company, 2011.

Bauval, Robert, and Graham Hancock. *The Master Game: Unmasking the Secret Rulers of the World.* New York: Disinformation Inc., 2011.

———. *The Message of the Sphinx: A Quest for the Hidden Legacy of Mankind.* New York: Three Rivers Press, 1997.

BBC News, Africa. December 22, 2000, 16:01 GMT.

Bebrens, J. E., *Knight Templar Magazine,* October 1983.

Benjamin, Daniel, and Steven Simon. *The Age of Sacred Terror.* New York: Random House, 2002.

———. *The Next Attack: The Failure of the War on Terror and the Stategy for Getting It Right.* New York: Henry Holt and Company, LLC, 2005.

Bruno, Giordano. *Dialoghi Filosofici Italiani.* Mondatori edition, 2001.

Cases, Count de la. *Memorial de Sainte-Helene.* Series title "Integrale." Paris: Éditions du Seuil, 1968.

Chevallier, Pierre. *Histoire de la Maçonnerie.* Paris: Librarie Arthème Fayard, 1974.

Collaveri, François. *La Franc-Maçonnerie des Bonaparte.* Paris: Payot, 1982.

————. *Napoléon: Franc-Maçon?* Paris: Jules Tallandier, 2003.

Curl, James Stephen. *The Art and Architecture of Freemasonry.* London: B. T. Batsford, 1991.

D'alton, Martina. *The New York Obelisk.* New York: The Metropolitan Museum of Art, 1993.

Eames, Andrew. *The Nile.* London: APA Publications, 1992.

Edges, Chris. "The Muslims' Wrath Doesn't Spare the Mummies." *The New York Times* (*Luxor Journal*), July 23, 1993.

"Egyptian Antiquities Become a Private Possession for Officials!" *Al Wafd,* August 5, 1993.

Egyptian Gazette, May 16, 1997.

El-aref, Nevine. "Zahi Hawass: A Hat Is a Hat." *Al-Ahram Weekly,* August 23–31, 2005.

Evans, Bros. Henry, Litt.D. "Masonry and Magic in the Eighteenth Century." *The Master Mason Magazine,* June 1927.

Fagan, Brian M. *The Rape of the Nile.* London: Myer Bell, 1992.

Fagiolo, Marcello. *Architettura e Massoneria.* Florence: Convivio, 1988.

Faucher, Jean-Andre. *Les Francs-Maçon et le Pouvoir.* Paris: Librarie Academique Perrin, 1988.

Fielding, Nick. "Egypt May Bar Pyramid Show." *The Sunday Times,* December 5, 1999.

Foreman, Laura, and Ellen Blue Phillips. *Napoleon's Lost Fleet: Bonaparte, Nelson, and the Battle of the Nile.* New York: Roundtable Press, 1999.

Fowden, Garth. *The Egyptian Hermes.* Cambridge: Cambridge University Press, 1986.

Gad, Emad. "Reconsidering Egypt's Identity." *Al-Ahram Weekly,* August 25, 2011.

Galtier, Gerard. *Maçonnerie Egyptienne: Rose-croix et neo-chevalierie.* Paris: Éditions du Rocher, 1989.

Genzlinger, Neil. "Chasing Mummies." *The New York Times,* July 13, 2010.

Girling, Richard. "King Tut Tut Tut." *Sunday Times Magazine,* May 22, 2005.

Hancock, Graham, and Robert Bauval. *Talsiman: Sacred Cities, Secret Faith.* New York: Penguin 2004.

Hawass, Zahi. *Secret Chamber.* Unaired documentary film by Boris Said, 1996–1997.

Hermes Trismegistus. *Hermetica: The Greek Corpus Hermeticum. Asclepius III.*

"Historical Decision to Question Farouk Hosni and the Jew Michel Jarre by the National Assembly." *Al Shaab,* January 4, 1999.

Hivert-Messeca, Gisele, and Yves Hivert-Messeca. *Comment la Franc-Maçonnerie vint aux Femmes.* Paris: Editions Dervy, 1997.

Hosni, Farouk (in an interview). "Israel Is Robbing the Pyramids as It Robbed Palestine." *Rose al- Yusef Weekly Magazine,* May 5, 1997.

Iversen, Erik. *The Myth of Ancient Egypt and Its Hierogyphs in European Tradition.* Copenhagen: GEC and Gad Publishers, 1961.

Jasnow, Richard, and Karl-Th. Zausich. "A Book of Thoth?" Cambridge: Seventh International Congress of Egyptologists, September 3–9, 1995.

Kerisel, Jean. *La Pyramide a travers les Ages.* Paris: Presse Ponts & Chaussees, 1991.

Kiessel, Willam C., Jr. *The Masonic Philalesist.* September 1983.

The Kneph. Volume III, no. 6, June 1883, 45.

Lacouture, Jean. *Champollion: Une Vie de Lumieres.* Paris: Grasset, 1988.

Legaret, Sylvie and Philippe Courtines. *Paris Story.* Paris: Denoel, 1977.

Malek, Jaromir. "Who Was the First to Identify the Saqqara Serapeum?" *Chronique d'Egypte Bruxelles 58,* 1983, 65–72, 115–16.

Mansfield, Peter. *Nasser.* London: Methuen, 1969.

Memri TV. Arabic Video, English Transcript. Broadcast February 11, 2009. www.memritv.org/clip/en/2049.htm

Miller, A. *Freemasonry in the Mind of the Islamist.* Hudson, N.Y.: Stonegate Institute, 2009.

Moorehead, Alan. *The Blue Nile.* New York: Penguin Books, 1983.

Morrow, Lance. "The Shoes of Imelda Marcos." *Time Magazine,* March 31, 1986.

Mostyn, Trevor. *Egypt's Belle Epoque.* London: Tauris Parke Paperbacks, 2006.

Mouilleseaux, Jean-Pierre. *Les Pyramides ephemeres de la Revolution Francaise.* Paris: Revue FMR 21, vol. VI, August 1989.

"The National Assembly Queries the Meaning Why a Golden Masonic Capstone Will Go on the Pyramid." *Al Shaab,* December 10, 1999.

Naudon, Paul. *Histoire Générale de la Franc-Maçonerie.* Paris: Office du Livre, 1981.

Nemah, Fuoad, trans. "Stealing of Egypt's Civilization." *Akhbar el Yom,* January 8, 1994.

Noakes, Aubrey. *Cleopatra's Needle.* London: H. F. and G. Witherby, 1962.

"Orders Issued to Halt Masonic Event at the Pyramids." *Al Shaab,* December 18, 1999.

Ovason, David. *The Secret Zodiacs of Washington DC.* London: Century Books, 1999.

Petrie, Sir William Flinders. "Historical References in the Hermetic Writings." *Transactions of the Third International Congress of Religions.* Oxford: Clarendon Press, 1908.

———. *Personal Religion in Egypt before Christianity.* New York: Harpers, 1909.

Plotinus. *Ennead* IV.8.1.

Ressner, Jeffrey. "Old World, New Tricks." *American Way,* June 15, 2011, p. 48.

Rodenbeck, Max. *Cairo: The City Victorious.* Cairo: The American University of Cairo Press, 1998.

Saudi Arabia's Curriculum of Intolerance. Hudson, New York: The Center for Religious Freedom of Hudson Institute with the Institute for Gulf Affairs, 2008. www.hudson.org/files/publications/saudi_textbooks_final.pdf.

Sinoué, Gilbert. *Le Dernier Pharaon: Mehemet-Ali, 1770–1849.* Paris: Pygmalion Gerard Watelet, 1997.

Smith, A. Robert, and Hugh Lynn Cayce. *About My Father's Business.* Virginia Beach: The Donning Company, 1988.

Strabo. *Geographica.* Isaac Casaubon, 1587.

Strathern, Paul. *Napoleon in Egypt.* London: Jonathan Cape, 2007.

Tigor, Robert L. *Egypt.* Princeton: Princeton University Press, 2010.

Vovelle, Michele. *La Revolution contre L'Eglise.* Paris: Complex, 1988.

White, Michael. *Isaac Newton: The Last Sorcerer.* Boston: Addison-Wesley, 1997.

Wistrich, Robert S. "The New Islamic Fascism." *The Jerusalem Post,* November 2001.

Wynn, Lisa L. "Shape Shifting Lizard People, Israelite Slaves, and Other Theories of Pyramid Building: Notes on Labor, Nationalism, and Archaeology in Egypt." *Journal of Social Archaeology,* June 2008: 272–95.

Yates, Frances A. *Giordano Bruno and the Hermetic Tradition.* Chicago: University of Chicago Press, 1991.

———. *The Rosicrucian Enlightenment.* London: Routledge, 1972.

Index

Abbas I (viceroy of Egypt), 122–23, 140

Abbas II (khedive), 155–58

Abduh, Muhammad, 155, 156, 162

Ahhotep I (queen), tomb of, 151

Ahmose Nefertari, 280, 282, 283

Aida (Verdi), 130, 151

Akhenaten, King, 171–72, 232, 305,
    307–9, 324–27, 328–29
  as Moses, 311

Al Ummah Party, 162

Al-Banna, Hassan, 174–75

Al-Nour Party, 4, 244–46

Alexander the Great, 75, 76

Alexandria, 14–18
  French attack on, 85, 87, 88
  Library of, 75

Amenhotep III, 307, 309, 316, 324–
    25, 326

American Research Center in Egypt
    (ARCE), 202–3

Amin, Qasim, 167

antiquities
  after the First Revolution, 168–72
  foreign destruction of, 100
  iconoclastic destruction of, 76–77,
    86, 99

looting during Revolution (2011),
    231–35, 236–37, 241
  protection of, 4–5, 98, 136–37,
    143–44 (*See also* Mariette,
    Auguste [Mariette Pasha])
  theft of, 41–43, 46, 96, 98–99
  trade in, 104, 116, 133

Apis (sacred bulls of Memphis), 137,
    141–42

Arab League, 180

Arab-Israeli War (1948), 56, 152,
    180–81, 183, 185

architecture, Masonic, 247, 248–49

Assembly of Delegates, 132–33,
    134

Association of Research and
    Enlightenment (ARE). *See* Edgar
    Cayce Foundation (ECF)

Atatürk, Mustafa Kemal, 173–74

Atlantis, 20, 21, 22, 58, 196, 210. *See
    also* Hall of Records

Bakr, Mohammed Ibrahim, 38–42,
    43–48, 204, 215

Baring, Evelyn. *See* Cromer, Lord
    (Evelyn Baring)

Bauval, Robert, 3, 8, 64–65, 205, 216, 300
family, 16, 17
Hawass and, 57, 58, 64, 334, 339, 341
life of, 334–40
Belzoni, Giovanni Battista, 120, 121–22
Bergé, Pierre, 264, 265
Borchardt, Ludwig, 171–72
Bouazizi, Mohamed, 225–26
British Museum, 55, 118, 120, 121
Bruno, Giordano, 80–81
Bulaq Museum, 144–46, 147

Cagliostro, Alessandro, 248, 253, 254
Camp David Treaty, 56
Carnarvon, Lord (George Herbert), 169–70, 171
Carter, Howard, 168, 169–70, 279, 280, 306. See also Tutankhamun, King
damage to Tutankhamun's body and, 312–13, 317, 322
Cayce, Edgar, 23, 24, 201
Cayce, Hugh Lynn, 20–23, 26, 198, 199, 200–1, 202, 203
Champollion, Jean-François, 91, 101–3, 116–17, 258, 259, 264, 265
Chasing Mummies (TV show), 302–4
Cheops. See Khufu, King
Cleopatra, 76, 280
Cleopatra's Needles, 116, 262–63
Constantinople, Sack of (1453), 80
Copernicus, Nicholas, 82

Copts, 16, 157
post-Revolution (2011) status of, 244
rights for, 163
corruption, government, 150, 183–84. See also Egyptian Antiquities Organization (EAO)
cotton, 112, 128, 130–31, 166
Cromer, Lord (Evelyn Baring), 153–57, 167

dam projects, 113, 154–55, 275
de Lesseps. See Ferdinand, viscount de Lesseps
demotic, 102
Denon, Vivant, 95, 104
Derry, D. E., 320, 321, 327–28
Discovery Channel, 281–84, 286, 313
Dormion, Gilles, 211–12
Drovetti, Bernardino, 119–20, 259

Edgar Cayce Foundation (ECF), 20–24, 28, 65, 196–208
Edict of Theodosius (391 CE), 76–77
Egypt. See also Tahrir Square Revolution
anti-semitism in, 66 (See also Israel; Zionism)
as cradle of civilization, 6, 74–75
Bible and, 9, 331–33
Europeanization of, 127, 128–29, 131 (See also Ismail Pasha)
feminist movement in, 166–68
French occupation of, 84–85, 88–90, 94–96, 106 (See also Napoleon I [Napoleon Bonaparte])

independence from Great Britain,
164, 165
military rule of, 194–95 (*See also*
Free Officers Movement)
population growth, 166
Egyptian Antiquities Organization
(EAO). *See also* Supreme Council
of Antiquities (SCA)
accusations of corruption in,
46–48
leadership of, 31–32
Egyptian language, ancient, 102–3
Egyptian Museum, 36, 147–48
gift shop, 238, 239, 240
laboratory, 281, 285–86, 313
looting of, 232, 234, 237, 241
Egyptology
Egyptians in, 149–51 (*See also*
Fakhri, Ahmed; Ikram, Salima)
origin of, 95–96
tomb robbery and, 139 (*See also*
antiquities)
El Saadawi, Nawal, 168
el-A'ss, Amr ibn, 85–86
Enfantin, Prosper, 125–26
European plundering of antiquities,
116, 117–22
eye, Masonic symbolism of, 70, 249–
50, 262, 268, 269

Fakhri, Ahmed, 295
Farouk I (king), 152–53, 161, 175–79,
187–88
Arab-Israeli War and, 181
death of, 186
feminism, 166–68

Ferdinand, viscount de Lesseps, 124,
126, 140, 143
First Revolution (1919), 162–64, 165
feminist movement and, 166–68
Fox TV, 2, 9, 219, 221–22, 282,
287–96
France. *See also* Napoleon I (Napoleon
Bonaparte)
creditor to Egypt, 132–33
pyramids in, 247–48
Free Officers Movement, 15–16, 29,
181, 183–86, 188–89
Freemasonry, 23, 27–28, 154. *See
also* Josephine, Empress of
France; Napoleon I (Napoleon
Bonaparte); Supreme Being
America and, 92–93
architecture and, 247–50
as revival of Gnosticism, 92
banned in Egypt, 24
conspiracy theories concerning,
60–64
in Egypt, 247–70
Jews linked to, 61, 63, 66–67,
72–73, 180–81, 268–70
symbolism of, 70–71, 269 (*See
also* eye, Masonic symbolism of;
triangle, Masonic symbolism of)
French Revolution, 85, 248
bicentennial, 69, 261
Freemasonry and, 92
Fuad I (king), 153, 159–61, 164–65,
175
Fuad II (king), 185

Gaddafi, Muammar, 38–40

Gantenbrink, Rudolph, 43–45, 213–16, 219, 296

Giza Plateau and Pyramids
Hawass oversight of, 19, 21, 23, 27, 28, 38–43, 195
repairs needed at, 209

Goidin, Jean-Patrice, 211–12

Great Britain, 89–90. *See also* Tripartite Invasion
creditor to Egypt, 132–33
occupation of Egypt by, 135, 152, 153–59, 161–64
support of Tewfik Pasha, 134–35
war with Ottoman Empire, 158
World War II and, 176, 178–79

Great Pyramid, 43–45, 210–22, 296–301
capstone and, 66–72, 248, 250, 262, 267, 268
closing of (November 11, 2011), 244, 269–70
Masonic architecture and, 248
millennium celebrations at, 66–74, 262, 267–69
possible hidden chambers in, 211, 215, 219
Queen's Chamber of, 43, 208, 211–17, 296–98 (*See also* Gantenbrink, Rudolph)
stellar alignments of, 296

Hall of Records, 20–24, 196–207, 209. *See also* Edgar Cayce Foundation

Hancock, Graham, 57, 58, 64

Hansen, Marjorie, 196–98

Harrison, R. G., 306, 307, 318, 319–21, 322, 328

Hatshepsut, 279–86, 313

Hawass, Zahi, 1–10, 12–50, 51–71, 193, 223
accusations against, 36–37, 229–30, 232–35, 241–42, 317
anti-semitism and xenophobia of, 9, 53–54, 56–61, 64–65, 206–7, 300
blog, 243–44
celebrity friends of, 224
clothing line, 230–31, 238, 240
education of, 18–19, 22–23, 28
Farouk Hosni and, 29–34, 36–38, 40–42, 49
Fox TV and, 2, 9, 219, 221–22, 282, 287–96
Giza oversight of, 19, 21, 23, 27, 28, 38–43, 195
Great Pyramid and, 212–22, 288
Hosni Mubarak and, 227–28
Indiana Jones image of, 1, 48–49, 243
Mohammed Bakr and, 38–42, 43–48
Muammar Gaddafi and, 40–42
National Geographic Channel and, 53, 217, 218, 288, 296–98, 312
Osiris tomb alleged by, 177–78
pyramid builders, theories regarding, 271–73
Revolution and, 3, 225–42, 340
Sphinx restoration and, 29–34, 273–77
Suzanne Mubarak and, 2, 34–38, 49, 238

Tutankhamun's death and, 305–24
youth of, 13–18
Herbert, George. *See* Carnarvon, Lord
(George Herbert)
Hermetica, 10–11, 77–83
hieroglyphics, 102
History Channel, 302–3
Hosni, Farouk, 29–38, 40–42, 46,
204, 262, 267–68, 310, 328–30
anti-semitism of, 63
complaints about, 36–37
press controlled by, 48

Ikram, Salima, 13, 285–86
Institut d'Egypte, 92, 93–95, 96, 106,
257
Islam
conversion of Egypt to, 86
covering/defacing antiquities and,
86, 88, 99, 245
Napoleon and, 255–56
Islamic Jurisdictional College, 73
Ismail Pasha, 126–33, 151
Auguste Mariette and, 146–47
desire to train Egyptian
Egyptologists, 149
financial crisis under, 131–32, 152
Israel, modern state of. *See also*
Zionism
Egyptian antipathy toward, 18, 56,
337
founding of, 179–81, 331
jubilee celebrations of, 68, 263,
267
wars with Egypt, 18, 52, 56, 152,
180–82, 189–90, 192

Jahoda, Joseph, 65, 200, 202, 203,
204, 207, 208, 209
Jarre, Jean Michel, 68–69, 70, 72,
261–62, 268–69
Jerusalem (El Quds), 18, 192
Josephine, Empress of France, 92, 95,
96, 251–52, 254–55
Freemasonry and, 92, 251–52,
258

Kadri, Ahmed, 28, 29–34, 38
Kamel, Hussein (sultan), 158, 159
Kamel, Mustafa, 156, 157
Khafre, King, Sphinx and, 205–6,
274
khamseen (sandstorms), 30–31
khawagas, 16, 166, 175, 334
anger against, 336–37, 338
khedive, the. *See* Ismail Pasha
Khufu, King, 218, 220
Killearn, Lord (Miles Lampson), 176,
178–79
Kitchener, Herbert, 155, 156, 158, 159
Kléber, Jean-Baptiste, 89, 257–58

Lampson, Miles. *See* Killearn, Lord
(Miles Lampson)
Lehner, Mark, 19–23, 196, 198–203,
218, 219–21
Lenormant, Charles, 114, 115–16, 259
looting of antiquities, 231–35, 236–
37, 241
Louvre, 119, 121, 143

Maat, 75
mafia, archeological, 46–48

Mamluks, 84, 88, 105, 255
   slaughter of, 107
Mariette, Auguste (Mariette Pasha),
   101, 136–51
   tomb of, 148
Maspero, Gaston, 147, 149, 150
Menkaure, sarcophagus of, 116
Metropolitan Museum (New York
   City), 262, 263, 306
millenium celebrations, 66–74
Ministry of State for Antiquities
   Affairs, 227, 229
Mirandola, Giovanni Pico della, 80
Monge, Gaspard, 93, 95, 257
monotheism, 7, 308, 326–27
Moses, 7, 311, 331, 333
Mubarak, Hosni, 67, 223
   protests against, 226–28 (*See also*
   Tahrir Square Revolution)
Mubarak, Suzanne, 2, 34–38, 42,
   223
Muhammad Ali, 14, 104–17, 118
   conflict with Ottomans, 108–9
   defeat of the Wahhabis, 108
   indifference toward antiquities, 110,
    113–15, 116–17, 140
   modernization of Egypt by, 110–13
   slaughter of the Mamluks, 107
   Société Secrète Egyptienne and, 259
mummies. *See also* Hatshepsut,
   alleged mummy of
   DNA testing of, 281–86
   golden, 222, 279, 291–96
   supposed medicinal value of, 100,
    294
   trade in, 100

Muslim Brotherhood, 4, 172–75, 179,
   189, 244, 246
   Nasser and, 191
Musri, Mohammad, 246

Naguib, Mohammed, 183, 184, 185,
   189, 194
Napoleon I (Napoleon Bonaparte),
   7, 51
   Egypt expedition, 84–85, 88–90,
    93–96, 252, 254–58
   Freemasonry and, 251–52, 257–58
   savants (scientists) of, 93–96, 257
Nasser cult, 190–91
Nasser, Gamal Abdel, 16–18, 52–53,
   152, 181–83, 190–93
   Free Officers Movement and, 183,
    189
   khawagas and, 336–37
   xenophobia of, 195
National Democratic Party, 32, 48, 149
National Geographic Channel, 53,
   217, 218, 288, 296–98, 312
National Geographic Society, 217,
   219, 238
   Hawass as explorer-in-residence,
    217, 218, 238, 239, 240
Nazli (queen), 160–61, 163
Nefertiti, bust of, 66, 171–72, 173
New Agers, 57–58, 290
Newton, Isaac, 83
Nur el-Din, Mohammed Abdel
   Halim, 38, 42, 72

Obeid, Makram, 163
obelisks in Paris, 259–60, 264

Opening the Lost Tombs, 221, 288–90

Opening the Tombs of the Golden Mummies, 222, 291–93, 295

Orabi, Ahmed, uprising of, 134–35, 152, 153

Osman, Ahmed, 3, 8, 65
 Hawass and, 305–24, 332–34, 341
 life of, 331–34

Ottoman Empire, 80, 84, 105
 British war with, 158
 defeat of, 173–74 (*See also* Muslim Brotherhood)

Pasha, the. *See* Muhammad Ali

Pharaoh (title), 333

Philalethes, 253

Protocols of the Elders of Zion, 61–64

Ptolemaic dynasties, 76

pyramids, builders of, 53–54, 58, 271–73, 297–98, 299–301
 alien theory of, 272, 289–90, 300

Ramses II, obelisk of, 116

Renaissance, 79–80
 Egypt as inspiration for, 83

Revolution. *See* Tahrir Square Revolution

Revolution Command Council (RCC), 189

Rosetta Stone, 55, 66, 96
 Hawass's demand for return of, 97

Rosicrucians, 27, 254

Sadat, Anwar, 181, 182, 183–84

Saïd Pasha, 123–24, 126
 concern for antiquities, 143–44, 146

Saint Laurent, Yves, 264

Saint-Simoniens, 125–26

Salt, Henry, 117–21

Schoch, Robert, 56, 204, 206

Schor Foundation, 209

Schor, Joseph, 28, 65, 207–8, 209, 210

Secret Chambers Revealed, 53–54, 218–19, 221–22, 296–301

Secret National Party, 156

Serapeum, 137–43
 destruction of, 77

Services des Antiquitées, 135, 146–47, 151, 168–69
 founding, 144

Sève, Joseph Anthelme (Suleiman Pasha al-Fransawi), 108, 160, 162

Shaarawi, Hoda, 167

Sharaf, Essam, 228–29, 236, 237, 242

Sharif, Omar, 1, 40, 302

Six-Day War (1967), 18, 192

Smenkhkare, Pharaoh, 324–25, 326, 328

Société Secrète Egyptienne, 259

Sphinx, 21–22, 28, 29–34
 chambers beneath, 199–200, 204–5, 208, 209, 210
 constellation Leo and, 205
 dating of, 56, 204, 205, 206
 excavations near, 199–202, 203 (*See also* Hall of Records)
 Khafre and, 205–6, 274
 nose broken off, 88, 99
 possible sabotage of, 33–34
 restoration of, 273–77

Stadelmann, Rainer, 213–15

Stanford Research Institute (SRI), 198, 199, 200, 201

Strabo, 136, 137–39, 141
Suez Canal, 18–19, 129–31, 140, 252
   British control of, 131, 165, 189–90
   building of, 124, 126–28
Suez War. *See* Tripartite Invasion
sun, deity of, 82
Supreme Being, 92, 93, 249–50, 256, 261
Supreme Council of Antiquities
   (SCA), 3, 9. *See also* Egyptian
   Antiquities Organization (EAO)
   corruption in, 37, 101
Supreme Council of the Armed Forces
   (SCAF), 4, 228, 229

Tahrir Square Revolution, 3, 4, 48, 97,
   226–42
   elections, 244–46, 269
   looting of antiquities in, 231–35,
   236–37, 241
Talleyrand, Charles-Maurice de,
   252–53, 257
Tantawi, Mohammad, 194, 228, 229
Tewfik Pasha, 133–35, 153, 154, 155
   Freemasonry of, 134
Thoth, 79. *See also Hermetica*
Thutmose I, King, 280, 282
Thutmose II, King, 280
Thutmose III, King, 280
Tiye, Queen, 325, 326, 332
tomb robbers and robbery, 75–76
triangle, Masonic symbolism of, 249,
   250, 251, 256, 268, 269
Tripartite Invasion (1956), 16, 52,
   189–90
Truman, Harry, Freemasonry of,
   180–81

Turkey, 174. *See also* Ottoman Empire
Tutankhamun, King
   antiquities stolen, 232–33
   death of, 305–24
   discovery of, 168–71
   ownership of, 170
   possible European roots of, 316–17
   relatives of, 324–30

United States
   as superpower, 180
   Freemasonry and, 92–93, 250
Upuaut II, 43–44, 45

vandalism, 76–77, 86, 99, 150. *See also*
   antiquities
veil, 167. *See also* feminism

Wafd Party, 162–63, 164–65, 167,
   169, 179
   Farouk I and, 175–76
Waseda University DNA tests, 309–
   10, 311
West, John, 56, 57, 58, 64, 204, 206, 208
Wingate, Reginald, 158–59, 160,
   161–62
World War II, 175–79

Yuya, 232, 325, 332–33

Zaghloul, Saad, 157, 158, 162–63,
   164, 167, 169
Zaghloul, Safiya, 157, 161, 168
Zionism, 264, 267
   purported connection to
      Freemasonry, 24–25, 268–70

BOOKS OF RELATED INTEREST

Black Genesis
The Prehistoric Origins of Ancient Egypt
by Robert Bauval and Thomas Brophy, Ph.D.

Moses and Akhenaten
The Secret History of Egypt at the Time of the Exodus
by Ahmed Osman

Lost Technologies of Ancient Egypt
Advanced Engineering in the Temples of the Pharaohs
by Christopher Dunn

The Giza Power Plant
Technologies of Ancient Egypt
by Christopher Dunn

The Giza Prophecy
The Orion Code and the Secret Teachings of the Pyramids
by Scott Creighton and Gary Osborn

Ancient Egypt 39,000 BCE
The History, Technology, and Philosophy of Civilization X
by Edward F. Malkowski

The Temple in Man
Sacred Architecture and the Perfect Man
by R. A. Schwaller de Lubicz

Lost Knowledge of the Ancients
A Graham Hancock Reader
Edited by Glenn Kreisberg

INNER TRADITIONS • BEAR & COMPANY
P.O. Box 388
Rochester, VT 05767
1-800-246-8648
www.InnerTraditions.com

Or contact your local bookseller